THE VICTORIA HISTORY OF SHROPSHIRE

WEM

Judith Everard, James P. Bowen and Wendy Horton

VICTORIA
COUNTY
HISTORY

First published 2019

A Victoria County History publication

© The University of London, 2019

ISBN 978 1 912702 08 4

Typeset in Minion pro
Published by the University of London Press
Senate House, Malet Street, London WC1E 7HU
https://london.ac.uk/press

Cover image: Wem in 1631, detail of map of the manor of Wem: SA, 972/7/1/49.
Back cover image: Eckford's Novelties, seed catalogue for Eckford's nursery, Wem, 1912.

CONTENTS

LIST OF ILLUSTRATIONS

Photographs by Wendy Horton unless otherwise stated. Images from SA reproduced with the permission of Shropshire Archives.

Figures

Maps

Tables

ACKNOWLEDGEMENTS

THE VICTORIA COUNTY HISTORY (VCH) has an impressive record in Shropshire. The first Shropshire volume was published as long ago as 1908. Six volumes were published between 1968 and 1988, including three topographical volumes covering large areas of the county including parishes in parts of the Severn Valley, the South Shropshire Hills and Telford. There are also thematic volumes on agriculture and administrative, political and ecclesiastical history. Until about 2000 the work of VCH was funded through a partnership between the University of London and Shropshire County Council, and latterly the University of Keele; activities in the county then went into abeyance.

Following publication of the VCH volume *Shrewsbury, General History and Topography* in 2014, the project was relaunched by Professor Richard Hoyle as Director and General Editor of VCH. Wem is the first history to be published by the new VCH Shropshire, thanks to the dedication of Professor Hoyle as chair of the county committee. We are very grateful to the chairman and the members of the committee, past and present, whose continuing efforts make this work possible.

To achieve its aims, VCH Shropshire depends upon the generosity of benefactors, principally the Jean Jackson Charitable Trust and the Walker Trust. This project has also benefited from the financial and material support of the Victoria County History Trust, the Friends of Shropshire Archives, Shropshire Archaeological and Historical Society, and South West Shropshire Historical and Archaeological Society, and the donations of individual supporters. We are pleased to acknowledge the interest and financial support of Wem Town Council.

It is a pleasure here to acknowledge the assistance of Mary McKenzie and the staff of Shropshire Archives. We are especially grateful to Ralph Collingwood for sharing with us research notes and publications on Wem by the late Dr Sylvia Watts. This book would have been longer in production and poorer without this resource. Tom Edwards generously shared his knowledge of Wem's history, both in many enjoyable discussions and through his collection of photographs and press cuttings, part of which is deposited at Shropshire Archives. Oliver and Shelagh Richardson offered valuable support and information, and kindly welcomed us to meetings of Wem Civic Society. At the beginning of this project David Spalding deposited at Shropshire Archives the papers of Samuel Garbet, which have proved invaluable. We are honoured to thank Lord Barnard for his kind hospitality, his interest in this project and his very generous assistance with access to the Raby Estate archive, and we are also grateful to Katrina Appleyard and other staff members at Raby Castle.

We are grateful to Keith Lilley of Queen's University Belfast, for his advice and support in undertaking the town plan analysis. Tinho Da Cruz, Map Librarian of the School of Environmental Sciences, University of Liverpool, assisted in producing the GIS maps that underpin the town plan analysis and Suzanne Yee, also of the School of Environmental Sciences, University of Liverpool, produced the maps. We are also grateful to Jeff Spencer of Clwyd-Powys Archaeological Trust for providing aerial photographs.

We are very grateful for the generous contributions, in addition to those named above, of: James Ballantyne, Martin Carruthers, Eirene Craney, Roger Foreman, Robert Ginder, Harriet Hunt, John Pinfold, the Revd Canon William Price, the Revd David Smith, Jeff Sumbler, Rosemary Thornes, Penny Ward and Sue Wilton-Morgan. Nigel Tringham read and commented on the whole draft.

Finally we would like to thank Adam Chapman and Jessica Davies Porter of VCH Central Office at the Institute of Historical Research, University of London, and Emily Morrell of University of London Press for their assistance with production of this book.

'There is history in all men's lives'
(*Henry IV, Part 2*, act 3, sc. 1)

IT WAS SHAKESPEARE WHO PENNED this truth. One of our own contemporaries, the social historian Dr Jonathan Healey sharpened it further when he said, 'If academics, even social historians, forget that most people in history have not been Kings, Queens, or celebrities, then we local historians might be the only ones holding on to this knowledge'.

The Victoria County History, founded in 1899, values this approach. Its ambition is to write the authoritative history of every English parish. It is the longest, possibly greatest, publishing project in English history, well known for its iconic 'red books'. A more recent initiative to help achieve its aims is the publication of single-place studies known as 'VCH Shorts', of which this is one. When it was established, the committee for Victoria County History Shropshire delighted those of us who live in the ancient town of Wem in the north of the county by selecting our parish as the one to research and publish as their first 'short'. In their own words, they describe the book that you now have in your hands as 'the first modern history of this intriguing small town'.

In doing this they build upon earlier attempts during the 18th and 20th centuries to write our local history. This 21st-century publication is in part a belated answer to the plea of the Revd Samuel Garbet (*c.*1685–1756) in his preface to his *History of Wem*:

> It has been long lamented, that Shropshire has produced no Author that has taken a Survey of it, and published its natural and civil History, its Antiquities, and present State ...

He sought to address this omission by making enquiries about Wem as time and opportunity allowed him, but his work was only published in 1818 long after his death. We are grateful to have it. Garbet's *History* is the foundation on which rests Iris Woodward's *The Story of Wem and Its Neighbourhood* (1952, 1976) with its later updates from John Dromgool and now this 'Short'. It is all history 'from the bottom up', not of kings and queens, landowners or celebrities, but of ordinary people and their endeavours.

This approach to local history well describes our town of Wem. It shows our independence of spirit and non-conformity in all senses and a strong and pervading sense of community and resilience. Indeed Wem is an acronym which I and others have used frequently when explaining to visitors what it means to live in this special place: **W**here **E**veryone **M**atters.

I feel very honoured to have been asked, as a representative of our community, to write a Foreword welcoming this important publication which will itself become part of our continuing historical record. I have also had the privilege of having a 'first glimpse' of this volume and learnt much as I read it. It is written in a clear, concise, scholarly and well-informed style. It clearly shows our community within the context of time and helps us discover how things are as we find them today. Further it may help us learn how we can meet today's challenges and in our turn leave the town and surrounding area in a better state for the generations which follow us. It is a book to read for pleasure, for profit and not just by Wemians, past or present.

As the researchers and writers for this book will testify, there is much more to be discovered about our town's past. It may be that it is this book that stimulates new researchers and further publications. The story of Wem continues to unfold and we, today's Wemians, are grateful to VCH Shropshire for their interest in our community and their efforts to bring this publication to a conclusion and to help us better understand ourselves.

Councillor Edward Towers
Mayor of Wem, 2011–12 and 2017–18

A NOTE ABOUT VICTORIA COUNTY HISTORY SHROPSHIRE

WHEN I WAS APPOINTED DIRECTOR and General Editor of the Victoria County History in April 2014, the brief I was given was an expansionist one. One part of it was to revive 'dormant counties', amongst which was Shropshire.

Shropshire had had a vigorous county office, financed originally by the County Council and then for a short period by the University of Keele. After that arrangement came to an end, VCH Central Office took over the management of the Shrewsbury volumes of the history and brought the first one to a triumphant conclusion. One of my first engagements as Director was to come to Shrewsbury to preside over the launch of this volume. The warm reception we received on that occasion, and the fact that James Bowen was already agitating for the revival of VCH in the county, made Shropshire an obvious county on which to direct our energy.

Five years on, we have the Wem 'Short' to show for our efforts. This is, therefore, an appropriate moment to mention those who have contributed so much to the endeavour. An energetic and supportive committee came together of Dr James Bowen, John Cherry, Linda Fletcher, Dr Chris Fountain (current Treasurer), Nigel Hinton (founding Treasurer), Professor Tim Jenkins, Sarah Lane (Secretary), Mary McKenzie, David Saunders, Nigel Semmens, James Parker, Penny Ward and Dr Jonathan Worton. The committee and I especially wish to thank Nigel Hinton who, with the help of David Saunders, piloted us through the necessary legal and financial arrangements and Mary McKenzie whose support and knowledge was indispensible. We were fortunate in finding two excellent locally-based researchers in Dr Judith Everard and Wendy Horton as well as a good number of volunteers in Wem and further afield. We received initial financial assistance from the Jean Jackson Charitable Trust, the Walker Trust and the Victoria County History Trust.

VCH Shropshire is now active on a number of fronts. Histories of the rural townships of Wem Rural are being prepared. Work continues on Shrewsbury. We have started work on a new history of Newport.

We welcome more volunteers, whether as committee members or as researchers and writers. But our biggest need is money. There is little or no local government money to fund us. All charities, in Shropshire as elsewhere, are under pressure from the many deserving causes that approach them for aid. We therefore need our supporters to contribute. Having shown with this volume what we can produce, we very much hope that they will.

Richard Hoyle
Chairman, Victoria County History of Shropshire

Figure 1 *Aerial photograph of Wem showing the castle mound, former market house, parish church and High Street.*

INTRODUCTION

WEM IS A SMALL MARKET TOWN, 10½ miles (17 km) north of Shrewsbury, at the centre of a regional network of north Shropshire market towns. The Old English name *Weme* is first recorded in Domesday Book, but modern-day Wem originated as a planted Norman castle-town with a motte-and-bailey castle, parish church and burgage plots. Wem had the characteristic features of a medieval small town including a diverse occupational structure, distinctive topography, social stratification, a degree of self-government, and cultural activities.[1] The built-up area did not develop beyond the medieval settlement until the 19th century. As the *caput* (head) of a barony and the centre of a large manor and parish, throughout its history Wem has been a centre for justice and local government, latterly as the headquarters of North Shropshire District Council.

Wem's pre-modern economy was based on pastoral agriculture and trading in agricultural produce, especially livestock and cheese, as well as leather and flax production. An endowed grammar school was founded in 1650 by Thomas Adams, a native of Wem who became Lord Mayor of London. During the Civil War, Wem was an outpost of the Parliamentarians in Shropshire; it was the seat of the Shropshire Committee until the fall of royalist Shrewsbury in 1645. Some of the buildings in the town centre, mainly of 16th- or 17th-century date, were destroyed or damaged in the great fire in 1677. The parish church was soon repaired; but the whole church, except the tower, was taken down and rebuilt between 1810 and 1813. In the 18th and 19th centuries Nonconformity flourished, with chapels drawing congregations from the town and surrounding rural townships, playing a role in the regional organisation of their denominations.

From the early 19th century, public subscription elementary schools, both Church of England and Nonconformist, provided education for the children of the town and wider parish. The town prospered from the opening of canal wharves at Edstaston and Quina Brook in 1805, with new building along the Edstaston road and the High Street. This also reflected an emerging sense of civic pride among Wem's property-owning classes, many owing their fortune and status to the legal and medical professions. Wem railway station, on the Shrewsbury–Crewe line, opened in 1858, and was retained despite threatened closure in the early 1960s and the demolition of the station buildings. At the turn of the 20th century the efforts of local councillors and incomers like Elijah Wood Bowcock, headmaster of the British Schools, and Edmund Bygott, solicitor, drove the formation of Wem Urban District (UD), which acquired the market rights from the lord of the manor and built a new municipal market and town hall. A new bank, free library and post office

---

1   For small towns in England, see C. Dyer, 'Small places with large consequences: the importance of small towns in England, 1000–1540', *Hist. Research*, 75, 187 (2002), 1–24.

added to Wem's urban amenities, and Wem gained renown as the home of modern sweet pea, cultivated by Henry Eckford at his Soulton road nursery.

During the 20th century employment in agriculture and most crafts and trades declined while others, for example, malting and brewing, became large-scale enterprises: the Shrewsbury & Wem Brewery, Isherwood's timber yard, and two cheese factories employed considerable numbers, until all in turn ceased trading in the 1980s–90s, since when most employment in Wem has been in the public sector. In recent decades Wem has proved a desirable place to live for all ages, with a strong sense of community and many recreational activities.

Wem's medieval past is not well documented. By contrast there are rich sources for the early modern period: a survey of landholding in the manor in 1561 and a large estate map of 1631, as well as further surveys of 1589, 1648 and 1805. The town's history was first studied by the Revd Samuel Garbet (d. 1756), an able antiquary, schoolmaster and curate of Edstaston, whose *History of Wem* was published posthumously in 1818.[2] Two hundred years after Garbet wrote, a new history was commissioned by Wem Town Council; Iris Woodward's *The Story of Wem*, first published in 1951 and updated to 2012. This new history of Wem draws together the material from these and a wide variety of other authoritative manuscript and published sources.

2   ODNB, s.v. Garbet, Samuel (1684/5–1751); Jones, *Mr Garbet*. Garbet's papers are deposited in SA, 9043.

LANDSCAPE, SETTLEMENT AND BUILDINGS

Boundaries and Township Origins

Weme WAS AN ANGLO-SAXON estate in Hodnet hundred: in 1086 it was assessed at four hides and encompassed what became Wem township as well as Tilley and Trench and probably Lowe and Ditches. The manor of Wem was formed from the conglomeration of *Weme* with the adjacent Anglo-Saxon estates of Aston, Coton, Edstaston, Horton, Sleap, Steel and Wolverley; it eventually extended about 6 miles (10 km) from north to south and 5 miles (8 km) from east to west.[1] The northern boundary, with Prees, was confirmed in 1228.[2] The former estates, along with areas colonised later, were recognised as townships within the manor: Aston, Coton, Edstaston, Horton, Lowe and Ditches, Newtown, Northwood, Sleap, Steel, Tilley and Trench, Wem and Wolverley. Wem township – the market town and its close rural hinterland – lay at the centre of the manor and the parish, which measured 13,900 a. and was coterminous with Wem manor plus two more small manors, Lacon and Soulton.

Wem township was approximately 1½ miles (2.4 km) from east to west and 1 mile (1.6 km) from north to south, comprising 1203 a. (487 ha.).[3] The southern boundary was the river Roden, whose tributaries formed the other boundaries except that to the east, between Wem and Aston, which was a 'cross pavement', presumably the 'stepping stones' on wet ground that gave their name to the fields there.[4]

The township lost its historical identity when Wem Urban District (UD) was created in 1900 from the built-up area, with a salient south of the Roden into the adjacent township of Tilley as far as the railway viaduct. The total area of Wem UD was just 452 a. (183 ha.). The remainder of Wem township remained in Wem Rural District (RD). Some of this rural area was regained in 1935 when Wem UD was enlarged to 901 a. (365 ha.).[5]

Landscape

The area around Wem is covered with deposits formed over the last two million years by glaciation, latterly the Devensian glaciation.[6] The bedrocks are clay, marl, mudstone and siltstone of the Lias group, the lower division of the Jurassic era. Bedrock is generally not exposed in the area. The town sits on a curving moraine of outwash sand and gravel deposited by glacial meltwaters.

3   Bagshaw, 317.
4   Garbet, 13–14. For 'Aston Stepping Stones', see, e.g., SA, 167/6, ff. 55v–56; SA, 1186/3.
5   SA, CP325/7/1/1, CP325/2/7/17; TNA, OS 38/1195/8.
6   P. Toghill, *Geology of Shropshire*, 2nd edn (Marlborough, 2006), 212, 235–8, fig. 9.

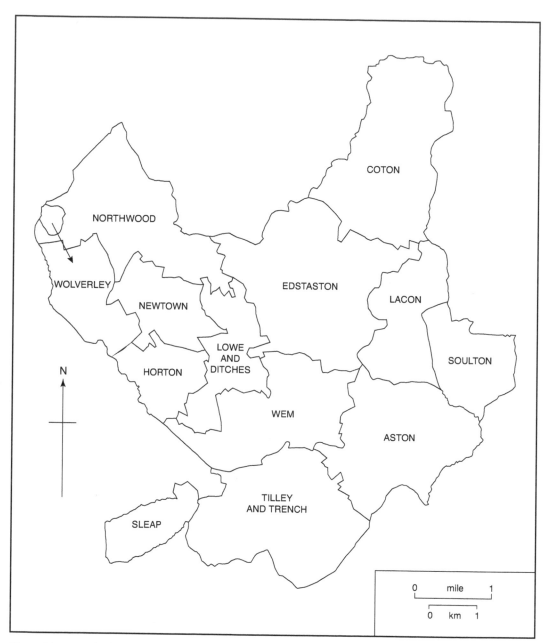

Map 1 *Wem parish, showing townships.*

The place name, from Old English '*wemm*' (filth, corruption), may refer to marshy ground. Nearby are Horton (OE *hohr*: dirt, for muddy ground), Lacon (OE *lacu*: streams or drainage channels) and Sleap (slippery place).[7] An alternative derivation of the place name could be from the sense of OE *wemm* as 'stain' or 'blot'; the soil of the township

---

7   Gelling and Foxall, *PN Salop.* I, 303, 160, 169, 273–4; Gelling, *PN Salop.* V, 239, 246, 252; Gelling, *West Midlands*, 5–6.

(apart from the river floodplain), was 'generally mould or mother earth, of a dark brown colour and pretty dry',[8] hence it may refer to the distinctively dark colour of the terrain.

Although not elevated relative to its hinterland, at 262–79 ft (80–5 m.) above sea level the town centre rises above its immediate vicinity, controlling the river crossing.[9] To the south-west of the town, prior to drainage and reclamation, lay Wem Pool, around 200 a. (81 ha.) of marshland fed by Wem Brook.[10]

Communications

Roads

An east–west route traverses the township on the higher ground north of the Roden, its course preserved in Soulton Road, Aston Street, High Street and Ellesmere Road. It probably pre-dates the town since construction of the castle appears to have altered its alignment, creating the bend in High Street west of the church. Wem is otherwise isolated from the major road system. The Roman road from Wroxeter to Chester via Whitchurch passed about 3 miles (4.8 km) to the east,[11] and during the early modern period routes from Shrewsbury to Chester went via Preston Brockhurst and Whitchurch to the east of Wem, or via Burlton and Ellesmere to the west.[12]

In 1710 a county map giving distances and purportedly showing 'great roads' depicted Wem as a market town with roads leading from it to Whitchurch, Hodnet, Shrewsbury and Ellesmere.[13] The north–south route from Whitchurch was turnpiked in 1756, passing through Wem to Harmer Hill where it joined the Shrewsbury–Ellesmere turnpike.[14] The east–west route was turnpiked, first eastwards, in 1769, as the Wem–Sandy Lane turnpike, and westwards in 1771, from Wem via Ellesmere to Bron-y-garth (Denbs.).[15]

Wem Highway District was formed in 1862.[16] Wem parish elected three waywardens annually, one each for Wem, Tilley and Wolverley.[17] By this time turnpike trusts were being wound up,[18] and proceeds from the remaining tolls and the sale of gatehouses in Wem parish were used to pave the town's footpaths with 'chequered bricks'.[19] Shropshire Constabulary in 1881 judged the main road from Wem to Shrewsbury 'fair'.[20] In 1888

---

8   Garbet, 14; E. Crompton and D.A. Osmond, *The Soils of the Wem District: Soil Survey of England and Wales, Wem, Sheet 138* (1954); C.P. Burnham and D. Mackney, 'Soils of Shropshire', *Field Studies* 2 (1975), 83–114.
9   Garbet, 15.
10 Below, Economic History.
11 I.D. Margary, *Roman Roads in Britain*, 3rd edn (London, 1973), 296–7, plate 12.
12 J. Ogilby, Scroll 1 plate 98, Scrolls 3 and 4 plate 57 (London, 1675).
13 B. Wood, *A New Map of Shropshire* (1710).
14 Harmer Hill to Whitchurch Turnpike Act, 29 Geo. II, c.23 (d).
15 Wem to Bron-y-Garth Turnpike Act, 11 Geo. III, c.95; *cf. Chester Chron.*, 2 Sept. 1796.
16 SA, QA/4/1/13/11/1–4; QA/4/2/2/2; QA/4/6/4; SA, P267/N/3/13; P295/C/1/2, Oct. 1862, Dec. 1862; SA, HB 13/D/1.
17 SA, P295/C/1/2, Mar. 1867 and passim.
18 SA, QA4/4/1/1.
19 SA, P295/C/1/2, Oct. 1870.
20 SA, QA/4/5/1/6.

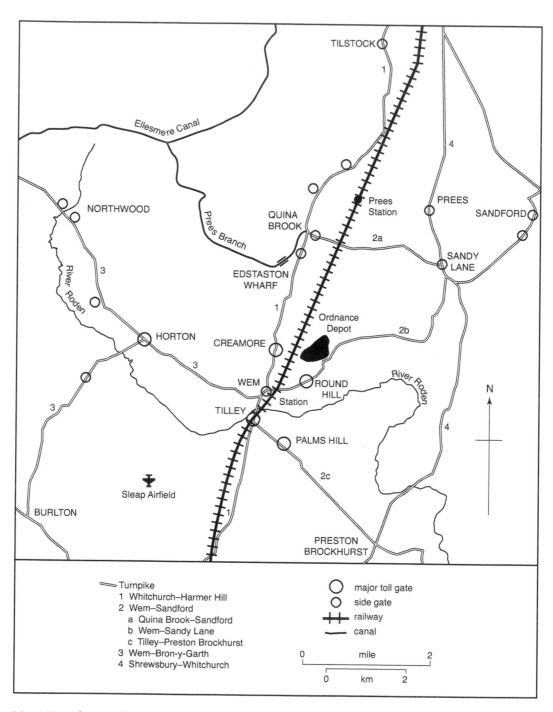

Map 2 *Turnpikes, canals and railways in Wem parish.*

Shropshire County Council (SCC) took over responsibility for main roads and bridges, and Wem parish council, from 1900 Wem UDC, became responsible for other highways in and around the town following the Local Government Act 1894.

Bridges

A bridge over the Roden was an element of the medieval planned town, while a smaller bridge at the western edge of the town crossed Wem Brook.[21] The Roden bridge was repaired at the lord's expense in 1409.[22] In 1631 a single-arched bridge crossed the northern channel (Back Brook) with a causeway crossing the mill dam.[23] In 1795 Quarter Sessions ordered that a new bridge should be erected and the road widened. Designed by Thomas Telford, the county surveyor, it was built by John Simpson of Shrewsbury in 1808 at a cost of £737 10s.[24] The bridge was 20 ft wide, with a span of 24 ft and a rise of 6 ft, having a single segmental arch of stone voussoirs with raised keystone, slightly splayed parapets, and square end piers with pyramidal capstones.[25] In 1941 the mill pond was filled in and the river diverted to the south of the mill, crossed by the present

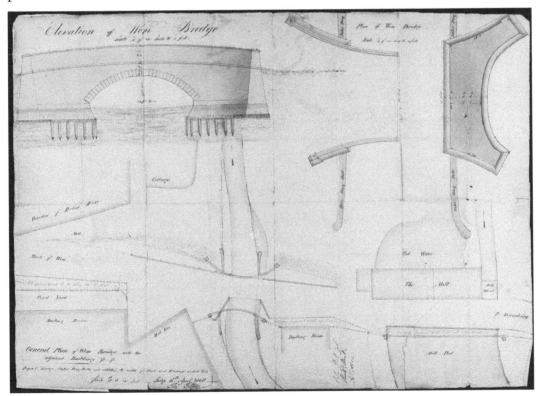

Figure 2 *Plan for new Wem bridge by Thomas Telford as county surveyor, showing Wem mill, 1808.*

21 Garbet, 245; labelled 'Bridge' on SA, 800 bdl 138.1.
22 ACA, MS W13.
23 Arundel map.
24 SA, DP199/2; *ODNB*, s.v. Telford, Thomas (1757–1834) (accessed 4 Mar. 2019).
25 SA, PH/W/8/5/2; SA, DP199/2.

causeway-style bridge with brick parapets. The causeway built in 1808 was then left on dry land, with the stone parapet on its upstream side intact.

Canal

The canal network came nearest to Wem via a branch of the Ellesmere canal terminating at Quina Brook,[26] with canal wharves at Edstaston and Quina Brook by 1806.[27] A substantial amount of Shrewsbury's commercial traffic thereafter passed through Wem: canal carriage from Edstaston was advertised by a Shrewsbury wharfinger in 1822, and by 1835 the canal wharf was served by two Shrewsbury road carriers operating daily;[28] one Shrewsbury carrier met 'the Fly Boats of Swanwick & Co.' from Liverpool and Manchester.[29] Wem's canal heyday ended in 1836 when the Shrewsbury canal was connected to the Shropshire Union canal at Norbury Junction (Staffs.), soon followed by the first railway services.[30]

Railway

From 1837 passengers and goods from Wem could gain access to the national railway network at Whitmore (Staffs.) on the Grand Junction Railway route from Birmingham to Warrington.[31] By 1849 there was a daily horse omnibus from Wem to Baschurch station on the new Shrewsbury–Chester line.[32] A railway line from Shrewsbury to Crewe via Wem opened in 1858[33] with a station about 500 m. east of Wem town centre, near the junction of Aston and Soulton roads, whose layout was altered to allow a single level crossing.[34] Station buildings, a goods depot and sidings were provided, along with a crane, wagon turntable and cattle pens.[35] The line was doubled in 1862.[36] In 1942/3 a short spur was constructed to the US Army ordnance depot at Aston Park.[37]

Initially four or five trains stopped at Wem daily, increasing to about eight by 1888. There was a further increase to ten or 11 per day following the introduction of diesel trains c.1960.[38] Proposed closure of the station in 1964 was resisted locally and the threat

26   R. Dean, 'The metamorphosis of the Ellesmere Canal', *Jnl of the Railway and Canal Hist. Soc.*, 28 (1984–6), 228–47; R.K. Morriss, *Canals of Shropshire* (Shrewsbury, 1991), 41.
27   B. Trinder, *The Industrial Archaeology of Shropshire*, 2nd edn (Logaston, 2016), 182–3.
28   SA, 6001/5042–6; *Pigot's Dir.* (1822, 1835).
29   *Pigot's Dir.* (1835).
30   *Pigot's Dir.* (1835); A. Jowett, *Railway Atlas of Great Britain & Ireland from Pre-Grouping to the Present Day* (Wellingborough, 1989), 57.
31   *Pigot's Dir.* (1842).
32   *Pigot's Dir.* (1849).
33   TNA, RAIL 410/814–16; R.K. Morriss, *Railways of Shropshire: A Brief History* (Shrewsbury, 1991), 27; R.K. Morriss, *Rail Centres: Shrewsbury* (London, 1986), 8–9.
34   B. Yate, *The Shrewsbury to Crewe Line: A Detailed History* (Nottingham, 2014); *Shrews. Chron.*, 26 Mar. 1858, 4; Woodward, 91.
35   Yate, *Shrewsbury to Crewe Line*.
36   Morriss, *Rail Centres: Shrewsbury*, 14–15.
37   M. Stratton and B. Trinder, *Twentieth-Century Industrial Archaeology* (Abingdon, 2000), 111.
38   Yate, *Shrewsbury to Crewe Line*.

Figure 3 *Wem station in 1963, showing the signal box at the level crossing.*

withdrawn,[39] but the station buildings were subsequently demolished and replaced by simple shelters and a ticket machine. The signal box was demolished in 2015.[40] In 2019 there were about 14 trains daily, a mixture of stopping and semi-fast services between Manchester and South Wales.[41]

Post, Carriers and Buses

The 17th-century post towns north of Shrewsbury were Ellesmere and Whitchurch,[42] but Wem was probably too close to Shrewsbury to be a staging post and was bypassed by the main routes to Chester. After the Post Office Act 1711, several Wem men gave their occupation as 'postman' or 'post': Robert Evans was 'inholder & postman' in 1735;[43] Henry Holbrooke, a 'post' by 1753, was licensed to carry letters between Wem and Shrewsbury in 1755;[44] William Deakin was postmaster *c.*1795 when post arrived

39   *Birmingham Daily Post*, 4 Sept., 8 Dec. 1964.
40   *Shropshire Star*, 10 Aug. 2015
41   Transport for Wales timetable (Nov. 2018).
42   R. Blome, *Britannia* (London, 1673), 15.
43   Wem Parish Registers: Charles Puliston (d. 1723), John Peacock (fl. 1727), Thomas Jones (fl. 1739, d. 1747).
44   Wem Parish Registers, baptisms 1753; SA, QS/1/3, f. 253r.

'from London' six days a week.[45] In 1822 a horse-post still passed through Wem twice daily, between Shrewsbury and Whitchurch,[46] whilst in 1829 a daily 'Post-office Car' service was established from Chester to Wem.[47] Service by mail carts continued into the 20th century, and a postal service by rail began apparently as late as 1880.[48] The post office was located at various High Street premises until 1908 when a new post office was built at 25 High Street. Designed by F.H. Shayler and stylistically 'a match for the Town Hall', it comprised a ground-floor post office counter and sorting room, a telephone exchange offering a continuous day and night service, and accommodation above for the postmaster.[49] In 1990, when post office services were relocated to the town's supermarket, it was converted to a public house.[50] In 1960 the telephone exchange moved to the redundant cheese hall and in 1974 to a purpose-built telephone exchange on Drawwell Lane.[51] Broadband internet became available from 2004.[52]

By the 1790s there were commercial wagon services from Wem to Manchester and Shrewsbury.[53] A goods wagon left from a Wem inn for Manchester every Tuesday. By 1822 this service had increased to three days a week, but had ceased by 1835, probably due to competition from the canal.[54]

By 1801 Wem was a staging post on the Shrewsbury–Chester coach route.[55] The 1820s saw intense competition between the landlords of Wem's coaching inns: Thomas Griffiths of the White Horse and Sarah and John Drury of the Waggoners and the Castle. In 1824 John Drury become a partner in the *Shropshire Hero* service, horsing the coach for the nine-mile stage between Wem and Whitchurch. After his death, in 1828 Griffiths threatened to put a rival coach on the road unless Sarah would agree to the *Hero* stopping at the White Horse on alternate stages. She refused, fell out with her partners and finally lost the business, leading to an episode – perhaps invented – in which she sent boys to drag the coach from the White Horse to the Waggoners.[56] The *Hero* was still in service in 1840. A new service commenced in 1835, extending the Cheltenham–Shrewsbury route to Liverpool via Wem and served by the *Hibernia*; it seems to have ended by 1842, but while it lasted there were two coaches in each direction calling at Wem daily.[57] By 1842 the growth of the railway network was causing changes to destinations, but the daily service between Shrewsbury and Chester via Wem continued with the introduction of the *Liver* and the *Salopian* coaches.[58] All stage coach services to Wem ceased with the arrival of the railway in Shrewsbury in 1848.

45   *Univ. Brit. Dir.*, 718.
46   *Pigot's Dir.* (1822).
47   *Chester Courant*, 1 Sept. 1829.
48   *Kelly's Dir.* (1909).
49   SA, DA14/700/9, no. 3; *Kelly's Dir.* (1913), 288; Newman and Pevsner, 676; Woodward, 99.
50   Below, Economic History.
51   SA, DA14/154/9; Woodward, 114.
52   Pers. comm. James Elder, Archives Manager, BT Archive, 2 Aug. 2019.
53   *Univ. Brit. Dir.* IV, 718; *Pigot's Dir.* (1822).
54   *Pigot's Dir.* (1822, 1835).
55   cf. *Univ. Brit. Dir.*, IV, 718. *Chester Chron.*, 19 June 1801; *Liverpool Mercury*, 21 Nov. 1817; *Pigot's Dir.* (1822).
56   SA, 1848, box 21, *Jacques v Drury*; box 22, Drury deeds. The cartoon described in Woodward, 51, is no longer in the possession of Wem Conservative Club (pers. comm., Apr. 2017).
57   Woodward, 51.
58   *Pigot's Dir.* (1822, 1835, 1842); *Robson's Dir.* (1840).

Bus services commenced in the early 20th century by both local firms and services from Shrewsbury and Whitchurch. The first was in 1908 (Chesworth of Whitchurch), and from 1916 Salopia Saloon Coaches of Whitchurch ran char-a-banc excursions picking up in Wem.[59] Percy Moss of Wem ran weekly bus services to local towns on market days in 1926 and Grocott of Wem was established in 1930. In 1949 they merged as M&G Motor Services, continuing market-day services and school runs until 1974.[60] From 1925 the Birmingham and Midland Omnibus Co. Ltd ('Midland Red') provided services from Shrewsbury.[61] In 2019 the Arriva Midlands bus service from Shrewsbury to Whitchurch (no. 511) stopped at Wem, with about ten services a day, Monday to Saturday, but no service on Sundays.[62]

Population

Just seven households in Wem township were assessed for the lay subsidy (having goods valued over 10*s.*) in 1327, out of 43 in the whole manor (Table 1).[63] Underlying this rather low figure is the likelihood that the majority of the townspeople lacked the level of wealth enjoyed by several dozen substantial landholders living in the rural townships.

When the poll tax was levied in 1381, 52 men and women were assessed in Wem township out of 187 in the whole manor, but this figure represents a minimum due to the probable high level of evasion.[64] The 1525 lay subsidy names 48 heads of household in the manor, but the low number recorded for Wem township is again suggestive of widespread evasion.[65] The figures for the 1543 lay subsidy are more plausible, and show that at that time just a quarter of the taxpayers of the whole manor were resident in Wem township.[66]

In 1561 there were some 60 burgages plus about 14 'messuages' in the town,[67] indicating around 74 households (Table 2). A diocesan survey in 1563 recorded 219 households in the parish,[68] which , assuming households averaged 4.3 persons, would give a population of 942,[69] rising to 1,416 (not counting children) in 1676.[70] In 1672 there were 110 hearth tax payers in Wem township, of a parish total of 292.[71] The hearth tax assessments give an estimated population of Wem parish of approximately 1,800 people

59   For Salopia Saloon Coaches Ltd, see A. Smith, 'The personal touch creates success', *Commercial Motor*, 10 Feb. 1950, 42–5.

60   N. Mercer, *Independent Buses in Shropshire* (Glossop, 2011).

61   Midland Red, Bus Map (1925), Official Timetable (1936); P. Gray and M. Keeley, *Midland Red: A History of the Company and its Vehicles up to 1940* (Glossop, 1979); Smith, 'The personal touch', 44.

62   bustimes.org.uk/operators/arriva-midlands-north (accessed 4 Mar. 2019).

63   *Shropshire Lay Subsidy Roll, 1327*, 143–5.

64   Fenwick, *Poll Taxes*, 378–9, 392–4.

65   Faraday, *Shropshire Taxes*, Table II and nos. 449–57, 465.

66   Ibid., 31 and nos. 939, 957, 959–65, 986–8.

67   *Survey 1561*, 20–47.

68   BL, Harl. MS 594, f. 160: 197 in the parish of Wem and 22 in the chapelry of Edstaston.

69   S. Watts, 'Some aspects of mortality in three Shropshire parishes in the mid-seventeenth century', *Local Population Studies*, 67 (2001), 11–25, at n. 2.

70   *Compton Census*, 442, 433. cf. Watts, 'Mortality in three Shropshire parishes', 12 ; S. Watts and R. Collingwood (eds), *Shropshire Hearth Tax Exemptions 1662–1674* ([editors], 2018), 12–13.

71   *Shropshire Hearth Tax Roll*, 47–8; below, Social History.

Table 1 *Population figures from medieval and Tudor taxation assessments.*

Township	Numbers of taxpayers assessed			
	1327	1381	1525	1543
Wem	7	52	4	34
Aston	4	34	4	*15*
Coton	4	26	7	17
Edstaston	6	30	8	*12–20*
Horton	5	19	3	8
Lowe and Ditches	5	11	4	8
Newtown	–	–	4	[illegible]
Steel	3	–	3	3
Tilley	4	14	5	12
Wolverley	5	12	6	[illegible]
Total	43	198	48	–

Notes: Missing or uncertain values are marked with a dash or italic.
1327: Lay subsidy levied on households with goods worth over 10*s*.: *Shropshire Lay Subsidy Roll*, 143–5.
1381: Men and women assessed for poll tax, probably 1381: TNA, E 179/242/34, rot. 1d, m. 4d.; Fenwick (ed.), *Poll Taxes*, 374–5, 392–4.
1525: Lay subsidy levied on households with goods worth over 40*s*. or annual income over 20*s*.: TNA, E 179/166/123 rot. 6d.; Faraday (ed.), *Shropshire Taxes*, nos. 401–528.
1543: Lay subsidy levied on households with property worth over 20*s*.: TNA, E 179/166/157 rot. 1 m. 1, E 179/166/167 rot. 1 m. 1; Faraday (ed.), *Shropshire Taxes*, nos. 939–987.

in 1672, suggesting that the population had doubled in 100 years. There were occasional episodes of unusually high mortality but apparently not of plague. Demographic analysis has identified crisis years including 1596, 1622 (both possibly dearth), 1643–4 (the Civil War, when the town was garrisoned), and the late 1720s.[72]

In a census conducted by the curate of Wem in 1800, the population of Wem township was 1,417 and that of the parish was 3,096,[73] close to the figure of 3,087 recorded in the first national census the following year.[74] In 1811 the population of Wem township was 1,395, increasing rapidly to 1,932 in 1841,[75] but in the next decade it decreased by nearly 10 per cent. This pattern matches developments in transportation; Wem prospered from the opening of canal wharves nearby in 1806, and the population decline after 1841 coincided with the loss of this business. Slow but steady population growth resumed after the railway arrived in 1858 (Table 3).

72   Data supplied by the Cambridge Group for the History of Population and Social Structure. Wem was one of the parishes whose population was studied in E.A. Wrigley and R. Schofield, *The Population History of England 1541–1871* (London, 1981). For the high mortality of the 1640s, Watts, 'Mortality in three Shropshire parishes'.
73   Wem Parish Registers, 778–9.
74   *VCH Salop.* II, 228.
75   See Yalden, 'Landownership', 5.

By 1901 the part of Wem township in Wem UD had a population of 2,149. After a boundary change enlarged the urban district, the population in 1951 was 2,409. If population growth since the mid 19th century had been slow, it took off in the post-war years, rising to 3,082 in 1968, an increase of around 25 per cent in less than two decades. The growth was attributed to ease of travel to Shrewsbury, plus the inexpensive cost of housing.[76] A prediction made in 1971 that the population in 1991 would be 4,800 proved accurate; it was 4,882, having doubled in 40 years. The 1971 prediction anticipated consistent growth at the same high levels but growth very soon stalled due to rising fuel prices and the general economic downturn of the mid 1970s.[77] Once population growth returned it was rapid, from 3,988 in 1981 to 5,142 in 2001. The 21st century has seen a slowing of the rate of population growth, reaching 5,435 in 2011.[78]

In the late 20th century almost 30 per cent of the population was aged over 65, reflecting the town's attraction as a place to retire at that time, with dedicated residential accommodation for elderly people in the town. Since the 1990s the figure has reduced to around 25 per cent, and in 2015 Wem had a lower percentage of residents aged 50 to 74 than the county average, but a higher percentage aged 75 and over (around 12 per cent) than the county average (around 10 per cent).[79]

Table 2 *Number of burgages in Wem.*

	1561 survey	*1589 survey*
High St	10	17½
Cripple St	7	6
Noble St	18½	17
New St	18	18
Leek Lane	3	8
Mill St/Parsons St	2½	1½
unlocated	1	
Total	60	68

Sources: Survey 1561, 17–33; TNA, LR 2/225, ff. 32–33.

76   M. Law, *Draft Wem Planning Policy & Advisory Plan* (County Planning Department, Shrewsbury, 1971), paras. 4 and 10.

77   NSDC, *Wem Discussion Paper* [1981]; *North Shropshire Local Plan 1991–2001, part 2: Proposals Maps* (NSDC, 1996), No. 48 'Wem'.

78   Ibid.; Wem Town Plan Steering Group, *Wem Town Plan* (WTC, 2007); WTC, *Shropshire Local Development Framework: Wem & Surrounding Area Place Plan*, version 20, 24 Jan. 2011.

79   *Wem Town Plan* (2007), 2; *Wem & Surrounding Area Place Plan* (2011), sec. 2.2; *North Shropshire Local Plan 1991–2001*, part 2: Proposals maps, Wem; Woodward, 125, 151; Shropshire Council, 'Wem Market Town Profile, Winter 2017/18': http://www.shropshire.gov.uk/media/9454/wem-market-town-profile.pdf (accessed 4 Mar. 2019).

Table 3 *Population of Wem, 1801–2011.*

Census year	Wem township	Wem parish
1801	1417*	3087
1811	1395	3130
1821	1555	3608
1831	1932	3973
1841	1932	4119
1851	1750	3747
1861	1770	3802
1871	1809	3880
1881	1882	3751
1891	1961	3796
	Wem UD	Wem Urban + Wem Rural **
1901	2149	3903
1911	2273	4176
1921	2172	4154
1931	2157	4095
1941	–	–
1951	2409	4320
1961	2606	4369
1971	3411	4984
1981	3988	5178
1991	4882	6057
2001	5142	6598
2011	5435	7094

Notes:
*   *Source:* 1800 survey of Wem parish (Wem Parish Registers).
**   After 1900 figures are no longer available for the whole of Wem parish. For comparison, the populations of Wem UD and Wem rural civil parish are added here to represent the whole ancient parish.

Settlement

Anglo-Saxon Period

Wem may have originated as a Mercian secular administrative centre. Archaeological finds are lacking, but there is evidence in the town's early layout and in the name of nearby Aston (OE Estune: 'east settlement').[80] By 1066 *Weme* consisted of four estates held by four individual free landholders. Urban development seems to have begun soon

80   J. Blair, *Building Anglo-Saxon England* (Princeton, 2018), 145, 147; Gelling and Foxall, *PN Salop.* I, 23.

after the Norman Conquest: before 1066 *Weme* was said to have been worth 27*s*. but the new Norman lord, William Pantulf, 'found it waste', yet by 1086 its value had grown to 40*s*. Edstaston too gained in value, from 7*s*. to 20*s*., although Aston, Coton, Horton, Sleap, Steel and Wolverley had all been worth the same or considerably more in 1066 than in 1086, when their average value was 8*s*. 6*d*., one-fifth that of *Weme*.[81]

Medieval and Early Modern Periods

Wem displays the characteristics of a Norman castle-town,[82] with the castle, protected by watercourses and marshes to the west and south, overlooking a crossing of the Roden. The land sloping to the river was the lord's demesne until the mid 17th century, preserved as open ground known as the Alleys.[83]

The town was planted to the north of the castle, with evidence of ambitious urban planning on a scale that did not fully materialise; the location of a 12th- or 13th-century pottery kiln, within the Norman town boundary, was apparently open space in the 17th century.[84] The curve of Noble Street probably marks the northern boundary of the planned town, whose western limit was Wem Brook, from where the boundary continued south-west of the castle, turned east across the Alleys, and crossed Mill Street just north of the Roden bridge. Completing the circuit in the south-east quadrant was Drawwell Lane, leading north-eastwards to close off two parallel streets running north (Chapel Street and Leek Street); the original boundary probably re-joined the High Street between them.

The Norman town was probably enclosed by an earthwork. The lord's steward incurred expenses for the town's enclosure ('in clausura ville de Wemme') in 1410, after Wem had been 'totally burnt and wasted by the Welsh rebels'.[85] Garbet's claim that Wem 'was demolished to the ground, with its walls and castle' in the reign of Henry VI has been cited as evidence for medieval town walls[86] but the source Garbet named, an annotation to 'Fabyan's Chronicle', has not been identified, and 'Fabyan's Chronicle' does not mention Wem.[87]

There were 'bars' at the three entrances to the town. Cripple Street, the name of that part of the High Street running from the castle down to the western bar until the early 18th century, may be 'crypel-geat', a low gate in a town wall,[88] but if that is the correct derivation it might equally refer to a gate at the castle. Two bars were at the points where Noble Street meets the High Street: the western at the grammar school and the eastern 'at the long stone near the pinfold'.[89] The southern bar was at the junction of Mill Street and

81 *Domesday*, 703–4.

82 K.D. Lilley, 'The Norman Conquest and its influences on urban landscapes', in D.M. Hadley and C. Dyer (eds), *The Archaeology of the 11th Century: Continuities and Transformations* (Abingdon, 2017), ch. 3.

83 D. Sylvester, *The Rural Landscape of the Welsh Borderland: A Study in Historical Geography* (London, 1969), 301–3; N.J.G. Pounds, *The Medieval Castle in England and Wales: A Social and Political History* (Cambridge, 1990), 224–31; O. Creighton, *Castles and Landscapes: Power, Community and Fortification in Medieval England* (London, 2005), 126–7; Garbet, 250–1; SA, D3651/B/151/9/1–5.

84 HER 31608, incl. H.R. Hannaford, 'An archaeological evaluation at Market Street, Wem, Shropshire', Shropshire County Council Archaeology Service, Report no. 87 (1996).

88 Gelling, *PN Salop*. V, 258; *Survey 1561*, 7–8, 26, 30, 32; Garbet, 236–7, 240, 245.

89 For 'the long stone', see Garbet, 201. Its position is marked on the 1631 Arundel map and the 'Longueville' map, SA, 800, bdl 138.1. For the manorial pinfold, *Survey 1561*, 22.

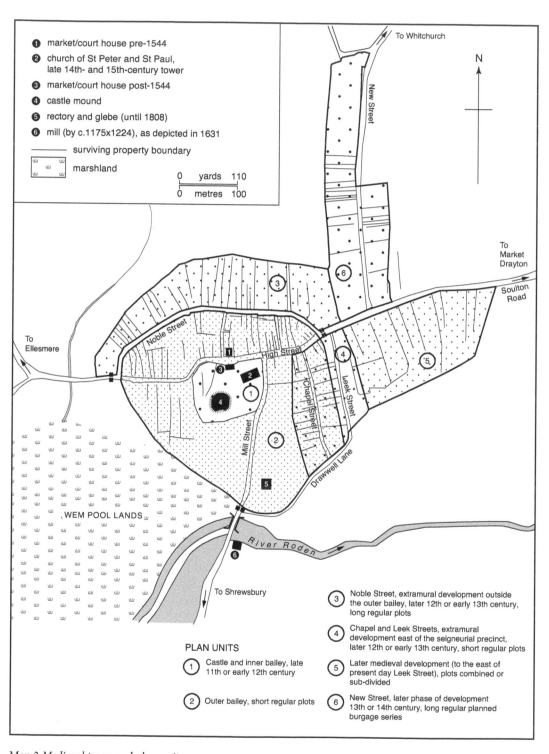

Map 3 *Medieval town and plan units.*

Drawwell Lane.[90] In 1514 four men were employed 'keeping the Barrs' at fairs or market days.[91]

Several plan units are distinguishable which give an indication of the sequential development of the medieval town.[92] The first would have been a seigneurial precinct with a motte-and-bailey castle,[93] constructed by *c*.1175 x 1224, when tenants of Hugh Pantulf, lord of Wem, were obliged to render aid (*auxiliantur*) at his *castellum*,[94] and called 'castr[um] de Wemme' in 1233.[95] The motte (or castle mound) survives and aerial photography shows the form of the bailey.[96] The roughly circular motte is located at the rear of 67 High Street and is now approximately 3 m. in height and 56 m. in diameter. In the first half of the 18th century it was 'about eight yards high', presumably before one recent owner had 'sunk the hill six feet' and the next had reduced it further in height and 'carried off several loads of stone'.[97] In the 19th century the motte's southern flank was removed and a curving brick and sandstone retaining wall constructed around its west and south sides. The motte was surrounded by a ditch, described *c*.1750 as 'a foss eight yards broad'. To the south-east it formed the rear boundary of adjacent burgages, and a section remains on the west side.[98] A sketch map by Garbet shows the ditch being supplied with water from a canal crossing the High Street.[99] The High Street in front of the castle formed the town's market place:[100] in 1561 Thomas Pontesbury had a burgage 'in High Street near the market place'.[101]

The rest of the planned town would have been divided into large blocks within which burgage plots were laid out. There is some evidence of plots measuring 24 yd (72 ft) wide based on a statutory perch of 16 ft. They are found within the medieval core and along the north side of Noble Street, examples including 11–15 Chapel Street, the site of Wem Senior Club in Chapel Street, the former Buck's Head inn in Mill Street, 2–4 Noble Street, 46–58 Noble Street and the plot east of the White Lion inn in Aston Street. The infilling of the enclosed area and the laying out of plots – for example, the development of built-up frontages and burgage plots along the adjoining streets – probably took place in the later 12th and early 13th century. The presence of burgage plots on the south side of Noble Street which are not aligned with those on the north side of the street suggests that the former were laid out at a later date. The area between High Street and Noble Street may have originally been a large market place, with the castle and church on its south

90 Garbet, 230–1. The absence of a north gate bears out the remarks below about the lack of a northern route in the early phases of the town's development. For Noble Street and Mill Street, *Survey 1561*, 22–4.
91 ACA, MS W14.
92 Lilley, 'Norman Conquest'.
93 E.g. *Survey 1561*, 24–5.
94 *Survey 1561*, 160.
95 *Excerpta è Rotulis Finium*, 237.
96 SA, PH/W/8/1/2.
97 HER 01135; NHLE, no. 1020287, Wem Castle (accessed 4 Mar. 2019); Garbet, 250.
98 HER 01135, see Central Marches Historic Towns Survey (CMHTS) record; Garbet, 250: *Survey 1561*, 25, 27.
99 SA, 9043, File W, 1. For the history of the castle site, below, Landownership.
100 Arundel map, sheet 5.
101 Garbet, 234–5; *Survey 1561*, 32–3. According to Garbet's calculations from the 1561 survey, Pontesbury's burgage was on the western corner of the (modern) Market Street junction: SA, 9043, File W, 9ab. For 'Market Street' as part of the High Street, e.g., Bagshaw, 325.

side, in which case Noble Street formed the northern edge of the market place and the
burgages north of Noble Street were the original foundation burgages. If so, this would be
further evidence of (over)ambitious town plantation.

Later phases of settlement can be distinguished; for example, the burgage plots along
Chapel Street (formerly 'Lik Lane')[102] and Leek Street, forming a plan unit to the east of
the seigneurial precinct, appear to be a single later phase of development, overlaying the
putative seigneurial enclosure, and so must date from a period when the boundary –
whether defended or not – was no longer maintained.

New Street was laid out beyond the eastern bar probably in a still later phase of
development in the 13th or early 14th century.[103] It is a single street running north, lined
with plots on both sides, and may have been designed as a suburb to enhance the north–
south route through the town. These large burgage plots, 13 to each side (26 in total),[104]
were 17–20 yd wide and 50–60 yd long, some held as multiple units. They are noticeably
shorter than the later Georgian plots.[105] Some properties running north as far as no. 49
may correspond with Garbet's 17–20 yd pattern, the plots having been retained even if
the buildings were demolished and rebuilt.

By the mid 16th century a number of messuages with associated land lay beyond
the bars. To the west, Lacons Hall, perhaps the 'mansion' of Rowland Lacon in 1589,
fronted High Street with farmland extending southwards to Wem Pool and the Alleys.[106]
An expansive suburb appears to have been laid out east of the town along Aston Street,
where a pattern of 14 ft units, equivalent to a customary perch, is laid over the 16½ ft
plot pattern, suggesting the settlement may have been redeveloped during the medieval
period.[107] It seems likely that these messuages can be equated with eight cottagers in
1436 and the eight copyholders 'without the bar' noted in 1589.[108] If these had once been
holdings of similar size, by the mid 16th century any regularity had been lost and in 1589
their landholdings in the open fields totalled 14½ nooks.[109] This suburb was sufficiently
inhabited to be enclosed within the Civil War defences in 1642.[110]

At its fullest medieval extent, the town had around 80 burgage plots:[111] 70 were
recorded in 1436, and about 60 in 1561, to which could be added a few more omitted
from the survey.[112] Most paid 1s. rent, and a valuation of the manor in 1589 included 80s.
in rents received from tenements, apparently burgages, obscurely abbreviated as 'nativ'
burgag'.[113] In 1589 there were 68 burgages in total, suggesting some had been combined

102 ACA, W14, last folio; *Survey 1561*, 28–32.
103 'Le Newstrete', 'in novo vico de Weme', *Survey 1561*, 20–3.
104 Ibid.
105 Ibid.; SA, 9043, File W, 1 and 8.
106 TNA, LR 2/225. Below, Landownership.
107 *Survey 1561*, 34–47.
108 TNA, C 139/76/34; *Cal. Inq. p.m.* XXIV, no. 495; TNA, LR 2/225.
109 TNA, LR 2/225. For nooks, see Glossary.
110 Garbet, 217, '… ran along the side of Sandland's yard …'; M. Charles, 'Wem, Aston Street', *West Midlands Archaeology* 50 (2007), 42–4.
111 Garbet, 146.
112 TNA, C 139/76/34, *Cal. Inq. p.m.* XXIV, no. 495; *Survey 1561*, 20–47.
113 *Survey 1561*, 17–33; Garbet, 146. Certain tenures ('Burgag ad voluntatem' and 'Burgag pro cop'') listed in the valor remain unexplained: TNA, SC 12/26/56.

(Table 2).[114] Some burgages paid lower rents, perhaps because they were not full size. For instance, in 1561 William Holbrooke paid 6*d.* for a burgage plot squeezed in between the lord's court house on the east and the former castle ditch on the west.[115] That several burgage plots were not built upon in 1561 suggests that the town remained too large for its population.[116]

The Civil War

The Parliamentarian occupation of 1642–5 left a legacy on the townscape, although the circuit of a 'Civil War rampart' and its four gates was marked by the Ordnance Survey with greater confidence than is warranted by the archaeological evidence.[117] Following Sir William Brereton's successful defence of Nantwich (Ches.) in 1643, a coalition of Parliamentary forces, including those from Cheshire led by Brereton himself, together with units recruited mainly in the Home Counties commanded by Parliament's general for North Wales, Sir Thomas Myddelton, allied to the Shropshire Parliamentarians Colonel Thomas Mytton and his captains Humphrey Mackworth, Andrew Lloyd and Thomas Hunt, entered Shropshire and occupied Wem in late August or early September.[118] Defences comprising a ditch, bank and palisade were hastily constructed around the town and crude wooden gates erected.[119] About 70 years later it was recalled that '[a]ll houses and buildings without the wall were burnt, to prevent their giving shelter to the enemy'. In particular, 'all the burgages were destroyed that lay north of Whitchurch gate, being thirteen or fourteen at least'.[120] Some 13 or 14 burgages were thus destroyed, probably having long-term effects on the development of New Street by opening the way for new building independent of the old burgage boundaries. The fortifications were further strengthened in the spring of 1645 under the direction of the mercenary military engineer Wilhelm Reinking.[121] An eyewitness to the first hastily constructed defences described a ditch 'little bigger than such as husbandmen enclose their ground with', whereas the surviving portion of the ditch in the 18th century was 'four yards wide and of a proportionable depth'.[122] Archaeological investigation has identified a contemporary ditch to the south-east of the town, 8.7 m. wide with a maximum depth of 1.4 m., suggesting that it was a substantial and broad earthwork feature.[123]

---

114 TNA, LR 2/225.
115 *Survey 1561*, 25, see also ibid., 27 (burgage of Richard Braban).
116 *Survey 1561*, e.g., 31.
117 OS Map 6", Salop. sheet XXI.NE and XIV.SE (1884 edn); HER 01637.
118 J. Worton, '"A crow's nest": The significance of Wem during the Civil War 1642–1646', *Salopian Recorder*, 86 (2016), 6–8; J. Worton, *To Settle the Crown: Waging Civil War in Shropshire, 1642–1648* (Solihull, 2016), 75, 118, 248.
119 *Reliquiae Baxterianae: Or Mr. Richard Baxter's Narrative of the Most Memorable Passages of His Life and Times* (London, 1696), 45; Garbet, 217–18; Worton, *To Settle the Crown*, 205, 218–19.
120 Garbet, 218, 243.
121 Worton, *To Settle the Crown*, 198, 219, 230.
122 Garbet, 217–18.
123 Garbet, 218; HER 01637, citing excavation report: 'Marches Archaeology. 1998. Land at Wem, Shropshire: a report on an evaluation excavation'. Marches Archaeology Series, 049; Charles, 'Wem, Aston Street'.

The Great Fire of Wem

The townscape of Wem owes much to the great fire of 1677, one of several that devastated towns in the region in this period.[124] It destroyed around 140 dwelling houses as well as the timber market house and almshouses on Mill Street, and badly damaged the medieval church,[125] although a pair of cottages in the path of the flames, now 40 and 42 Noble Street, escaped destruction.

Garbet wrote a detailed account of the fire, apparently based on eyewitness testimony and the 'brief' issued in aid of those who had suffered loss.[126] The flames ran west from Chapel Street along the High Street as far as the grammar school. The headmaster's house was destroyed but the schoolhouse was spared. Southwards the fire burned about halfway down Chapel Street and down the west side of Mill Street to the barns of the (then) rectory. A change in wind direction to the south-west meant that the fire was carried along Noble Street, on whose north side it was brought under control at Drawwell House.[127] The fire extended along the south side of Noble Street and as far on the High Street.[128]

Although there seems to have been only a single fatality – Richard Sherratt died when the market house collapsed on him – the fire devastated Wem's urban core: on three adjoining plots on the north side of High Street, belonging to Thomas Jebb and John Shenton, both mercers, and Hugh Bate, cordwainer, only Shenton's house had been rebuilt, a year later.[129] The town made do with a temporary market house until 1702, and the headmaster of the grammar school, with his family, had to move in to the upper storey of the schoolhouse.[130]

18th Century to the Present

Wem retained its medieval urban form well into the 19th century. Garbet's descriptions and sketch maps provide unique insight into the town's urban development from the mid 16th to the mid 18th century.[131] Beyond the bars, the township had a rural aspect. The Aston Street suburb contracted: in the early 18th century there were 'some good houses' with 'considerable' farms east of the bar but further east, beyond New Street, 'the private houses are mean and ruinous'.[132] Fields and gardens occupied the abandoned spaces; Mrs

---

124 E.L. Jones, S. Porter and M. Turner, *A Gazetteer of English Urban Fire Disasters, 1500–1900* (Norwich, 1984).

125 Garbet, 224–5, 234–5.

126 Garbet's account of the fire was published in a pamphlet: *An account of the dreadful fire of Wem, in Salop, by which nearly the whole town was consumed on the third of March, 1677; by the Rev. Samuel Garbet. With an interesting address to the inhabitants by the Rev. Andrew Parsons, M.A. their minister of the Established Church* (Shrewsbury and Wem, 1802), an extract from his *History of Wem* (Garbet, 223–6) which was then unpublished. The brief is SA, 484/240.

127 Garbet, *Account of the Dreadful Fire*, 6; Garbet, 224–5, 239; HER 16817.

128 Garbet, 226, 213.

129 SA, 741/27, deed of 1 Feb. 1678.

130 Garbet, 235, 200.

131 SA, 9043, File W, 1, 9ab; Jones, *Mr Garbet*, 53.

132 Garbet, 234.

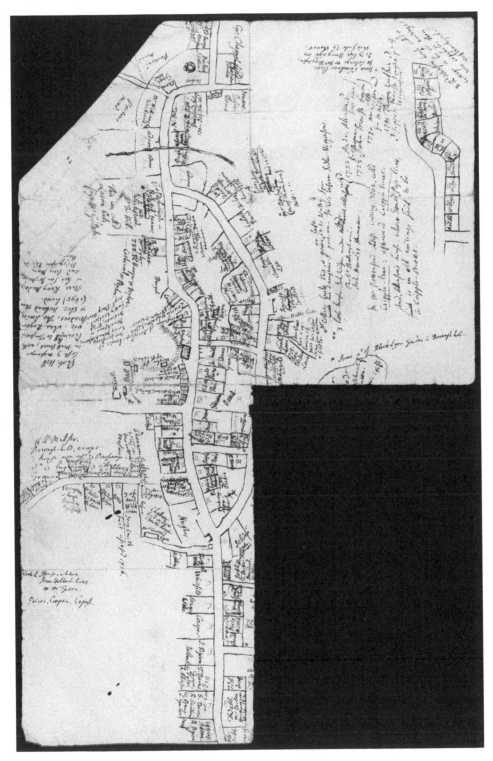

Figure 4 *Sketch map of Wem by Samuel Garbet, one of several among his papers, showing streets, property boundaries and the names of successive owners. It is orientated with North to the right.*

Drury owned a garden on the south side of Aston Street in 1805 and 1834, adjacent to one of her fields.[133]

Since *c.*1800 Wem has developed eastwards away from the medieval core; an important element being the replacement of the lord's market/court house (now 'the old town hall') with the current town hall further east along the High Street. The shift originated with new transport and trading activities connected with the turnpike roads and the canal, to the north-east, while the arrival of the railway at the eastern limit of the township also attracted both residents and industry in that direction.[134] As a consequence the western end of the town declined. Around 1800 the western continuation of the High Street – Cripple Street and the Horse Market – was a busy place, with the grammar school, the parish poorhouse, the fire engine house and lock-up, public houses, residential tenements, a chapel and tan yards, but in the 1830s it became more industrial: a gas works was constructed, the tan yards expanded, and the old parish poorhouse was converted into maltings. The small houses deteriorated and most were demolished, with an early exercise in slum clearance in 1844.[135] In 1857 the old lock-up was condemned as being in 'a very isolated situation in the very worst part of town' and soon afterwards it was relocated to Chapel Street.[136] These and other changes towards the end of the 19th century, notably the closure of the tan yards on Wem Brook, made the area more salubrious, to the point that by 1902 The Grove, set back from the High Street in wooded grounds, became a girls' private school.[137]

As the west end of the town declined, the northern end of New Street developed as a polite suburb of large houses, a major development of the late 1820s known as 'Islington', which attracted the professional classes. Commerce was still largely contained within the area of the medieval town, but new housing was built on greenfield sites further out. In 1866 Shrewsbury Freehold Land and Building Society offered 17 lots of desirable building land close to Wem railway station.[138] New houses were being built on Aston Street in the 1890s.[139] Beyond the level crossing, there were only two houses on Soulton Road in 1901, one being Edward Bygott's residence, 'Forncet'.

In 1890 Wem Rural Sanitary Authority (RSA) took responsibility for street naming and the numbering of houses, applying new street name plates throughout the town.[140] The first new street in the town was Barnard Street, developed in 1895–6 by a local builder, Thomas Jervis,[141] on land, formerly the Alleys, which had been sold by the Walford estate in 1865. Around the same time, Station Road was developed by C.H. Kynaston north of his rail-side maltings.[142] The pair of cottages nearest to the former maltings site has a date-stone 1895, and 25 houses had been built by 1901. Edward Bygott

133 SA, 8611/3/1; SA, 167/47; SA, 800, bdl 138, 1.
134 Below, Economic History.
135 Woodward, 55–6; *Eddowes's Jnl*, 12 July 1843.
136 *Shrews. Chron.*, 23 Oct. 1857, 6. Below, Local Government.
137 Below, Social History.
138 *Shrews. Chron.*, 13 Apr. 1866.
139 SA, DA27/994/1/2, May 1891, June 1892; DA27/994/1/3, Nov. 1892, Jan., Apr. 1893, July, Aug., Sept. 1894.
140 SA, DA27/994/1/2, Jan. 1890.
141 SA, DA27/994/1/3, Aug. 1895; *Wellington Jnl*, 2 May 1896, 7; 14 May 1898, 4; 1 July 1899, 8.
142 *Wellington Jnl*, 22 Oct. 1898, 2.

purchased land there from Kynaston in 1904 to build six more houses, a contemporary describing the area as 'Klondike', apparently in reference to the profits to be made.[143] Summerfield Road, leaving the Whitchurch Road near the Hawkestone Arms, was also a dead-end until it was connected to Station Road, which was formally laid out and adopted by Wem UDC in 1907.[144] After the First World War, the northern end of the road was built up and by 1926 there were houses along most of the length of the new Station Road: the later ones, towards Summerfield Road, include stylish private houses by local builders, including Thomas Jervis and F. & E. Tommy.[145]

House building for most of the 20th century took the form of municipal housing schemes. Wem UDC initially approved the immediate construction of 26 houses in Shrubbery Gardens in 1919, with a total of 56 planned.[146] A small estate of 28 houses was built in 1935 at the end of Barnard Street, on land formerly part of the grounds of The Grove which had been acquired by the county council. In 1936 a survey under the 1935 Housing Act found that out of 477 houses surveyed 13 (2.7 per cent) – five of them cottages on Leek Street – were overcrowded, and seven should be demolished as slum clearance. There was a need for 16 new houses, not including housing for people on the council waiting list.[147] Before the end of the Second World War the council was planning both the Lowe Hill Road and The Grove estates, both designed by Hind and Brown of Stoke-on-Trent (Staffs.); the first houses were completed in 1947 and 1950, respectively.[148] When completed, The Grove estate had 42 houses and 24 flats (in Grove Court) and the Barnard Street estate (1953) had 50 houses. Bungalows were added to the Lowe Hill estate in 1966. In 1954, 24 houses were built in Queensway, off Shrubbery Gardens. The Cordwell Park estate was commenced in 1955 and by 1967 consisted of 62 houses and 27 flats. Between 1951 and 1971, 307 houses, bungalows and flats were built in Wem UD, most of them by the council. In 1950 Wem UDC had 130 houses or flats; 312 properties in 1960 and 346 in 1966.[149] In 1955, 55 per cent of the housing stock was council owned, rising to 73 per cent in 1971. Just 31 new private houses were built between 1975 and 1981. One of the few examples of private house building from this period is the Roden Grove estate, on the site of Tilley House (latterly The Grove School). Demand for housing was driven by post-war population growth and by decreasing household sizes, from an average of 3.3 persons per dwelling in 1951 to 2.75 in 1968.[150]

During the Second World War a large ordnance depot was constructed at Aston Park, east of the town, in Wem RD. It was a prototype storage base for the United States Army, constructed in 1942–3, occupying 180 a. (72 ha.), including a camp for 1,250

143 *Wellington Jnl*, 21 July 1906, 12. Below, Local Government.
144 OS Map 25" Salop. sheet XIV.15 (1901 edn); SA, DA14/100/3, 36–7, 62. See also E.W. Bowcock, 'Wem of the past', *Border Counties Advertizer*, 20 Feb. 1935.
145 OS Map 25" Salop. sheet XIV.15 (1926 edn).
146 SA, DA14/100/5, 892, 943, 945, 949.
147 SA, DA14/135/4.
148 Woodward, 98; SA, DA14/100/8, 109, 207, 387–8, 422, 515, 577, 583, 751, 857, 950.
149 *Municipal Yearbook 1950*, 1375; *Municipal Yearbook 1960*, 1340; *Municipal Yearbook 1966*.
150 Law, *Draft Wem Planning Policy & Advisory Plan* (1971), par. 10; NSCD, *Wem Discussion Paper* [1981], 3; Woodward, 114; *The Shropshire Magazine*, Oct. 1958, 17–21.

personnel.[151] Part of the site was also a prisoner of war camp, in use until 1948.[152] After the war, the site became an outstation of the Royal Army Ordnance Corps' Donnington Central Ordnance Depot.[153] Permanent married quarters were built off Soulton Road around 1947.[154] When the depot closed in 1966, it was intended that the 23 a. nearest the town should become a storage/light industrial area, the remainder returned to agriculture.[155] However, the eastern part was developed as a holiday park and the western part as an industrial area.[156]

In 1971 it was recommended that in general there should be no further development east of the railway, due to the lack of capacity of the railway level crossing.[157] The industrial use planned for the redundant ordnance depot would proceed, but heavy goods vehicles were (and still are) encouraged by signage to approach it from the B5065 road at Prees Green. This policy has preserved the area east of the railway as a residential suburb in a rural setting. Instead, farmland north of the town was built over.[158]

In 1981 it was proposed that the majority of new housing in North Shropshire District was to be in the market towns of Ellesmere, Market Drayton, Wem and Whitchurch, which were to provide land for a total of 1,550 to 1,800 new houses. NSDC immediately recommended that land should be made available for 300 dwellings in Wem by 1991, but also recommended that the character of the town centre be protected by designation as a conservation area.[159] In contrast with the period prior to 1980, house building was almost entirely by private developers, with 122 houses built in 1987/8, and a total of 382 houses between 1985 and 1990. The first large-scale private housing development was to the north of the town, the Wemsbrook estate, with access from the new Pyms Road.[160] This was followed by house building on land between Station Road, Whitchurch Road and the railway. Concern having been expressed at rapid expansion in recent years, the North Shropshire Local Plan 1991–2001 permitted just 250 more houses, including the Foxleigh development (60 houses); the former Isherwood's timber yard near the station (up to 65 houses); Fothergill Way (20 houses); and Love Lane (ten houses).[161] Although these large-scale extensions of the suburban area are unlikely to be repeated in the near future, there remains pressure to identify sites for new housing.

---

151 Law, *Draft Wem Planning Policy & Advisory Plan* (1971), par. 22; Stratton and Trinder, *Twentieth-Century Industrial Archaeology*, 111.
152 R.J.C. Thomas, *Twentieth-Century Military Recording Project. Prisoner of War Camps (1939–1948), Project Report*, English Heritage (Swindon, 2003), 49.
153 shropshirehistory.com/military/camps.htm (accessed 4 Mar. 2019); A.H. Fernyhough, *History of the Royal Army Ordnance Corps 1920–1945* (London, n.d. ?1967), 416.
154 SA, DA14/700/7, Plan no. 467 (15 May 1947).
155 SA, SCC1/K/7 TP70; Law, *Draft Wem Planning Policy & Advisory Plan* (1971), par. 22.
156 Woodward, 112; *Shropshire Star*, 28 Jan. 1985, 5.
157 Law, *Draft Wem Planning Policy & Advisory Plan* (1971), par. 14.
158 Ibid., par. 30.
159 NSDC, *Wem Discussion Paper* ([1981]), sec. 2.3.
160 Woodward, 114–15, 125–6.
161 *North Shropshire Local Plan 1991–2001*, part 2: Proposals maps, Wem.

The Built Character

With a large number of surviving historic buildings, on first impression Wem is largely a late 18th- and 19th-century town,[162] but exposed 16th- and 17th-century timber framing on some houses reveals much earlier buildings behind brick façades. There are also substantial 20th-century buildings, but these are less apparent: the modern shopping precinct, for example, emerges onto the High Street only at Talbot House. The importance of preserving the quality of this built environment was recognised by the creation of Wem Conservation Area in 1990, incorporating the medieval extent of the town, New Street and Aston Street.[163] The parish church, which dominates the entrance to the High Street, is conspicuously too large for its site, having originated, apparently, as a chapel within the castle precinct.[164] It is less evident that the open aspect of the church is a modern feature; in past centuries buildings clustered between the church and street, and the church yard was much more restricted in size.

Medieval and Early Modern Periods

Timber cruck construction is evidenced in Shropshire from the late 13th to the mid 16th centuries; none is recorded in Wem town, although one may survive in the White Horse hotel (see below).[165] No tree-ring dating has so far been undertaken in Wem, but two box-framed houses in the nearby hamlet of Tilley have been dated 1579–80 and 1604 19.[166] West of the town is The Ditches, a timber framed house with a date of 1612 on the door latch.[167] Wem took part in the major rebuilding that occurred across England in the late 16th and early 17th centuries, a process presumably accelerated in Wem by the great fire of 1677. Cruck buildings were often replaced by box-framed buildings, as, for example, 76 and 81 High Street.[168] Other examples of box-framed houses of this date are found across the town centre. The Old Hall (so named from c.1880) in New Street is an early 17th-century timber-framed gentry house. The symmetrical two-storey house has a central three-storey gabled porch, close-studded and jettied, with ogee motifs on the sides and a carved frieze on the jetty bressumer, and a mosaic floor made of knuckle bones. The chimneys with circular shafts may be contemporary with the early 19th-century south cross-wing.[169] The property was mortgaged in 1740 as a capital messuage with maltkiln, stables, barn and orchard.[170] Astley House, 4 Noble Street, has a double-

---

162 Newman and Pevsner, 673.

163 Director of Planning Services, *Wem Conservation Area Appraisal* (NSDC, [2003]).

164 Below, Landownership, for the castle chapel.

165 HER 12511; NHLE, no. 1175748, former White Horse Hotel (accessed 4 Mar. 2019).

166 Vernacular Architecture Group, 2000 (updated 2018), Dendrochronology Database: https://archaeologydataservice.ac.uk/archives/view/vag_dendro/ (accessed 4 Mar. 2019).

167 M. Moran, *Vernacular Buildings of Whitchurch Area and Their Occupants* (Logaston, 1999), 219–22; Newman and Pevsner, 677; Woodward, plate 3.

168 Moran, *Vernacular Buildings*, esp. ch. 3 for construction techniques.

169 Newman and Pevsner, 676; Historic England, cards 5115/56–7, photographs of interior and exterior, c.1962: https://historicengland.org.uk/images-books/photos/englands-places/gallery/ (accessed 4 Mar. 2019) and available at SA, PH/W/8/7/15 and 16.

170 SA, 6000/19479–82; SA, 4791/1/1, policy no. 216; SA, 167/47.

Figure 5a *40 Noble Street. Part of the timber framing survived the great fire of 1677.*

pile plan with two gables at each end and a large central stack with clustered diagonal shafts. The building has a large front gable with canopied entrance below but the blocked Tudor-arched doorway to the left is probably the original entrance. The timber-framing of the north gables can be seen in a photograph of *c.*1950, but has since been rendered over. An 18th-century staircase has been recorded inside.[171] The Castle inn, situated prominently on the High Street, is 18th century in appearance, but the right-hand front room has deeply chamfered ceiling beams supported on corbels, which are probably 17th century; the beams rest against an earlier box-framed partition, now open, which bears carpenter's marks. This partition is aligned with the cellar and may mark the former street frontage, which would have been several metres north of the current alignment.[172]

Other 17th-century box-panelled houses which have been demolished include Well House and Well Cottage in Drawwell Lane.[173] The former was of two-and-a-half storeys,

171 Newman and Pevsner, 676; Woodward, plate 5; HER 12529; Garbet, 239.
172 Visit 16 Dec. 2016, Landlord, pers. com.
173 HER 12507, incl. RCHME (Historic England), Field Survey Report, 1962; HER 12287.

Figure 5b *70 High Street. Exposed timbers show the development of the houses prior to being re-faced with brick.*

with a T-shaped plan with the hall in the upright section and parlour and service room in the cross-range; a service range contained a small dairy.[174] The home of James Forgham in 1796, the curtilage was just over 2 a. (0.8 ha.) with 'barns, gardens, folds, crofts, tan house etc.'.[175] Wem Senior Club is on the site of 25–29 Chapel Street, a timber-framed range of *c.*1600 which was partly fronted in brick and raised to two storeys.[176] The Talbot inn, demolished *c.*1970, was a two-storey, box-panelled building, its lobby-entrance suggesting an early to mid 17th-century date.[177] Although an inn by 1805, it was probably originally a dwelling house.[178]

Timber-framed houses continued to be constructed after the great fire in 1677. The house Samuel Garbet had built in New Street in 1717 re-used the timber frame of a house from Edstaston which was at least 40 years old, although Garbet had the box frame filled with brick and the roof tiled.[179] Dial Cottage, 93 High Street, is a timber-framed house with the date 1677 inscribed on one of the two decorative attic dormers.[180] In the early 19th century it became a service building of The Grove estate and was divided into two

174 Ibid.; Mercer, *English Arch. to 1900*, 153; Whitehead, *Wem*, 66–7.
175 SA, MI6508/1A.
176 HER 12500.
177 SA, PH/W/8/6/42.
178 SA, 167/47; SA, 8611/3/15.
179 Jones, *Mr Garbet*, 34–6.
180 Woodward, 57 and fig. 7; Newman and Pevsner, 676; Whitehead, *Wem*, 56.

Figure 6 *Astley House, Noble Street.*

Figure 7 *The Talbot Hotel, Wem, in 1965; on the site of the present Talbot House.*

Figure 8 *Hazlitt House, Noble Street.*

cottages; the '1974' on the other dormer is the date when the property was restored.[181]
A box-panelled house at 2 Market Street, recorded in advance of its demolition, formed
the rear wing of 62 High Street. The two-and-a-half storey, two-and-a-half bay house
had a central entrance and staircase, with hall to right and parlour to left; adjoining the
end of the parlour was a small structure, possibly a dairy or service unit. The house was
dated, on the basis of its ovolo-moulded detail, to the early 17th century, and was clearly
a building of some prestige. An additional bay at the south end has been replaced by the
street range of no. 62; this bay would have fronted the High Street, though not necessarily
on the current alignment.[182] This was probably 'the commodious house' built by Joseph
Smith soon after the great fire in 1677.[183]

Many of the box-panelled houses in Wem were re-fronted or completely encased in
brick in the 18th or early 19th century. Some were also raised in height, evidence for
which is visible in the framing of gable ends, for example, 40 and 42 Noble Street.

Hazlitt House in Noble Street is probably early to mid 18th century. Of brick
construction, now painted, the irregular two-storey four-bay front is lit by casement

181 Woodward, 113.
182 HER 16817; HER 12512, incl. RCHME (Historic England), Field Recording, 1980s; HER 31609,
     incl. Gifford & Partners, 'Archaeological Recording Work at 2 Market Street', 1995; photographs of
     demolition in possession of Tom Edwards.
183 Garbet, 234, 235. Below, Local Government.

windows with leaded panes. To the right of centre is a taller bay with hipped roof and pilaster strips, left of which is the doorway under a canopy. The house was built by George Tyler after his appointment as curate of Wem in 1727. After Tyler's death in 1747, the house was purchased for the manse of the Presbyterian chapel[184] and was occupied by the Revd William Hazlitt from 1787 to 1813; his son William, the essayist and critic, lived there until 1799.[185] The interior is reported to contain 17th-century panelling with a fluted frieze, said to have come from the parish church, and a moulded stone chimney piece.[186]

The White Horse hotel is mainly early 18th century, but may have an encased cruck on the first floor at the north end of the rear wing, and three pairs of upper crucks on the second floor are probably a structural device for supporting the high lateral walls.[187]

Late 18th to Early 19th Century

The townscape of Wem is distinctly Georgian in character, with red-brick buildings under slate roofs with stone dressings, sash windows and Neo-classical detail. Georgian buildings include The Hall/Park House (1784), the old rectory (1808), Thomas Telford's Wem bridge (1808), the mill (c.1818) and the 'Islington' development on New Street (c.1830).

Façades were built across the gaps between buildings to form a consistent, continuous and polite new streetscape. A spirit of improving and beautifying the town in the late Georgian style is seen in the rebuilding of the church and the enhancement of its surroundings. The demolition of three old houses on Mill Street enabled enlargement of the church yard in 1822. The south and north entrances to the church yard were rebuilt in a formal, Classical style.[188] On the north side of the church crowded old houses and shops, which occupied the entire High Street frontage from Mill Street almost to the market house, were demolished in the late 1820s. They were replaced by the Union Buildings (1830, demolished 1943), designed by the London architect Charles Ferdinand Porden, a deliberate exercise in achieving a harmonious neo-classical appearance.[189]

Adjoining the western side of the market house, 67 High Street has an ashlar façade and good neo-classical detail including the forecourt boundary railings. Internally, it has a simple 18th-century staircase with stick balusters and column newels, along with moulded plaster ceiling cornices and original joinery.[190] The Congregational chapel was re-fronted in ashlar in 1835.[191]

184 Garbet, 171–2.
185 *ODNB*, s.v. Hazlitt, William (1737–1820); Hazlitt, William (1778–1830) (accessed 4 Mar. 2019); Woodward, 47–9; SA, PR/2/526: cutting from the *Border Advertizer*, Apr. 1907; 'Wem's house of history', *Shropshire Star*, 13 Aug. 1977, 16–17.
186 HER 12536.
187 HER 12511; NHLE, no. 1175748, former White Horse Hotel; fieldwork 11 Sept. 2016.
188 Below, Social History; Religious History.
189 See Woodward, plate 7. Below, Economic History. A. Brodie, *Directory of British Architects, 1834–1914*: Vol. 2 (L–Z) (London, 2001), 392.
190 HER 12519; Newman and Pevsner, 675.
191 Below, Religious History.

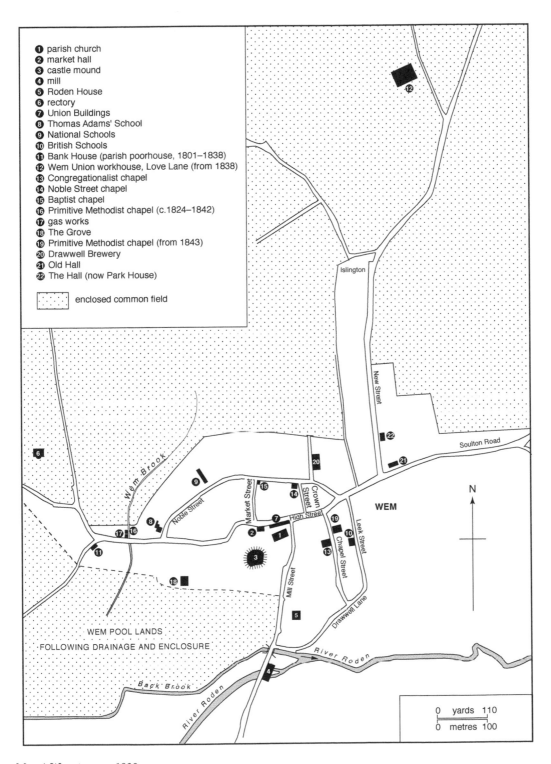

1 parish church
2 market hall
3 castle mound
4 mill
5 Roden House
6 rectory
7 Union Buildings
8 Thomas Adams' School
9 National Schools
10 British Schools
11 Bank House (parish poorhouse, 1801–1838)
12 Wem Union workhouse, Love Lane (from 1838)
13 Congregationalist chapel
14 Noble Street chapel
15 Baptist chapel
16 Primitive Methodist chapel (c.1824–1842)
17 gas works
18 The Grove
19 Primitive Methodist chapel (from 1843)
20 Drawwell Brewery
21 Old Hall
22 The Hall (now Park House)

:::::::: enclosed common field

Islington

New Street

Soulton Road

WEM

N

Market Street

Noble Street

Crown Street

High Street

Leek Street

Chapel Street

Drawwell Lane

Mill Street

Wem Brook

WEM POOL LANDS
FOLLOWING DRAINAGE AND ENCLOSURE

Back Brook

River Roden

River Roden

0 yards 110
0 metres 100

Map 4 *Wem town, c.1830.*

Figure 9 *Park House (formerly The Hall), New Street.*

Park House, formerly The Hall, was built by Thomas Dickin between 1781 and 1784 at a cost of over £4,000.[192] A square-plan three-storey brick house with fine Neoclassical detail, the west entrance front has a central bay set forward, the stone pediment bears a prominent coat of arms with swags combining the Dickin arms with those of Thomas's wife, Sarah, *née* Acherley.[193] The stone-carving may have been executed by the Shrewsbury sculptor John Nelson.[194] The east garden front has a large full-height bow to the centre, and the interior originally had particularly rich ceiling decoration with egg-and-dart, florette and vase ornamentation.[195]

192 SA, 306, box 3d, 'An Account of the Expences on Building the New House in Wem', within a book of accounts of Thomas Dickin, 1770s–1805.
193 Newman and Pevsner, 676–7; Woodward, 56–7.
194 The building account includes payment of 'Mr Nelson's bills' on 24 Oct. 1784.
195 Newman and Pevsner, 676–7; NHLE, no. 1308007, Park House (formerly listed as the Hall, New Street) (accessed 4 Mar. 2019).

A new rectory in the neo-classical style was built on Lowe Hill road, c.1808.[196] The glebe on Mill Street was sold to the attorney John Walford (1774–1836), who replaced the old 'parsonage house' with Roden House, an elegant ashlar-faced villa set back from the road. It has a stone porch on classical-style columns and a garden front with an open ironwork porch of distinctive shape.[197] In 1804 Walford had married Dorothy, a daughter of Thomas Dickin of The Hall. The property continued in the ownership and occupation of the Walford family until the death of Mary, widow of John Henshaw Walford, in 1908.[198]

Grove End House, 91 High Street, has a three-storey front dominated by full-height bows flanking the entrance, which were added by 1834.[199] These were perhaps inspired by the full-height bows on the garden fronts of the rectory and The Hall; full-height bows flanking the entrance are also a feature of the early 19th-century front elevation of 32–34 Chapel Street. Well-executed detail on Grove End House includes sash windows with stuccoed heads decorated with paterae and a stone door-case with round-arched entrance.[200] The arrangement is not symmetrical – the eastern bow is narrower – suggesting modification of an earlier house.[201]

An early 18th-century owner of Lacons Hall, William Wickstead, 'built a high tower of brick, for no visible purpose' at some distance from the street, which was known as Wickstead's folly.[202] In 1827 the property was a 'dwelling house' formerly called the Folly,[203] but had been known as The Grove since at least 1807.[204] The medieval Lacons Hall must have been replaced with the entrance gate and tree-lined drive to the new house, which was set back from the High Street, possibly on the site of Wickstead's folly. In 1826 The Grove was 'a messuage or mansion house' with just over an acre of gardens and 'spacious avenues beautifully ornamented with elm and other trees'.[205] It was described as a house with pleasure grounds and gardens in 1842.[206] An early 20th-century photograph shows a two-storey brick house roughly Georgian in style, with four round-headed windows arranged symmetrically on the upper floor and corresponding windows on the ground floor, the symmetry interrupted by the position of the front door in the place of one of the lower windows. At the time the photograph was taken, however, the entire front elevation was incongruously decorated to resemble black and white timber framing.[207]

Other examples of Wem's Georgian domestic architecture are found on Market Street, a narrow street which was an 'obscure', unnamed alley with no houses until c.1700, when it was paved and improved by the Revd John Collier, whose garden adjoined its east side,

196 Below, Religious History.
197 Newman and Pevsner, 676.
198 *Shrews. Chron.*, 11 Dec. 1857, 1 May 1908, 1; *Wellington Jnl*, 28 Dec. 1907, 10; cf. Woodward, 71–2, 99.
199 HER 12521, incl. C. Giles, RCHME (Historic England), Field Survey Report, 1992; Woodward, 158. Newman and Pevsner, 676; SA, TP15, map of Wem by John Wood, 1834 (photocopy).
200 Mercer, *English Arch. to 1900*, 204.
201 HER 12521.
202 Garbet, 237. See SA, 112/1/2452.
203 SA, 3651/B/151/6.
204 Woodward, 65–6.
205 *Gore's Liverpool General Advertiser*, 23 Mar. 1826.
206 SA, 8611/3/15; SA, P295/T/1/9.
207 SA, PC/W/6/30; Whitehead, *Wem*, 64; see also Woodward, 57, 99.

and was for a time called (new) Cripple Street. In the mid 18th century there were 'three new houses' on the west side.[208] Eckford House, a tall, three-storey, sash-windowed house on the western corner of Noble Street and Market Street, was the home of Henry Eckford from 1888 to 1905.[209] The house has a central pedimented doorcase fronting Noble Street, now blocked.[210] Eckford's nursery was located on Soulton Road, but he purchased the three adjoining houses on Market Street for warehousing and packing operations.[211]

Drawwell House, set back from Noble Street, survived the great fire in 1677.[212] It was later rebuilt in brick with a two-storey, three-window front, and then extended by two bays to the east, all placed under a new roof. The house later became the offices and brewery tap of the Shrewsbury & Wem Brewery Co.[213]

Gentry houses and terraces with gardens were built along New Street, perhaps taking the place of burgages destroyed during the Civil War, with ownership concentrated in the hands of a few landowners.[214] Around 1830 a development of fashionable houses was realised at the northern end of New Street, informally renamed Islington and with an inn called the Angel (later the Hawkestone Arms).[215] A contemporary observed: 'That portion of the town, designated New Islington, leading to Whitchurch, has been lately increased and beautified, by the addition of many excellent houses and smaller dwellings; for these additions the town is chiefly indebted to Mr Walter Gough.'[216] Gough, the Baptist minister of Wem from 1825, headed a consortium of local investors interested in improving the town.[217] Brunswick House was ready for letting in 1832 and others were offered for sale in 1833 as newly erected dwellings occupied by respectable tenants.[218] By 1842 both Brunswick House and Islington House belonged to Thomas Ireland.[219] Islington Villa was the home of the Revd Joseph Pattison, minister of the Congregationalist chapel until his death in 1866, and his daughters, who ran a private girls' school there.[220]

The Islington houses share a similar Neo-classical design of symmetrical two-storey, three-window fronts and are of brick with stone dressings under hipped slate roofs. Most have a central stone portico supported on columns, sometimes with a decorative architrave to the window above, and sash windows. The individual houses are set back from the road with carriage driveways, large gardens and outbuildings. The Crescent fronts the road and consists of six substantial three-storey properties. No. 61 has a

208 Garbet, 240–1, 208.
209 Below, Social History.
210 SA, PH/W/8/6/14.
211 P. Stamper, *Historic Parks and Gardens of Shropshire* (Shrewsbury, 1996), 108–9.
212 Garbet, 224–5, 239.
213 Below, Economic History.
214 SA, 8611/3/1; SA, 167/47.
215 SA, 7577/36/8, 19 Apr., 6 Dec. 1831; *Shrews. Chron.*, 14 Sept. 1832, 3.
216 C. Hulbert, *The History and Description of the County of Salop*, vol. 2 (Providence Grove [Hadnall], near Shrewsbury, 1837), 124.
217 SA, 8611/3/1; SA, 167/47; SA, 1848 box 167, 'Abstract of Conveyance of land in New Street for the Revd. Gough to secure £1000' (draft); *The Baptist Magazine for 1825*, XVII (London, 1825), 487.
218 *Shrews. Chron.*, 24 Feb. 1832, 3; *Salopian Jnl*, 11 Sept. 1833, 1.
219 SA, P295/T/1/9.
220 P. Edwards and T. Edwards, *A History of the Methodist and United Reformed (Congregational) Societies in Wem* (Wem, 1995), 19. Below, Social History.

stable block adjoining the rear boundary wall of the garden, which had accommodation and a hay loft in the upper storey.[221] At the northern limits of the town, a newly built farmhouse on Love Lane was acquired by Wem poor law union in 1837, and converted into the union workhouse.[222]

Many of the properties on the west side of New Street are well preserved, their long gardens backing onto Drawwell Walk. Fields beyond Drawwell Walk, some planted with ornamental trees, were also included in the premises of The Crescent houses.[223] These properties therefore had gardens which were considerably larger than the medieval burgages.[224] Gardens as well as houses were a signifier of status, as indicated by the large gardens of houses in New Street such as The Hall and The Shrubbery. Although there was limited room for expansion in the town centre, some residents acquired pleasure gardens nearby, such as on Aston Street.

Some property boundaries in and around the town centre may have been replaced in red sandstone at this time. Such walls are a characteristic feature in north-central Shropshire, the stone from the Grinshill, Myddle and Harmer Hill quarries.

Later 19th and 20th Century

The Baptist chapel in Market Street, the mortuary chapel of the Aston Street cemetery designed by Richard Dodson (1853), and the chancel of the parish church designed by G.H. Birch (1886) are examples of buildings influenced by the mid to late 19th-century Gothic style of architecture.[225] The main contribution of the Victorians to Wem town centre was the insertion of shop fronts, which disrupted the consistent Georgian character of the townscape. Most of them are late 19th-century, some with narrow pilasters, such as 37 High Street. Typical Victorian terraces also appeared in the suburbs: in Barnard Street and along Aston Street, Station Road and other locations close to the railway station (1858). The station building, now demolished, was constructed of black engineering brick and, like other larger stations on the Shrewsbury–Crewe line, was a symmetrical two-storey structure with main range and flanking wings.[226] The end of the century saw a hint of the Elizabethan revival style in the mortuary chapel of the Whitchurch Road cemetery (1891)[227] and the Birmingham District and Counties (latterly Barclays) Bank (1889).[228] Nos. 58–62 Aston Street were remodelled in terracotta to form shops with accommodation over, the decorative timber-framed gables dated 1898. Next door, no. 56 is dated 1893, constructed of brick and stone, with decorative doorheads flanking the shop window, over which is a prominent half-dormer in stone.[229]

The Arts and Crafts style was adopted for several public buildings in the early 20th century: the town hall, Morgan Library and post office. Grove Villa, High Street

221 Inf. from Malcolm and Hazel Adkins, 2016.
222 Below, Social History.
223 Inf. from Malcolm and Hazel Adkins, 2016.
224 SA, 9043, File W, 1. Cf. Garbet, 243.
225 Newman and Pevsner, 674, 675; Woodward, 92. Below, Religious History.
226 Mercer, *English Arch. to 1900*, 262–3; SA, PH/W/8/9/5.
227 SA, P295/B/8/2/5 and 9.
228 Below, Economic History.
229 Mercer, *English Arch. to 1900*, 258–60.

(opposite Stanier Hall), is an example of the style in domestic architecture,[230] as are semi-detached houses in Station Road (nos. 84/86 and 90/92) designed in 1922 by F.H. Shayler, the architect of the Morgan Library.[231]

In the second half of the 20th century a number of public buildings were built in a Modern, or at least utilitarian, style. These buildings are inconspicuous from the High Street, whether by design or because the High Street was fully built up. The exception is Talbot House, 3 High Street, the site of the former Talbot inn, constructed as a supermarket and laundrette c.1970, but since 2001 the county branch library. At the western end of the High Street is Thomas Adams School's Stanier Hall, built in 1969 on a former industrial site long owned by the school.[232] Of similar design and construction is the Butler Sports Centre off Pyms Road (1971–5).[233]

Architecturally more ambitious, but particularly inconspicuous being set back from Lowe Hill road, is the lower school of Thomas Adams School, completed in 1958 as the secondary modern school.[234] Off New Street are two more public buildings: Edinburgh House, built in stages between 1971 and 1989 as the local authority headquarters, and the NHS medical practice (1991).[235]

In recent decades several redundant historic buildings have been converted into residential houses or apartments. These include Wem Mill, the former Baptist chapel on Market Street, the Noble Street maltings and Grove End House, and the former police station, Oddfellows Lodge and Primitive Methodist chapel, all on Chapel Street. One of the most prominent is The Hall (now Park House), which was let during the mid 19th century, one tenant being Sir John Bickerton Williams (d. 1855).[236] Advertised for sale in 1902 as a 'family mansion with about 10½ acres of grassland', stabling for eight horses and coach house,[237] it was offered in 1919 to Wem UDC, which declined to pay the asking price of £3,750.[238] The same year, Wem Motor Co. Ltd commenced trading in the coach house and negotiations began to divest the grounds to the rear for a public recreation ground. In 1920 the house was divided in two, and a single-storey extension was built on the north side to provide a kitchen and service area for one of the dwellings.[239] A public road, Park Street, was opened between The Hall and the coach house c.1929, to create vehicle access from New Street to the recreation ground and Shrubbery Gardens housing estate. In 1938 The Hall, now known as Park House, was once more offered for sale to Wem UDC, this time for £550, but the council again

230 SA, DA14/700/20.
231 SA, DA14/700/13.
232 Woodward, 116, plate 18.
233 Woodward, 115, plate 16.
234 Below, Social History.
235 Below, Social History; Local Government.
236 *Extracts from the Diary of Sir John Bickerton Williams ... Edited by his Grandson, Robert Philip Williams* (London, 1896); London, National Portrait Gallery, D22458; *ODNB*, s.v. Williams, Sir John Bickerton (1792–1855) (accessed 4 Mar. 2019); SA, 306; SA, D3651/D/20/1792. Below, Social History, and see Woodward, 57.
237 *Wellington Jnl*, 1 Nov. 1902. For the land to the east of the Hall, incorporated in the extensive grounds c.1811, see SBT, MS DR 36/182–202.
238 SA, DA14/100/5, 940–2.
239 SA, DA14/700/11/5; Woodward, 99.

declined.[240] Wem Motor Co. Ltd built a new motor vehicle showroom in front of the house, *c*.1939.[241] Park House was converted into flats in the 1970s.[242]

A Georgian building that has not survived was The Grove. A private girls' school from 1902 to 1938,[243] the vacant house was requisitioned in June 1940 to accommodate wartime evacuees from Liverpool. By the time it was derequisitioned in 1945 the house was vacant and derelict; having been purchased by Wem UDC for post-war housing development, it was demolished in 1946 and the trees felled.[244] All that remains today is the former eastern boundary wall, of substantial sandstone blocks, which crosses Barnard Street from north to south.

240 SA, DA14/100/7, 20 Dec. 1937, 5 Apr., 26 Apr. 1938.
241 See SA, DA14/100/5, 940–1, 1012; DA14/100/7, 90, 139; DA14/700/11/8.
242 *Whitchurch Herald*, 25 Jan., 1 Feb. 2019: https://www.whitchurchherald.co.uk/ (accessed 4 Mar. 2019).
243 Below, Social History.
244 SA, DA14/100/7, 276, 324–5; DA14/100/8, 8, 38, 54, 69, 79, 107, 207, 222, 240, 281, 515, 583.

LANDOWNERSHIP

Pattern of Landownership

IN 1066 THE ADJACENT ESTATES of Aston, Coton, Edstaston, Horton, Sleap, Steel, Wem and Wolverley were held separately by various Anglo-Saxon free men and women.[1] All were held by one Norman lord, William Pantulf, in 1086. By the mid 13th century these estates had been gathered together to form the large manor of Wem, which thereafter descended as a single manor. If property was required, for example, for dower or to reward a retainer, it was found in other manors, or at least in the outlying parts of Wem manor. A watermill at Wolverley was given to Lilleshall abbey by William Pantulf II, but the grant appears to have been revoked in the next generation.[2] Sleap and parts of Wolverley, Edstaston and Coton were granted at an early date to hereditary tenants to hold in fee farm and even by military service, the peripheral situation of these estates proving the rule.[3] This policy had the effect of preserving the territorial integrity of the lordship. The manor was held by some of the great baronial families, including the earls of Arundel, and the Lords Dacre, Bradford and Barnard;[4] after the 14th century the lord was not resident. The pattern of landholding established in the Middle Ages continued into the 16th century when it was recorded in surveys made in 1561 for Lord Dacre and in 1589 on the attainder of Philip Howard, earl of Arundel (d. 1595).[5]

There were few freehold tenements in the township until the enfranchisements of the mid 17th century. The Coteman family held a hereditary estate, granted by the lord of the manor probably in the 13th century, which by the 15th century included burgage plots on Noble Street, agricultural land and a weir and fishery on the Roden. By 1561 this estate was held by John Thurleigh, who was also a tenant of the lord's demesne in Lowe and Ditches.[6] Of similar antiquity was the Lacon estate, consisting, in Wem township, of several burgages and a house (Lacons Hall) and pasture land west of the town.[7]

Tenants within the bars had borough rights. In 1561 burgages were normally held by copy of court roll. Several burgages on Noble Street, however, had long been transferred by charter and were deemed freehold, although still subject to the manorial customs of

---

1   *Domesday*, 703–4.
2   Probably 1227 x February 1233: *Cart. Lilleshall Abbey*, no. 87, confirmed in 1265 (ibid., no. 260), but there is no further evidence of Lilleshall or any other monastery having possessions in Wem (see, e.g., ibid., Appendix B, 1330).
3   *Survey 1561*, 93–7, 161.
4   Below, Landownership.
5   *Survey 1561*, 17–53; TNA, LR 2/225, ff. 18–37v. passim.
6   *Survey 1561*, 16–19, 53; Garbet, 258–9.
7   Garbet, 237. Below, Landownership.

borough-hold.[8] By 1673 it was claimed that no borough-hold properties were held by copy of court and all were sold by private deed – apparently a case of the tenants escaping the discipline of the manor.[9] The suburban area beyond the east bar was essentially an agricultural settlement of copyhold messuages.[10] There were also copyholders who held land without buildings; some of these held residential tenements and land in other townships of the manor.

The lord retained substantial demesne within Wem township. In 1561 the former castle enclosure was held at will by the rector, John Dacre, with 8 a. of pasture land, known as the Alleys, between the castle enclosure and the river, and a further 16 a. of riverside meadow and pasture in Tilley township.[11] Wem Pool, two mills and a windmill were leased by Lord Dacre in 1553 to six tenants who were to undertake the drainage and enclosure of the pool.[12] The demesne of Creamore, 100 a. of pasture in 1436, lay to the north of the town and spread into Edstaston; that of New Pool was on the western edge of the town.[13] The other manorial perquisites, noted in 1589, were two annual fairs where the lord took a toll on all goods worth above 12d. sold by strangers and tenants (but not burgagers) and the profits of the courts.

Neither of the 16th-century surveys gives much detail on tenure other than showing that most tenants of the manor held by varieties of copyhold. Two custumals describe the custom of the manor in more detail. The first is undated but is probably of the late 15th century; the other, of 1566–7, was printed by Garbet and survives in a broadly contemporary copy.[14] The custom of the manor was copyhold of inheritance with the usual common law rules of descent. Fines were arbitrary but could be no more than a single year's rent. The tenants had the right to take timber from their tenements and common of pasture in the lord's woods and to make leases for three years without licence. They claimed a right of free common in Wem Pool but in 1561 had recently been excluded from this due to enclosure.

Wem and the other Shropshire estates of the earl of Arundel were isolated from the family's core estates and lacked a house or other facilities which might prove attractive, hence it was one of those selected for sale in 1641 when the earl ran into financial difficulties.[15] The Alleys was sold to the executor of one of the earl's creditors, a clerk named William Petty, in 1643,[16] however, the majority of sales were delayed until after the Civil War.

8   *Survey 1561*, 16–17 (William Coteman to Richard Waring, 1418), 18–19 (Randulph Mainwaring to Richard Cowper of Creamore, 1544). For burgages, see above, Landscape, Settlement and Buildings.
9   Garbet, 122–3.
10 Above, Landscape, Settlement and Buildings. For the estate west of the bar, see below, Landownership..
11 *Survey 1561*, 49; Garbet, 251.
12 *Survey 1561*, 53.
13 TNA, C 139/76/34, *Cal. Inq. p.m.* XXIV, p. 348; *Survey 1561*, 51.
14 JRL, MS GB 133 PHC/3 (undated, the head of the MS is missing); Garbet, 110–22. SA, 6000/5384 is an early but incomplete copy. Garbet (110) gives the date incorrectly as '1564, 9 Elizabeth'. Since he adds that the custumal was made by a commission of the Court of Wards, it must date from the minority of George, Lord Dacre (1566–9), hence the date 9 Elizabeth, 1566–7, is to be preferred.
15 ACA, MS MD59 is a register of sales made by the trustees for sale, beginning with the conveyance to them and a tabulation of the earl's debts.
16 ACA, MS MD59, p. 51; SA, D3651/B/151/9/1.

In 1648 Thomas Duckett made a survey of the saleable assets of the manor covering the demesne estate but not the copyhold tenements. It therefore covers the parks and woods, and the few leasehold farms, but also cottages built on encroachments in Northwood and Wem, and shops in Wem. The survey contains elaborate calculations as to what each asset would be worth at 20 years' purchase. Duckett calculated that the properties he surveyed would be worth in total £33,130 and the standing timber a little under £26,000; with a small allowance for the value of buildings he offered a projected value of £59,089. He also suggested that the copyholds would be worth £18,000 on enfranchisement. He did not place a valuation on the sale of the manor but included the rectory which he valued at £1,400.[17] Rents on demesne properties were raised from 1650, perhaps to encourage the tenants to purchase.

The sum raised by selling parcels of the demesne was about £17,000, but most of this came from the sale of Edstaston Park (£2,000) and Wem Brockhurst (£8,140). It therefore seems unlikely that all the property identified for sale by Duckett was sold while the Arundels retained possession of the manor. When the manor was sold in 1665, Daniel Wycherley acquired property whose sale had been contracted for but had not yet been completed, worth £5,200, giving a total of about £22,200. The sale to him also included the rectory and Trench Farm.[18] The trustees' register records 50 enfranchisements in the manor but does not give the considerations paid. The land enfranchised had a rental value (as opposed to a rack-rent value) of £20 17s. 0d.,[19] hence it is not possible to say how much was raised by enfranchisement. Nevertheless it seems most likely that the majority of copyholders in the manor declined to buy the freehold of their tenements.

Where the Arundels saw the manor as an asset whose value could be realised, Wycherley saw it as an asset whose value could be improved.[20] He launched a more rigorous and personal manorial administration than the tenants were used to. He was alleged to have sat in the manor court, where he selected juries himself and used his own servants to affeer amercements (assess fines for wrongdoing). His own son George, the rector of Wem, complained that Wycherley had used the rectory house to hold courts, impanel juries, collect rents and fines, and host fair dinners, all at the rector's expense.[21] Wycherley sought to increase the rate of fines paid by the copyholders on the descent and alienation of copyhold land, and he demanded heriots of the tenants. He claimed to be ignorant of the manorial customs because the court rolls and other evidences had been lost or fraudulently removed before he purchased the manor, although it was alleged that Wycherley had himself removed them from the pentice adjoining the court house to his house at Clive. In 1673, 43 tenants of copyhold and borough-hold launched a suit in the Exchequer complaining of Wycherley's administration of the manor. He denied some of the allegations, including improper involvement in the court.[22] The evidence gathered included instances of Wycherley demanding fines far in excess of the customary single year's rent.[23]

17   ACA, MS 508, the calculations at f. 41, rectory at f. 35v.
18   ACA, MS MD59, 77. Trench does not seem to have been surveyed by Duckett.
19   No details are given in one instance so the figure is a minimum.
20   The following account, except where otherwise stated, is based on Garbet, 69–84.
21   SA, 6000/18101; see also deposition of George Chambre of Loppington: TNA, E 134/26Chas2/Mich48.
22   TNA, E 134/26Chas2/Mich48.
23   Depositions of Richard Mather of Wem, Richard Basnett of Baschurch and John Payne of Old Marton: ibid.

Wycherley commenced a cross-suit and in May 1675 the court ordered that the points in contention should go to a trial at common law. In the autumn Wycherley's counsel argued against this, but a trial in Easter term 1676 found that the practice of alienating borough-hold lands without a surrender was a good custom. On 1 June, after the customs declared in 1566/7 were read, the barons of the Exchequer found for the tenants on seven of the customs claimed by the tenants and left six others undecided. This decision was confirmed at a hearing in November, with the proviso that the tenants should enjoy the six undecided customs in perpetuity unless the court was satisfied of their non-existence within seven years.[24]

The question of the rate of fines was tried in 1677 and the court again found for the tenants. Wycherley, having staked so much on his right to arbitrary fines, refused to accept this verdict and demanded a new trial. According to Garbet, at this point he bribed Mr Felton, the tenants' agent, to betray them. When this was discovered, Felton was dismissed by the tenants but retained the evidences they had entrusted to him.[25] The story was more complicated, however. William Felton, gent, of the Lowe was one of the original tenant plaintiffs and had been acting as 'chief agent' on their behalf. In the summer of 1679, perhaps despairing of resolving the dispute with Wycherley, Felton sought a 'friendly ending' to the disputes over the rate of fines. By making this approach he conceded that the tenants' fines were arbitrary. An agreement was reached in which, for the abolition of future fines on Felton's copyholds in the manor, he undertook to pay an enhanced annual rent of £10 on his copyhold tenements: £4 in Lowe and Edstaston, £3 in Horton and £3 on his copyhold in Aston. Other lands in Edstaston would continue to pay arbitrary fines. Felton also released to Wycherley the £95 in costs that had been awarded to the tenants. At the manorial court held on 4 September 1679 Wycherley admitted Felton to lands in Aston and Edstaston and the agreement between them was formally made on 15 September. Two other tenants entered into similar agreements, but otherwise the tenants appear to have remained robust in the defence of their rights and Felton, as Garbet supposed, was disowned by them.[26]

By this time Wycherley had run out of money and, although his agreement with Felton discharged him of the £95 in costs awarded against him, he could not pay this sum, which may mean that Felton's action was condemned by the Exchequer and the damages reinstated. Wycherley managed to keep the suit in the Exchequer alive, and commenced a new suit in Chancery. In June 1681 he reopened the whole matter by paying the £95 in costs to the tenants. By this time some of the tenants had suffered losses in the great fire of 1677, their case had been badly damaged by the loss of some of their evidences, and some of them had made private settlements with Wycherley. On a subsequent trial on whether the fines were fixed at a single year's rent, in 1682, a jury found for Wycherley. Regarding the six customs left undetermined in 1676, as the seven-year deadline approached, Wycherley returned to the court, producing large quantities of manor court rolls and books in evidence. On 6 December 1683 the barons of the Exchequer made a decree absolute in favour of the tenants unless Wycherley should show cause to the contrary at the start of the next term. Evidently he was unable to do so.[27]

24   SA, 484/241.
25   Garbet, 79, 81.
26   Abstract, mm. 6–8; Garbet, 79–82.
27   SA, 484/241–2, copies of memoranda of the Exchequer orders on the customs, dated 8 Feb. and 18 June 1684.

Instead, Wycherley put the manor up for sale.[28] Although the tenants eventually succeeded on all counts apart from the assessment of fines, the litigation had cost them £3,000. There appears to have been no further litigation over customs, except an early 18th-century suit over the earl of Bradford's right to the goods of suicides and felons.[29]

At the beginning of the 18th century substantial areas of copyhold survived in the manor, including in Wem township.[30] More important were the burgage rents, but both were eclipsed by the rents drawn from the leaseholds, presumably the lands bought by George, Lord Jeffreys, and Henry Newport, earl of Bradford. The total of free and customary rents was £15 12s. 9½d.; the leaseholds were worth £25 6s. 0d. By 1770 – in the period when the manor was being administered by Sir William Pulteney on behalf of John Newport – the 'small rents' were worth just £11, suggesting that some enfranchisement had taken place under one or other of the earls of Bradford. By this time no distinction was made between burgage rents and copyhold rents. In the absence of a full estate archive, it is hard to ascertain the pace or chronology of enfranchisement. A letter was circulated in 1810 inviting the tenants to enfranchise. In 1811 it seems that enfranchisement was available more or less on demand provided a price could be agreed.[31] By 1820, the chief rents payable by Wem amounted to £10 10s. 5d. A printed notice giving the earl's terms for enfranchisement was published in 1824. However, in the mid 19th century much of the land offered for sale was still copyhold.[32]

Enfranchisements of copyholds were made under the supervision of the Copyhold Commissioners in the last quarter of the 19th century but were mostly of small parcels of land. By 1891 the copyhold rental of Wem township had dropped to £6 17s. 11½d.[33] Around 1911 the manorial steward compiled a list of lands still held by copyhold. This named around 20 copyhold tenants in Wem township but the area of land held by them was small. Elsewhere in the manor there were eight holdings of more than 20 a. which remained copyhold with a total acreage of around 425 a.: the total acreage of copyhold in the manor was less than 500 a.[34] The 1940 manor accounts show that even at this very late date the bailiff received a fine and heriot of £1 13s. 3d. (a guinea for the heriot and 13s. 3d. for the fine). In Wem nine tenants paid a total rent of 11s. 4½d. The total income from rents in the manor was £3 1s. 3½d. With arrears collected, the total income came to £13 11s. 4½d. The fees of the steward and bailiff totalled £13 11s. 0d. The balance due to Lord Barnard was therefore ½d.[35]

From the mid 17th century the majority of the tenants of the manor were de facto freeholders, whether actually freehold or by two forms of tenancy which were tantamount to freehold: borough-hold and copyhold. There were also large numbers of tenants: in 1711 there were 90 tenants, although this may involve some double

28   Below, Landownership.
29   TNA, E 134/10Wm3/Mich27; E 134/11Wm3/Hil30.
30   SA, 3607/III/A/10 (rental, 1711). This discussion considers the decline of the manorial interest in Wem (urban) and not the manor as a whole.
31   SA, Sprott II (acc. 2495), 56/63 and 59/95: also various items of correspondence in those boxes about enfranchisements; SA, 1502/11.
32   E.g. SA, 1186/51, 52: auction catalogue of the Dickin estate in Wem, 1865.
33   SA, unlisted archive from the Barnard estate office, accounts Lady Day 1820, Lady Day 1891.
34   SA, 1709, box 192.
35   SA, 1709, box 192/ II/10.

counting.[36] This situation might have been reversed if a figure had appeared who wished to invest in land in Wem, create an estate and perhaps even live in the manor. It is possible that George, Lord Jeffreys, thought along these lines; he was ennobled as Baron Jeffreys of Wem and bought property in the manor (although not necessarily in Wem township) in the short period between his purchase of the manor and his fall from grace and death while imprisoned.[37] Sir William Pulteney was the largest single landowner in Wem township in the 1798 land tax, paying 12.4 per cent of the township's land tax, but the estate was sold by the earl of Cleveland in 1809.[38] No other predominant landowners emerged in Wem township, although the Dickin estate rivalled that of the manorial lord.

Of the large numbers of property holders, many had no more than their dwelling or workshop.[39] In 1700 there were 108 individual ratepayers in Wem quarter. Of these, 46 (43 per cent) paid less than 6d. and a further 32 (30 per cent) less than 1s.; 30 paid 1s. or more, just five of whom paid over 3s. The Pool lands were assessed separately but only four of the 15 tenants there paid 2s. or more.[40] In 1798, 120 individuals paid the land tax contributing in total just under £127; 46 paid less than 5s. each (showing the large number of houses assessed for the land tax); 90 paid less than £1 each; and the 14 highest taxpayers, paying more than £2 each, paid 58.5 per cent of the total land tax.[41]

In 1805 there was still a high level of distribution of landholding in Wem township, and inequality between those who owned agricultural land and those whose tenements were no more than urban dwellings or workshops. There were 138 landowners, of whom the top 20 held 56.6 per cent of the total rateable value of the township; 48 held some agricultural land. The largest single landowner, Thomas Dickin, held land worth just under 7 per cent of the total.[42]

In 1841 there were 161 landowners in Wem township, of whom 110 owned only a house or houses, commercial buildings or property held by trustees (the schools and chapels) without significant areas of land attached to them. Thirty-four landowners held between one and 20 a., nine between 20 and 50 a., and eight more than 50 a. In total the eight largest landowners held 674 a.; as the township then measured 1203 a., these eight held only 56 per cent of the area of the township, suggesting a low level of concentration of ownership.[43]

The basis of this fragmentation was the 80 medieval burgages, plus subsequent encroachments; in 1648 Duckett noted the existence of 18 small encroachments on which cottages or shops had been built.[44] With no authority concerned to regulate the building of housing or the subdivision of tenements, it appears to have been relatively easy to rent or even build a house in the town, with rows of cottages built to rent.[45]

36   SA, 3607/III/A/10.
37   Garbet, 95.
38   SA, 6000/12498.
39   Yalden, 'Landownership'.
40   SA, P295/B/3/11 (unfoliated).
41   TNA, IR 23/71, ff. 54v–58. These figures exclude the land tax levied on tithes.
42   Yalden, 'Landownership'.
43   TNA, IR 29/29/334.
44   ACA, MS 508, f. 36.
45   TNA, IR 29/29/334.

Wem had the landholding characteristics of a borough but never developed the legal institutions of elected officers or borough courts and so remained a market settlement in the context of a manor. House property was held by a local form of burgage tenure. This, coupled with the fact that the prevailing form of tenure in the manor was either freehold or copyhold, made for a wide distribution of property, but it also encouraged poverty by giving workers and the poor the opportunity of renting housing. Much followed from this, and it determined Wem's character into the 20th century.

Wem Manor

Wem was held by William Pantulf in 1086 as tenant of Roger de Montgomery, earl of Shrewsbury, and from *c*.1102 as tenant-in-chief; the manor then passed in its entirety to successive lords who held in chief.[46] On William's death in 1112 his cross-Channel estate was divided, the Norman lands descending to his eldest son and the English lands to a second son, Robert (fl. 1130).[47] There were just five successive Pantulf lords of Wem from the Conquest to 1233: William (d. 1112), Robert (fl. 1130), Ivo (d. 1175), Hugh (d. 1224) and William II (d. 1233).[48] William Pantulf II left two daughters by his wife, Hawise, a daughter of Fulk FitzWarin III of Whittington, who was awarded custody of his granddaughters and their inheritance.[49]

By 1242 the surviving heiress, Maud, had married Ralph le Botiler of Oversley (Warws.).[50] After Ralph's death in 1281,[51] Maud married the royal justice Walter of Hopton. By a settlement of 1283, the entire barony was to pass to Maud's heirs with Walter holding the manor of Tyrley (Staffs.) and an annuity from Wem for life.[52] Predeceased by her eldest son, William le Botiler, Maud (d. *c*.1289) was succeeded by her grandsons: first Gawaine (d. 1290) and then his younger brother, William.[53] Another long period of stable lordship ensued under this William le Botiler (d. 1334) and his son William (d. 1361). The latter's son, the third William le Botiler (d. 1369),[54] left an adult daughter, Elizabeth, as sole heiress.

---

46   Garbet, 18–108, provides an account of successive lords of the manor with pen portraits of the lords from Arundel to his own day.

47   *ODNB*, s.v. William Pantulf (d. 1112?) (accessed 4 Mar. 2019).

48   Eyton, *Antiquities*, IX, 157–68; I.J. Sanders, *English Baronies: A Study of Their Origin and Descent, 1086–1327* (Oxford, 1960), 94–5.

49   *ODNB*, s.v. William Pantulf (d. 1233), Hugh Pantulf (d. 1224), baron (accessed 4 Mar. 2019); Eyton, *Antiquities*, IX, 168–9; *Excerpta è Rotulis Finium*, 237.

50   TNA, C 60/38, m. 5 26/266, https://finerollshenry3.org.uk/content/calendar/roll_038.html, no. 266 (Apr. 1242) (accessed 4 Mar. 2019).

51   TNA, C 133/27/9, *Cal. Inq. Edward I*, II, 229.

52   *ODNB*, s.v. Sir Walter of Hopton (*c*.1235–1295/6) (accessed 4 Mar. 2019); *Cal. Close*, 1279–88, 203, 233–4; TNA, E 133/57 No. 3; 'Calendar of Final Concords or pedes finium, mixed counties (including Staffordshire) Ed.I and Ed.II, 1272–1327', *SHC* (1911), 109. See F.R. Twemlow, 'The manor of Tyrley in the county of Stafford', *SHC*, 3rd ser., 68 (1945–6).

53   TNA, E 133/57, no. 3; E 149/1. *Cal. Inq. p.m.* II, 470, nos. 773, 774; Garbet, 35, 37. For Walter of Hopton's exploitation of the barony during the wardship, see *Welsh Assize Roll*, 106–8.

54   TNA, C 135/38/31; C 135/157/4; C 135/206/15. For the Botiler lords of Wem, Eyton, *Antiquities*, IX, 169–79.

Elizabeth le Botiler's husband, a younger son of Robert Ferrers of Chartley (Staffs.), was summoned to parliament as Robert Ferrers of Wem in 1375.[55] Styled baroness of Wem, Elizabeth outlived her second and third husbands: John de Say and Thomas Molington, the latter styled baron of Wem (d. 1408). She also survived her eldest son, Robert Ferrers of Oversley, her heiresses on her death in 1411 being Robert's two daughters.[56] The barony passed to the elder, Elizabeth, and the manors of Oversley and Tyrley to the younger, Mary.[57]

Elizabeth Ferrers married John of Greystock, baron Greystock, and their eldest son, Ralph, succeeded in 1436 to the baronies of both Greystock and Wem.[58] Ralph (d. 1487) survived his eldest son and was succeeded by his granddaughter, Elizabeth, who married Thomas, Lord Dacre, of Gilsland (Cumb.).[59] The Wem estates thus became incorporated with those of Dacre. Elizabeth's eldest son, William, succeeded as Lord Greystock and baron of Wem on her death in 1516, and as third Lord Dacre ten years later;[60] he commissioned a survey of the manor of Wem in 1561.[61] William's successor in 1563 was his son Thomas, fourth Lord Dacre (d. 1566). Thomas's son, George, fifth Lord Dacre, was a minor at his inheritance and his wardship was acquired by Thomas Howard, duke of Norfolk, who married Thomas Dacre's widow. When George died in an accident in 1569, a specially convened tribunal found that the inheritance of the Dacre estates lay with Thomas Dacre's daughters rather than his elder surviving brother Leonard, even though he was indisputably the heir male. While a younger brother lived into the 1630s, the Dacre brothers were never able to recover their estates from the Howards.[62]

After Thomas Howard, duke of Norfolk, was executed in 1572 the dukedom went into abeyance, his eldest son Philip taking the title of earl of Arundel from his mother's family.[63] The two surviving Dacre sisters were married to sons of the duke of Norfolk: Anne to Philip and Elizabeth to William, Lord Howard. The Dacre estates were partitioned between them in 1583 and the Shropshire estates – principally Wem, Loppington and Hinstock – together with estates in Cumbria formed the Arundel share.[64] Philip, earl of Arundel, was received into the Roman Catholic Church in 1584; the next year he attempted to flee abroad but he was intercepted and returned to England. Imprisoned after his trial in 1586, he was tried a second time in 1589, when he was attainted and sentenced to death. His estates, including those held *jure uxoris*, were

55   R.A. Wilson (ed.), *The Registers or Act Books of the Bishops of Coventry and Lichfield, Book V, being the Second Register of Bishop Robert de Stretton AD 1360–1385, An Abstract of the Contents*, William Salt Archaeological Soc. (Stafford, 1905), 47; Garbet, 40–1.

56   *Cal. Inq. p.m.* XIX, no. 824; *ODNB*, s.v. Beaufort [married names Ferrers, Neville], Joan, countess of Westmorland (1379? –1440) (accessed 4 Mar. 2019).

57   Garbet, 42.

58   *ODNB*, s.v. Greystoke family (per. 1321–1487) (accessed 4 Mar. 2019).

59   *ODNB*, s.v. Dacre, Thomas, second Baron Dacre of Gilsland (1467–1525) (accessed 4 Mar. 2019).

60   *ODNB*, s.v. Dacre, William, third Baron Dacre of Gilsland and seventh Baron Greystoke (1500–1563) (accessed 4 Mar. 2019).

61   *Survey 1561*, 13, 15.

62   R.A.A. Brockington, 'The Dacre inheritance in Cumbria, 1569–1601', *Trans. Cumberland and Westmorland Antiquarian and Archaeological Soc.*, 3rd ser., 14 (2014), 291–8.

63   *ODNB*, s.v. Howard [*née* Dacre], Anne, countess of Arundel (1557–1630), noblewoman; Howard, Philip [St Philip Howard], thirteenth earl of Arundel (1557–95) (accessed 4 Mar. 2019).

64   For the lands of the earl of Arundel in Shropshire, see TNA, SC 12/26/56.

seized by the crown, but Wem, at least, was restored to Lady Arundel on her husband's death in 1595 and she retained it for the rest of her life.[65] Styled Anne, dowager countess of Arundel, she did not remarry but dedicated herself to personal piety as well as the recovery and improvement of her estates.[66] She entailed the inheritance, in 1611, on her grandson, James, Lord Maltravers (d. 1624) with remainders to his younger brothers.[67] On Anne's death in 1630, however, her son, Thomas Howard, earl of Arundel, took possession of the manor for his lifetime, treating it as his own, rather than passing it to Henry Frederick, Lord Maltravers, under the terms of the entail. In 1631, having newly taken Wem into his own hands, Arundel commissioned a lavish map of the manor.[68] Possessing vast estates, Arundel nevertheless lived far beyond his income; by 1641 he was £93,234 in debt and transferred lands, including Wem, into a debt trust for sale. After the Civil War the two surviving trustees, William Playters and Richard Onslow, sold extensive tracts of demesne and copyhold land in Wem, and in 1665 disposed of the manor to Daniel Wycherley.[69]

Of a minor gentry family long established at Clive, near Wem,[70] Wycherley, a lawyer by training, acquired a substantial fortune as estate steward to the marquess of Winchester, much of which he invested in land in Shropshire. He bought Wem on mortgage: the manors of Wem and Loppington were remortgaged in 1681 for £4,000.[71] Wycherley viewed the manor as ripe for improvement and imposed a rigorous manorial regime to increase his profits, which embroiled him in protracted litigation with the tenants at punishing expense to both parties. Perhaps as a consequence, in 1684 Wycherley sold the manor to the Lord Chief Justice, George Jeffreys, created Baron Jeffreys of Wem in 1685.[72] Losing office upon the overthrow and exile of James II, in 1688 Jeffreys settled most of his property on his wife and his eldest son, John. Still a teenager when his father died in 1689, his father's friends succeeded in protecting the estate for him. Sir Robert Clayton and Henry Pollexfen served as trustees, hence the Wem manor court was held in their names from 1689 to 1694.[73] George Jeffreys is not known to have visited Wem, but his heir was once entertained at Lowe Hall, later known as 'Judge Jeffreys's house'.[74] With a reputation as a drunk and a rake, John, second Lord Jeffreys,

65   SA, 6000/2639; TNA, LR 2/225, ff. 18–37v. is an incomplete survey of the manor made on 11 Oct. 1589 after the lands were confiscated.

66   *ODNB*, Anne, countess of Arundel (1557–1630); Howard, Philip, thirteenth earl of Arundel (1557–95) (accessed 13 Mar. 2019); Garbet, 57–9; TNA, E 134/JasIMich20/5. Deeds of title upon successive conveyances of the barony of Wem and Loppington from this time until the early 19th century are in the possession of Lord Barnard at Raby Castle (Shropshire and Staffordshire deeds, box 6 (formerly box 1), bdl 1). The account given here draws on a very full 18th-century abstract of title to be found with the deeds (Abstract).

67   Abstract, m. 1.

68   1631 survey: SA, 972/7/1/49.

69   *ODNB*, s.v. Howard, Thomas, fourteenth earl of Arundel, fourth earl of Surrey, and first earl of Norfolk (1585–1646), art collector and politician (accessed 4 Mar. 2019): for the scale of his debts, ACA, MS MD59, f. 7. For the debt trust and sales, ACA, MS 508, and MS MD59, pp. 25–45, 51–7; Garbet, 62, 64, 68.

70   Wycherley is described by Garbet, 68–87. See also SA, 6000/18101.

71   Abstract, m. 10.

72   *ODNB*, s.v. Jeffreys, George, first Baron Jeffreys (1645–89) (accessed 4 Mar. 2019).

73   SA, 167/15.

74   G.H.F. Vane, 'Judge Jeffryes's house at Wem', *TSAHS*, 3rd ser., 2 (1902), 291.

died in 1702[75] and the manor descended to his daughter, Henrietta Levisa (or Louisa) (b. 1698).[76] In 1711, however, Wem was sold to Henry, Lord Newport, after a private act for the sale of estates had been obtained to clear her father's debts.[77] Lord Newport made a ceremonial entrance to Wem soon afterwards.[78]

Henry, Lord Newport, succeeded as third earl of Bradford on the death of his father in 1723 and died in 1734 without a legitimate heir.[79] His younger brother Thomas, fourth earl, suffered some form of brain injury in childhood and was judged to be incapable of managing his estate. He was the subject of a commission of lunacy in 1735, after which the estate was placed in the hands of trustees.[80] It may have been his brother's mental frailty which encouraged the third earl to disinherit him, bequeathing all his estates to an illegitimate son by one Ann Smyth, a boy called John Harrison, who took the name Newport, with the remainder in the estates vested in Smyth.[81] John Harrison too was the subject of a commission of lunacy in 1742[82] and died without issue in 1783. The third earl's will was contested in Chancery and consequently it appears the fourth earl had a life interest in the Newport estates conferred on him. Garbet took him to be lord of the manor c.1750: about the same time the earl (or his trustees) commissioned a survey of Wem (which appears to be lost).[83] It seems that John Harrison *alias* Newport had to wait until the fourth earl's death in 1762 to inherit, although his mother Ann had already bequeathed the reversion of the estates to her alleged lover, William Pulteney, quondam Secretary of State for War and from 1742 earl of Bath.[84]

Pulteney lived to 1764 without entering the estates and his future interest passed to his brother, General Harry Pulteney.[85] General Pulteney himself died without issue in 1767 and left his lands to his cousin Frances and her husband William Johnstone, who then took the surname Pulteney, with successive remainders to their male heirs, and a further remainder to a cousin, Henry, earl of Darlington. Frances Pulteney died in 1782; her husband, now Sir William Pulteney, became lord of Wem on the death of John Harrison *alias* Newport in 1783. When Sir William died in 1805, the estates devolved upon William Henry Vane, third earl of Darlington, created earl of Cleveland in 1833 (d. 1842). The main interests of the Vane family lay in County Durham around the ancestral estate of Raby Castle and in 1809 the (then) earl instructed his agent to sell off the Wem estates except for the manorial rights, which included the market rights and advowson.[86] The descent was then through his three sons, successively second, third and fourth earls

75 *ODNB*, s.v. Jeffreys, George, first Baron Jeffreys (1645–89) (accessed 4 Mar. 2019).
76 *ODNB*, s.v. Fermor, Henrietta Louisa [*née* Jeffreys], countess of Pomfret (1698–1761) (accessed 4 Mar. 2019).
77 Abstract, mm. 32–9; Garbet, 102; Statutes of the Realm, vol. IX.
78 Garbet, 105–6.
79 For the following, see E.R.O. Bridgeman and C.G.O. Bridgeman, 'History of the manor and parish of Weston-under-Lizard in the county of Stafford', *SHC*, new ser. 2 (1899), 188–93.
80 TNA, C 211/2/B74. Garbet blamed Bradford's mental condition on a failed love affair, but cf. Bridgeman and Bridgeman, 'Weston-under-Lizard', 193.
81 For Bradford's will, TNA, PROB 11/669, ff. 25v–28v.
82 TNA, C 211/17/N19; SA, 6000/6316.
83 Garbet, 108–9. For extracts from the survey of 1752, SA, 3607/III/A8.
84 *ODNB*, s.v. Pulteney, William, earl of Bath (1684–1764), politician (accessed 4 Mar. 2019), but cf. 'The Newport Estates', *The Daily Advertiser*, 30 Mar. 1780.
85 Bridgeman and Bridgeman, 'Weston-under-Lizard', 191.
86 SA, 6000/12498.

of Cleveland, none of whom had legitimate issue. The earldom and the Vane family's other titles became extinct on the death of the fourth earl in 1891. The fourth earl could not bring himself to bequeath the estates to his heir at law; instead he bequeathed them by will in trust for a descendant of the first Lord Barnard who could take the title. A distant cousin, Henry de Vere Vane, whose claim to the Barnard title was allowed by the House of Lords in 1892, succeeded to Raby and the other estates not specifically bequeathed by the fourth earl.[87] The succession was then through the barons Barnard to the present Lord Barnard, Henry Francis Cecil Vane, who succeeded his father in 2016.[88]

Castle and Manor Site

The site of the Norman castle was known as the manor place (*scitus manerii*) by the 16th century.[89] Ralph le Botiler, lord of the manor in the mid 13th century, evidently had lodgings there, which he used for entertaining, and a garden.[90] The castle was termed both *forcelettum* and *castrum* in an inquest of 1281.[91] 'Forcelettum' has been interpreted as a diminutive term, a 'fortlet', but it may simply refer to a fortress.[92] It was certainly defensible, as military service at Wem castle was due from other members of the barony, including Eyton-on-the-Weald Moors, Harcourt, Sleap and Tibberton.[93] Several suits of armour and weapons, as well as chapel ornaments, were said to have been taken from Wem castle by Walter of Hopton, *c*.1290,[94] and in that year the castle was said to be in ruins.[95] Nevertheless, in 1304 a tenement in Wolverley owed labour service at the castle, and in 1314 Hugh FitzAer held part of Great Wytheford by the service of providing a man with a lance to serve at Wem for 20 days when there was war with Wales, but 'if the garrison leave the castle he shall remain to guard the fire'.[96] William le Botiler I and Alice de Montgomery, the widow of his elder brother, both kept houses in Wem,[97] and in 1336 the grant of Harcourt to Robert Corbet by William le Botiler II still included the duty of castle guard at Wem.[98] By the time of William's death in 1361, however, the lord's 'capital messuage' in Wem was deemed to be of no value, although he possessed a garden and dovecotes.[99] In 1436 the castle site was said to be worthless, having been 'devastated of old by the Welsh'.[100] A survey in 1589 found an 'ancient castle … now wholly decayed'.[101]

---

87   The fourth earl's will, abstracted in *The Times*, 27 Nov. 1891, and the report of the House of Lords decision, 31 May 1892.
88   *The Times*, 13 June 2016.
89   *Survey 1561*, 24; Garbet, 250.
90   *Cal. Inq. p.m.* II, nos. 37, 390; TNA, C 133/27/9.
91   TNA, C 133/27/9, *Cal. Inq. p.m.* II, 229.
92   Ibid.; C.L.H. Coulson, *Castles in Medieval Society* (Oxford, 2004), 60.
93   *Rot. Hund.*, II, 56, 58; SA, 6000/2651, 'Slepe Magna'; SA, 322/2/117.
94   TNA, KB 27/130, extracted in 'Plea rolls of the reign of Edward I', *SHC* 6, part 1 (1885), 205.
95   TNA, C 133/27/9; Eyton, *Antiquities*, IX, 173–4.
96   *Survey 1561*, 92–3; *Cal. Inq. p.m.* V, no. 470.
97   Below, Social History.
98   SA, 322/2/117.
99   TNA, C 135/157/4; *Cal. Inq. p.m.* XI, no. 37; TNA, C 135/206/15, *Cal. Inq. p.m.* XII, p. 324.
100 *Cart. Lilleshall Abbey*, 199–200 (citing TNA, E 179/15/78, E 179/166/37); TNA, C 139/76/34; *Cal. Inq. p.m.* XXIV, p. 348.
101 See E. Gibson (ed.), W. Camden, *Britannia; or a chorographical description of Great Britain and Ireland…*, I (London, 1753), 654; TNA, LR 2/225.

As the lords were seldom if ever resident after the mid 14th century, there was no reason for the medieval castle to develop as a seigneurial residence. In 1553 it was still contemplated that William, Lord Dacre or his heirs might 'lye and kepe house within the lordshipe of Weme',[102] but instead Lord Dacre redeveloped the old castle site. Around 1540 he constructed a new court/market house on its north side (now occupied by the old town hall) which remained the property of the lord of the manor until 1920.[103] He let the remainder of the castle site and the adjacent Alleys to his kinsman, the rector.[104] A windmill was placed on top of the castle mound c.1570, according to witnesses in 1589, but this too may have been the work of William, Lord Dacre.[105]

Although the Alleys was sold in 1643[106] – apparently the first of the demesnes sold to defray the debts of Thomas, earl of Arundel – access to the premises conveyed was from Mill Street, rather than High Street, and there is no record of the sale of 'the manor site' as such. It was however occupied and apparently owned as freehold by Ralph Wilson, an attorney, and after his death c.1735 by his daughter and heiress, Beatrice, and her husband, John Henshaw (d. 1763).[107] The inheritance was apparently shared between two of their daughters: Beatrice, married to Daniel Wycherley (d. 1764), the eponymous heir to the remaining Wem estates of the sometime lord of the manor, and Rebecca, the wife of George Walford, a Wem timber merchant.[108] In 1783 Beatrice sold her half share to Walford, who had also latterly acquired the Alleys,[109] and the four houses then on the site were replaced by two,[110] now 67, and possibly 69, High Street. In 1815 one of the houses was sold as a freehold 'dwelling-house near the centre of the market in Wem with two shops in front, offices, yard [and] garden', let to Messrs Walmsley and Ireland, mercers.[111] The property, now 67 High Street and named Castle Mound House, has since remained a shop and private dwelling with the castle motte in its back garden.[112]

Other Estates

Lacon

Taking his family name from a small manor within Wem parish which his ancestors had alienated by marriage in the 14th century, Richard Lacon of Willey (Salop.) retained freehold tenements in the manors of Wem and Loppington. In Wem township, the property included burgages with cottages and shops in High Street, Noble Street and New Street (perhaps the site of the Old Hall) and also farmland lying west of the

---

102 *Survey 1561*, 53.
103 Below, Local Government.
104 *Survey 1561*, 49; Garbet, 251.
105 TNA, LR 2/225; below, Economic History.
106 SA, D3651/B/151/9/1.
107 Wem Parish Registers; Garbet, 250; SA, 327/2/2/47/2; SA, 5981/B/1/145. Above, Landscape, Settlement and Buildings; below, Economic History.
108 SA, D3651/B/151/9/3; Garbet, 250.
109 SA, 731/2/3255–6, 3260–70; 1805 survey, Wem, lots 9, 142–4; the Alleys: SA, D3651/B/151/9/3.
110 SA, 731/2/3266–8.
111 SA, MI1278/2.
112 Above, Landscape, Settlement and Buildings.

Alleys.[113] The latter, a freehold tenement with the 'mansion' known as Lacons Hall, extended over a large area from the western bar, along the south side of the High Street, with pasture land down to Wem Pool.[114] Richard's heir, Rowland Lacon of Kinlet, apparently did not respond to the 1561 survey for his tenements in Wem township, but produced a charter dated 1322 as evidence for his title in Wolverley, and another dated 1356 which purported to grant in fee the office of forester of the lord's woods with land in Edstaston and Coton.[115] The Lacon estate was sold to John Goldisbrough in 1618,[116] and some of the Wem tenements were then sold off, Lacons Hall to Thomas Adams, the school founder, c.1640.[117] Renamed The Grove c.1800, the freehold can be traced thereafter to its acquisition by Wem UDC for social housing in the mid 20th century.[118]

Dickin

In the absence of resident lords of the manor, the Dickin family was at the apogee of Wem society from the late 18th century.[119] Thomas Dickin, a younger son of Thomas Dickin of Loppington, held the copyhold estate of Aston Hall in Aston township, where he resided from c.1731 to his death in 1779.[120] His son, another Thomas Dickin, married Sarah Atcherley, a wealthy heiress, and in 1774 purchased the freehold property now known as the Old Hall on New Street.[121] Adjacent to the old house he built, at great expense, 'The Hall' (now Park House), adding the copyhold Piper's Pool to complete grounds extending to 11 a. (4.45 ha.).[122] He also acquired large and valuable farms and parcels of agricultural land, both freehold and copyhold, in Wem and Loppington[123] and by 1805 the Dickin estate was the largest landholder in Wem township. Around 1825 Thomas's son and heir, Major Thomas Dickin, moved to Loppington, and after his son, T.A.M. Dickin, succeeded in 1857 the Wem estate was sold off in parts,[124] The Hall in 1878 to Henry Calveley Cotton.[125] Nevertheless, Dickin still held copyhold tenements in Aston which were enfranchised in 1897,[126] and he continued to be active in Wem affairs.[127] The Old Hall remained in the ownership of the Dickin family until at least 1949.[128]

113 *Survey 1561*, 19, 23, 25–6, 31, 33; TNA, LR2/225. The Old Hall: SA, 306 box 2a: indenture, 30 Sept. 1747, Richard Goldisborough to William Tyler.
114 Garbet, 237.
115 *Survey 1561*, 94–5, 112–13; TNA, LR2/225.
116 Garbet, 268; Arundel map.
117 SA, 6000/3411, 6000/15401, 6000/15405.
118 Above, Landscape, Settlement and Buildings; below, Social History.
119 E.g. *Chester Chron.*, 16 Jan. 1829.
120 SA, 306 box 2a: lease 26 Aug. 1731: Thomas Dickin of Loppington to Bartholomew Ebrey of Aston; TNA, PROB 11/1054/152.
121 SA, 306 box 2a.
122 SA, 306 box 2a; SBT, DR 36/183–9, 197–8. Above, Landscape, Settlement and Buildings.
123 See SA, 306, 1186; SA, 1709 box 192. For the copyhold estate in 1858: SA, 1186/50.
124 *Eddowes's Jnl*, 16 Dec. 1857, 3; SA, 1186/40–6, 51–2.
125 SBT, DR 36/202.
126 SA, 1709 box 192.
127 E.g. SA, DA27/994/1/1, 22 Aug. 1872; SA, DA14/100/2, 16 Mar. 1904.
128 SA, DA14/100/8, 670, 728.

ECONOMIC HISTORY

CLOSELY TIED TO ITS AGRICULTURAL hinterland, Wem was a centre for collecting, processing and marketing agricultural produce and raw materials; activities included cheesemaking, tanning, milling, malting, brewing and dealing in timber. The town offered marketing and retailing, legal and financial services and plenty of public houses.

Farming

Agricultural Landscape

In 1648 the lordships of Wem and Loppington were described as 'a fair country', neither too flat nor too hilly. The tillable land was of good quality and its rental value was much the same as meadow and pasture; wheat and barley flourished. The worst pasture was 'moorish' (wet) but could be improved by draining, and there was an abundance of marl which improved the ground where it was used. Peat or turf grounds supplied fuel, and a great deal of woodland and hedgerow wood remained. It was a mixed agrarian economy, with arable production but also cattle and sheep. Wem was well located for the markets at Chester and Shrewsbury, with easy access to the river Severn.[1]

The agricultural landscape of the manor was not in any sense homogenous.[2] Wem township was described in the mid 18th century as having 'pretty dry' soil (apart from Wem Pool), which was mostly arable and best for growing 'muncorn', rye and barley.[3] By 1841 the agricultural land usage was 37 per cent arable, with meadow and pasture in equal amounts (28 per cent each), and 5 per cent classed as arable and meadow or arable and pasture. There was no woodland but 9.5 a. (1 per cent) of the area was used for plantations.

Medieval Period

In 1086 the estate named *Weme* was assessed as having arable land for eight plough teams, although only two were available.[4] In the late 13th century and mid 14th the lord of the manor of Wem held between three and five carucates in demesne.[5] By the

---

1   ACA, MS 508, f. 42. See also Garbet, 8.
2   For agriculture generally, see *VCH Salop*. IV and P. Stamper, *'The Farmer Feeds Us All': A Short History of Shropshire Agriculture* (Shrewsbury, 1989).
3   Garbet, 14.
4   *Domesday*, 703–4.
5   TNA, E 149/1, *Cal. Inq. p.m.* II, 470; TNA, C 135/157/4, *Cal. Inq. p.m.*, XI, 27.

Table 4 *Agricultural land use in Wem township c.1840.*

Land use	Acres
Arable	367.11
Arable and meadow	46.60
Arable and pasture	5.66
Meadow	283.10
Pasture	285.03
Plantation	9.56
Total	997.06

Note: Calculated from the Wem tithe apportionment (TNA, IR 29/334) taking all holdings with more than 1 a. of agricultural land (so house property and other buildings are excluded). The total area of Wem township given in the summary of the tithe survey is 1202 a. 2 r. 3 p. The balance is buildings of various sorts with their curtilages, public roads, water etc. The tithe agreement is dated 6 Nov. 1841: the data describes the situation in 1839 or 1840.

15th century this had increased markedly to eight carucates (or 100 a. and 118 nooks) in demesne in Wem township, and about 15 carucates (or 244 nooks) in the rest of the manor.[6]

In 1281, 14 yardlands (*virgate*) in the manor were held 'in villenagio' for 10s. per yardland with the obligation to work at Wem castle at the lord's will.[7] In that year the 'free rents' of £13 4s. 8d. were almost double the revenue from the land held 'in villenagio'.[8] By 1290 'assessed rents' had increased to £36 6s. 3d. per annum and customary tenants (*custumarii*) were also subject to tallage.[9] In 1362 the rents from both free and unfree tenants (*libere* and *natiui*) were worth £50, increasing to £80 in 1370. By 1436 the situation was reversed; rents due to the lord were not specified, but a much reduced revenue is detailed from the large parts of the manor held in demesne, totalling £23 4s. 4d. from arable land and £5 7s. 4d. from urban or residential plots.

Wem township had three open fields lying on the drier ground to the north of the town.[10] The names of the fields reflect the pre-Reformation landscape. North-east of the town was Cross field, its name possibly derived from a wayside shrine; Chapel field, to the west and crossed by the road to Ditches Hill, was named after the wayside chapel of St John; Middle field lay between the two and included a large area of land on the west side of the Edstaston road.[11] Traces of the former open fields were still apparent in 1631 in the form of curvilinear field boundaries and field names.[12]

6   TNA, C 136/14/11.
7   TNA, E 149/1. The figures in this paragraph are for the whole manor.
8   TNA, C 133/27/9.
9   TNA, E 149/1.
10   *Survey 1561*, 16–17: 'in campis de Weme'. Cf. D. Sylvester, *The Rural Landscape of the Welsh Borderland* (London, 1969), 302; Rowley, *Shropshire Landscape*, 136–49.
11   Garbet, 253. The field names 'Chapel Field' and 'Middle Field' survived in some enclosed fields in 1631 (Arundel map, sheet 5).
12   Arundel map, sheet 5; SA, 9043, file W, 12, showing Middle Field; HER, PRN 28265 and PRN 32651. Lidar imaging reveals traces of ridge-and-furrow in the location of the open fields.

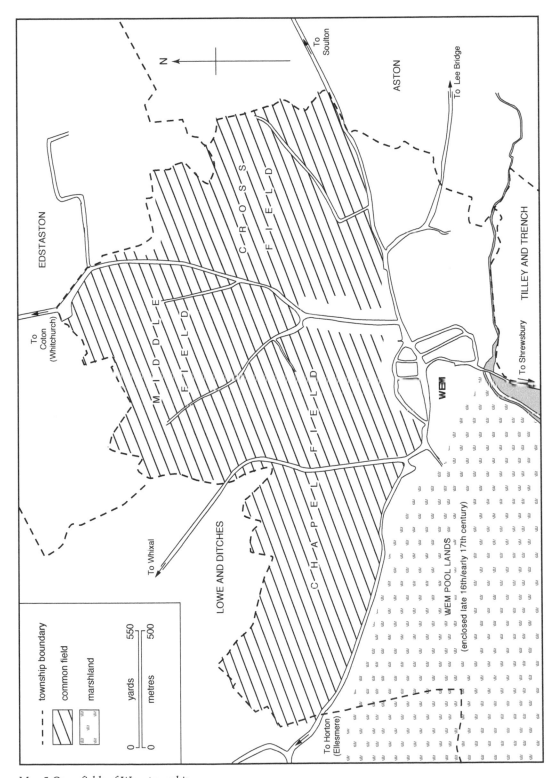

Map 5 *Open fields of Wem township.*

The standard tenement of arable land was a nook, notionally 9 a. (3.65 ha.), but by the mid 16th century there was considerable variation in the size of landholdings. The largest landholders in 1561 were Thomas Pontesbury and William Cowper with 50 and 30 a. of land in the open fields, respectively; the majority of tenants held between 9 and 18 a., such as Richard Watkis, who had 'certain arable lands lying dispersed in Cross Field and Middle Field' totalling 4 and 7 a. respectively, and Humphrey Jebb, who had a messuage outside the bars with 'two nook of land lying scattered in the common fields of Wem' (18 a.).

By the later Middle Ages there was no productive woodland in Wem township, although there was plenty in other parts of the manor, including Brockhurst, the old park (Tilley), the new park (Edstaston) and Northwood. Wem Pool was low-lying marshy land to the south-west of the town, 'about two miles in compass', containing about 200 a. (81 ha.) of unenclosed pasture,[13] where the tenants of Wem township enjoyed a customary right of free common pasture.[14]

Post-Medieval Period

In 1561 the demesne and customary (copyhold) lands of Wem township totalled approximately 318¼ a. (129 ha.) of arable (51 per cent), 251½ a. (102 ha.) of pasture (40 per cent), and 58 a. (23.5 ha.) of meadow (9 per cent), amounting in total to 627¾ a. (254 ha.). There were also small crofts and an orchard of 1½ a.[15]

Enclosure of the Open Fields

Some open-field land had already had been turned into pasture closes by 1561, when six closes 'lately enclosed' held by John Wright included 20 a. of pasture and meadow and a further 7 a. of arable land lying dispersed in the common fields. Wem's open fields were fully enclosed by agreement c.1585, when the tenants requested that 'certain copyhold and customary arable lands lying dispersed in three arable fields belonging to the town of Wem' should be divided and allotted to the tenants 'for their better commodity and profit'. John Heynes of Condover, 'being a man expert in measuring and dividing lands', was engaged by the lord's steward to undertake the operation and the enclosed parcels of land were then allocated to the tenants.[16] The process was complete by 1631.[17]

Drainage and Enclosure of Wem Pool

In 1553 six men were granted a 21-year lease of the lord's mills and of Wem Pool ('one ground or maresse called Weme's old pole'), paying 9d. for every acre 'drawne and maid drye'.[18] Some parcels had been enclosed by 1564.[19] Around 1586, the lord's steward undertook further drainage by cutting a large drainage channel or 'strind' and enclosing the reclaimed land in several parcels.[20] Anne, countess of Arundel, later invested in

13   TNA, E 134/20Jas1/Mich5; Garbet, 14, 251.
14   SA, 167/48.
15   *Survey 1561*, 35–53.
16   TNA, C 2/Eliz/W12/58.
17   Arundel map, sheet 5.
18   *Survey 1561*, 52–3; *VCH Salop. IV*, 123.
19   SA, 167/48.
20   Garbet, 252, 365; TNA, E 134/20Jas1/Mich5, esp. deposition of Laurence Welshe; ACA, MS 508, f. 3.

further reclamation work, and by 1622 it was estimated that just 8 or 9 a. remained to be 'improved'.[21]

In 1648 Thomas Barnes and others held 'the Pooles lands' in several parcels totalling 225 a. The land was described as 'quabby': soft, wet, muddy and prone to becoming overgrown with rushes. The surveyor blamed the overflow of water being held back to drive a mill, and recommended the mill be removed, the brook (the strind?) lowered and cross trenches cut. The land was worth 9s. 3d. per acre, but with further improvement it would be worth £1 per acre.[22] The Pool Lands were subsequently sold.[23] The church rates, starting in 1684, record 'Pool lands' as a distinct part of Wem quarter, with 15 or 16 individual owners. By the early 18th century the Pool Lands were 'divided into a great number of rich meadows and pastures'.[24]

Farms in Wem Township

The tithe award for c.1840 records 21 holdings in the township of between 10 and 20 a., and 14 of more than 20 a., but not all of these holdings had dwellings, suggesting the practice of land being farmed by farms outside the township was already well established.[25] In 1851 at least 12 farmers were resident in Wem.[26] The number of holdings found by the agricultural census in Wem UD fell from 51 in 1900 to 20 in 1940, six in 1980, and seven in 1988, but the seven were only farming 311 a., and the remainder was being farmed from outside the 'parish'.[27] In 1941 most of the holdings in Wem UD were not farms but rather parcels of grazing. For example, the headmistress of The Grove School made a return for the 6¾ a. of grounds around the school although she also had milch cows and poultry. There were six holdings of more than 20 a., of which the largest was Mr Bowen's Landona farm in Love Lane, at 105 a., with 53 cattle and 2,000 head of poultry. The farmers of the other large holdings were usually part-time farmers with other occupations: Messrs Griffiths at Wembrook farm, with 47 a., were also coal merchants, and Wilfred Hall of Roden Villa (28½ a.) a haulage contractor.[28] This remained the case in the 1980s. In 1988 six of the seven 'farms' in Wem urban civil parish were of less than 30 ha. (approximately 75 a.), only one was as big as 50 ha. (124 a.). One was a specialist dairy farm, another specialised in cattle and sheep, and the other five were part-time holdings.

Agricultural Association

Shropshire Agricultural Society held its annual show at Wem in 1886[29] and Wem and District Agricultural Association was founded in 1901. Within 18 months it had 250 members and held its first agricultural show – at Pankeymoor in July 1902 – with

21   TNA, E 134/20Jas1/Mich5; Garbet, 58–9, 252.
22   ACA, MS 508, ff. 3v–4r.
23   ACA, MD 59, pp. 73–4.
24   SA, P295/B/3/11; Garbet, 252.
25   Based on an analysis of the tithe commutation survey, TNA, IR 29/29/334.
26   Bagshaw, 327.
27   Wem data contained in TNA, MAF 68/257 (1870); 713 (1880); 1283 (1890); 1853 (1900); 2423 (1910); 2987 (1920); 3577 (1930); 3954 (1940); 4324 (1950); 4694 (1960); 5190 (1970); 5716 (1980); 6125 (1988).
28   TNA, MAF 32/642/254.
29   Wellington Jnl, 15 May 1886.

great success, with classes for horses (agricultural, hackney and hunter), cattle, sheep, pigs, dogs, poultry, eggs and cheese. In the 'miscellaneous' section 'many of the local tradesmen showed examples of their manufacture and creative genius'.[30] A report of the fifth show in 1906 noted the positive influence of the Association; there was greater interest in cattle-breeding and the standard of cattle entered in the show had improved each year.[31] In 1909 a horticultural show was added.[32] The Association also organised a shire horse stallion to tour the area around Wem to improve the local stock, a scheme that ended in 1944. After a hiatus during the Second World War the show was revived in 1951 and was 'an annual summer event taken for granted by everyone in the district'. The 50th show, held in 1962, was the last, however, as diminishing popularity had made the shows financially unviable. Instead, the Association organised an annual 'Farms Competition' for farms within a ten-mile radius of Wem town hall, which flourished at least until the mid 1970s.[33]

Dairy Farming and Cheesemaking

Cheesemaking on farms – for domestic consumption and as a commodity to be traded – was a feature of the agricultural economy by the 16th century, with an early cheese factory being established at Wem in the 1870s, yet it has always been carried on as part of a mixed farming regime. In his eulogistic description of agriculture in the manors of Wem and Loppington in 1648, Thomas Duckett did not mention dairy farming, merely referring to the raising of such 'cattle as oxen, kine and sheep … of an indifferent large size'.[34] Nearly a century later Garbet wrote that 'the pastures and meadows' of North Bradford hundred 'generally produce good grass and hay and thereby maintain great dairies, which supply the markets with plenty of butter and the factors with great quantities of cheese, in goodness not much inferior to those of Cheshire', but, like Duckett, he also acknowledged the extent of the arable cultivation in the area, seeing it as '[no] less fruitful and productive of grain', holding that its root crops were 'equal to what [is] grown in other parts' and that its potatoes were 'the best in England'.[35] Pigs fed on whey were often an adjunct of cheese production, but when praising the pigs of North Bradford hundred, Garbet attributed their superior quality to 'their being fed on peas'. Garbet also remarked on the large numbers of pigs sold in the autumn months at Wem's weekly market and at the November fair.[36] Around 1840 it was noted that '[Wem] is a great dairy parish and almost everything is subordinate to the dairy',[37] yet the mixed nature of land usage in the township at this time is shown in Table 4.

30   *Wellington Jnl*, 2 Aug. 1902; *Shrews. Chron.*, 30 Jan. 1903.
31   *Wellington Jnl*, 28 July 1906, see also 18 Aug. 1906.
32   *Wellington Jnl*, 7 Aug. 1909.
33   Woodward, 102–3, 118–19; 'Official Programme. 49th Annual Show, 15th July 1961' and inf. from Tom Edwards, June 2017; *Birmingham Daily Post*, 22 Oct. 1965, 6.
34   ACA, MS 508, f. 42.
35   Garbet, 8, 227–8.
36   Garbet, 9, 227, 228.
37   TNA, IR 18/8327.

Farmhouse Cheese

Farmhouse production of cheese (and butter) was an answer to the problem of preserving milk, which was perishable and – before the railways – could not be transported over long distances. Stocks of farmhouse cheese appear in many 16th- and 17th-century Wem probate inventories, and from their price and description these were small cheeses.[38] For example, in 1588 Edward Banister left 43 cheeses worth £1 1s. 6d. (6d. each) and 30 more 'of a smaller sort' (3d. each). These were quite different in character to the 'Cheshire cheeses' made for the metropolitan market which appeared in the late 17th century and which had an optimum weight of 20–24 lb. Ralph Harrison of Wem, who had £40 of cheese in stock when his inventory was made in 1698, is probably representative of the new style of farming which saw its prime objective as being the production of 'Cheshire cheese' for London.

Farmhouse producers required middlemen or factors to buy their cheese and sell it where it would be consumed. Thomas Dickin of Aston was a cheesefactor in the 1730s, and his son Thomas carried on the same business from 1768 to 1780, sending large quantities of cheeses produced by local Wem farmers, mainly to Bridgnorth, and dealing with Bristol merchants.[39] W. Jenks was trading as a cheesefactor in Wem by 1815 but was bankrupt in 1833.[40] Two cheesefactors were listed in Wem in 1851: John Edwards and Thomas Vaughan, both of whom appear to have been general traders who dealt in cheese rather than specialist factors. By 1841 a Cheshire farmer and cheesefactor named John Dobell was living at Bellevue, a gentleman's residence on the Ellesmere road in Lowe township;[41] he founded an important and enduring local enterprise.[42] Two of Dobell's sons, Joseph and Samuel, were in partnership as cheesefactors in Manchester by 1834,[43] probably employing their younger brother, Thomas,[44] and between 1841 and 1851 Thomas Dobell moved from Manchester to join his parents on a farm at Northwood. After John Dobell and his sons Joseph and Thomas died in 1852,[45] the family cheesefactoring business returned to Bellevue when Joseph's widow, Sylvia, leased the property in 1855. In 1856 she married John Platt, the son of a colleague of Samuel

---

38 For dairying, see P.R. Edwards, 'The development of dairy farming on the north Shropshire plain in the seventeenth century', *Midland History*, 4 (1976), 175–90 and for Cheshire, C.F. Foster, *Cheshire Cheese and Farming in the North West in the 17th and 18th Centuries* (Arley Hall, Ches., 1998). See also *VCH Salop.* IV, 150–61; J. Thirsk (ed.), *The Agrarian History of England and Wales, IV 1500–1640* (Cambridge, 1967), 103–4.

39 SA, 306, box 14e, appointment of Thomas Dickin of Aston as chief constable of Bradford hundred for 1739/40; box 3d, account book of Thomas Dickin of Wem.

40 SA, 1848, box 167 (1815); *The New Monthly Magazine and Universal Register* (London), Vol. 3, Jan.–June 1815, 91; *The Spectator*, vol. 6, 1833, 624.

41 TNA, IR 29/29/334; *Census*, 1841

42 Postcard, 'Platt & Swain 49th annual farmers' dinner at Wem, March 1925', 'Platt & Swain, Cheshire Cheese factors, est. 1832': SA, 8540, Wem album no. 2.

43 *Pigot's Dir.* (1834); *Slater's Dir., Lancashire* (1848); *Manchester Courier and Lancashire General Advertiser*, 30 Dec. 1843, 6; 1 Mar. 1848, 5. Samuel Dobell & Co.: *Slater's Dir. of Manchester* (1895), 432; *Manchester Courier and Lancashire General Advertiser*, 30 Dec. 1843, 6; 1 Mar. 1848, 5.

44 In 1841, Thomas Dobell, cheesefactor, aged 25, was residing with John Platt, cheesefactor, aged 30, at Chorlton upon Medlock, Manchester: Census 1841.

45 *Leeds Intelligencer*, 3 Apr. 1852, 8; *Manchester Courier*, 17 July 1852, 11; 16 Oct. 1852.

Dobell,[46] who moved to Wem and devoted his career to the Platt & Dobell firm. In time, John Dobell, the son of Joseph and Sylvia,[47] joined his stepfather in the business.

In 1910 the Wem Dairy Farmers Society was established with the object of promoting regular cheese fairs and holding an annual dairy show. Wem UDC, keen to support local cheese production, offered the Society free use of the town hall and provided the staff and equipment for moving and weighing the cheeses, levying a toll of 5s. per ton of cheese, of which the Society received a share.[48] The quantity of cheese offered at the fairs increased steadily and by June 1914 Wem UDC was considering how to improve the accommodation available for the fairs, in 1925 removing the fire engine shed to make space in the town hall yard. The council then acquired adjacent land, a former maltings on Noble Street, for a dedicated 'cheese hall', erected in 1928.[49]

Despite its success, Wem's cheese fair remained one of the smaller ones in the region. The tonnage offered for sale at the various fairs in 1925 was: 1355½ tons at Whitchurch, 950 at Nantwich, 750 at Market Drayton and 713 at Chester, but just 525 at Wem and about the same at Ellesmere. It was estimated in 1926 that about 10 per cent of the cheese produced was offered through these fairs,[50] but by 1941 farmhouse cheese production had virtually disappeared, and with it the Wem cheese fairs.[51]

Commercial Cheese Production

Platt & Dobell were pioneers in the factory production of cheese, their Bellevue cheese factory being one of the first in Shropshire, operating by 1876.[52] The firm collected milk from local farmers which was either made into cheese or despatched fresh to cities by rail; in 1898 John Platt was prosecuted for sending milk to London which was adulterated with boracic acid, used as a preservative.[53] In 1882 the milk of 600 to 800 cows was made into cheese daily, with the whey being used to feed 200 pigs through a mechanical feeding system.[54] From 1879 Platt & Dobell also leased a warehouse in Wem High Street, on the site of the present Stanier Hall.[55] In the mid 1880s their cheeses were exhibited and commended at agricultural shows at Wolverhampton and in Cheshire.[56]

After John Dobell died in 1894, Platt recruited Percival Swain, from Leicester, as his business partner and successor, trading as Platt & Swain even after Platt's death in

46   SA, 1848, box 101 'Wrench': 26 Oct. 1855, Henry Wrench to Mrs Sylvia Dobell, widow; 1 Nov. 1856, Wrench to John Platt of Bellevue, cheese factor, lease of Drakey Field, Bellevue.
47   *Census*, 1861.
48   SA, DA 14/100/3, 278, 285–6, 309, 326; *Shrews. Chron.*, 18 Nov., 25 Nov. 1910.
49   SA, DA 14/100/3, 620, 623; DA14/100/5, 1265; DA14/100/6, 25, 28, 154. For 'the maltkiln site', see, e.g. SA, DA 14/100/3, 314; DA14/700/9, no. 9 (May 1912).
50   *Manchester Guardian*, 16 Feb. 1926.
51   Reported in *Liverpool Daily Post*, 6 Feb. 1941, 6; *Chester Chron.*, 8 Feb. 1941, 4.
52   SA, DA27/994/1/1, 184.
53   *Eddowes's Jnl*, 28 July 1886; *Cheshire Observer*, 3 Sept. 1887; *Wellington Jnl*, 14 May 1898; *Shrews. Chron.*, 15 Feb. 1907, 8; 21 May 1909; *Staffordshire Advertiser*, 10 Aug. 1935; *Wellington Jnl*, 15 Oct. 1898.
54   *Yorkshire Post*, 10 Mar. 1882, from the *Agricultural Gaz.*
55   SA, 1416, box 45 Adams Grammar School; *Eddowes's Jnl*, 24 Mar. 1880; *Wellington Jnl*, 29 Oct. 1898; SA, DA 14/100/3, 21.
56   *Eddowes's Jnl*, 28 July 1886, 7; *Cheshire Observer*, 3 Sept. 1887, 2.

1910.[57] Described in 1911 as 'cheese factor and maker', Swain exhibited his cheeses at the Leicestershire Show and the London Dairy Show[58] and was an active member of the Wem Dairy Farmers Society.[59] In 1935 a new cheese curing room was constructed at the Bellevue factory.[60] At its height the firm was said to be making 2,000–3,000 cheeses a week. Platt & Swain was sold in 1938 to United Dairies, which in future would supply the cheese factory with milk from its dairies at Ellesmere and Whitchurch.[61] Swain died in 1977, shortly after the factory had ceased production, although it continued to be used for a time as a warehouse for maturing cheese. Most of the factory buildings have since been demolished.[62]

The milk factory on Aston Road was initially built by Cheshire Milk Producers Depots, a farmers' company which became the Cheshire and Shropshire Milk Depots Ltd in 1920. It was opened at the beginning of 1921 as a dual-purpose facility, capable of processing 3,500 gallons of milk per day for cheesemaking and 2,000 gallons for other purposes.[63] The company was always undercapitalised (the Wem factory was not fully funded when it was launched) and went into voluntary liquidation in 1925.[64] It was relaunched in April that year by a farmers' consortium under the chairmanship of the Wem solicitor, Edward Bygott.[65] The new company saw itself as upholding the price of milk in the face of the larger dairies 'and preventing the exploitation of the milk producing industry', but it seems to have had no greater success than its predecessor and by 1935 the factory belonged to a company called Single Services Containers which held patents for the production of milk cartons. It was one of the first factories to be taken over by the Milk Marketing Board. Initially the Board paid the factory to process milk on its behalf, but in June 1935 it agreed to purchase the assets of Single Services Containers (which seems to have been substantially in debt) for £6,000. At this stage the factory apparently specialised in cheese,[66] but repairs were undertaken and a whey tank installed in 1936–7. A new laboratory was built in 1938–9 and a new building erected in 1940 to process the skimmed milk and whey produced there and at other Milk Marketing Board creameries into skimmed milk powder and whey powder.[67]

In the 1960s Wem creamery manufactured Cheshire cheese, and less often Cheddar, drawing on the milk from 150 farms within a 20-mile radius and processing up to 13,000 gallons of milk a day in the spring and early summer peak. It made six tons of Cheshire a day, but the cheese was ripened for a minimum of just three weeks before being graded

57   *Shrews. Chron.*, 15 July 1910; 'Reminiscences of the cheese factory in the 1930s and '40s (an interview with Miss Sylvia Platt)', http://www.wemlocal.org.uk/wempast/memories/swain.htm (accessed 4 Mar. 2019).
58   *Shrews. Chron.*, 8 Oct. 1909, 6; *Grantham Jnl*, 29 May 1915; *Nantwich Guardian*, 22 Oct. 1915, 8.
59   *Nantwich Guardian*, 30 July 1915, 5.
60   SA, DA27/710/2/26; 'Reminiscences of the cheese factory'.
61   *Financial Times*, 29 Oct. 1938.
62   Woodward, 112–13; loc. inf. and pers. obs. 2017.
63   *Manchester Guardian*, 9 Oct., 11 Nov. 1920; *Dairy World*, 16 Dec. 1920, 300; 16 Feb. 1921, 350; *Wellington Jnl*, 22 Jan. 1921.
64   *Lond. Gaz.*, 5 June 1925, 3829.
65   *Whitchurch Herald*, 24 Apr. 1925.
66   TNA, JV 2/17, no. 47, paras 2–25; JV 2/1, 25 June 1935, 25 Sept. 1935.
67   TNA, JV 2/1, 25 Nov. 1935, 13 Dec. 1938; JV 2/25, no. 142, paras 13–14, no. 145, paras 16–20. For plans of the development of the site in 1935, see Cumbria Archive Service (Carlisle), DB 6/Plans2/127.

and sold.[68] The Milk Marketing Board closed the factory in 1976, following the opening of its new creamery at Bangor-on-Dee (Flints.).[69] The site was subsequently developed as a business park for light industrial use, with some of the creamery buildings retained.

Dairying

The late 19th century generally saw the development of both factory-produced cheese and also dairies, often co-operatives, which handled the milk from many farms and arranged its transportation into the industrial towns and the metropolis; this was true of both of Wem's cheese factory/creameries. By 1887 'purveyors of milk' were registered by Wem RSA; three were based in Wem town.[70] Dairies selling fresh milk continued in and around Wem into the mid 20th century,[71] when Brook House farm was supplying milk to the town's schools.[72]

Mills

The lord's water mill with its dam is mentioned *c*.1175 x 1224 when Richard of Sleap's tenants were obliged to grind their grain at the lord's mill in Wem, as well as help with maintenance of the millstones and the mill pond.[73] In the late 13th century the lord of Wem had two watermills worth £2 13*s*. 4*d*. per annum and a windmill worth 10*s*.,[74] but in the 14th and early 15th centuries only one watermill was in the lord's hands.[75] By 1561 there were two watermills and a new windmill in demesne.[76] All three mills were then leased to Richard Mylward, Humphrey Mylward and others for £8, with the corn of Lord Dacre to be ground free of charge if he should reside in Wem.[77] There was a newly erected horsemill and watermill in 1589, and a windmill on top of the old castle mound.[78]

In 1631 Wem mill sat on the south bank of the Roden, with a waterwheel against its north elevation. The mill was in the tenancy of William Adams in 1648, when two rye mills and a wheat mill occupied a building of four bays.[79] Around 1688 a Mr Dolman, who also held a portion of the nearby Pool lands, acquired the mills from Benjamin Arnold.[80] In 1722 William Jeffreys of Newhall (Ches.) purchased the parish mills from Thomas Dolman of Staffordshire and John Chettoe of Wem. In 1736 there were 'three

68   *Wem Creamery* (Milk Marketing Board leaflet, 196-?), Museum of English Rural Life, University of
      Reading, dairy pamphlet 4370 MIL 23543.
69   *Shrews. Chron.*, 6 Dec. 1974.
70   SA, DA27/994/1/2, July 1887, Feb. 1892.
71   *Strong's* (1925); P. Green, 'A Georgian rectory', *The Shropshire Mag.*, July 1981, 40–1
72   Inf. from Tom Edwards.
73   *Survey 1561*, 160–1.
74   TNA, C 133/27/9; TNA, E 149/1.
75   Garbet, 349; TNA, C 133/27/9; C 135/157/4; C 135/206/15; C 139/76/34; ACA, MS W13.
76   TNA, LR 2/225 also mentions a horse mill near the castle site in 1589.
77   *Survey 1561*; TNA, LR 2/225.
78   TNA, LR 2/225; depicted there in 1631 (Arundel map, sheet 5).
79   ACA, MS 508, f. 4.
80   SA, P295/B/3/11.

rye mills and a treble wheat mill', with a newly erected windmill on the mill dam and a 'brick house or mill house'.[81] In 1780 the mill with malt house adjoining, all brick and tiled, was insured for £50.[82] In a plan of the projected new bridge by Thomas Telford in 1808, the mill is shown as a long rectangular building on a dam, with a wheel pit at the south end over a watercourse and a small block to the north.[83]

The mill in its present form is constructed of handmade red brick on a sandstone plinth, with a moulded stone eaves cornice and raised kneelers. It was built in two parts: a long narrow four-window, four-storey range on the dam, and a three-window, three-storey block to the north. Archaeological investigations during the mill's conversion confirmed that the south range was constructed first, although stylistic similarities would suggest the north block was added soon afterwards.[84] The south range has outer doorways to each storey under gabled hoist canopies and cast-iron windows with small-pane glazing. The north block has a central loading door to each storey, including the attic, and sash windows. Its north entrance front is symmetrical with a raised central doorway. Internally, the south range of the mill had open working floors with full-length spine beams supported on cast-iron columns. The north range originally had offices on a raised ground floor, and a basement storey lit by windows cut through the sandstone plinth.

In 1819 the miller, John Boughey, announced his intention to install a steam engine.[85] A long building over a watercourse, labelled 'Mr Boughey', is shown on Wood's map of 1834; in 1851 Boughey's steam and water mill was 'an extensive modern brick building, the machinery of superior construction'.[86] In 1886 the premises consisted of a corn mill, warehouse, boiler house, engine house, mill dam, mill pond, sluices and watercourses, as well as two cottages on the site of a windmill adjoining the mill dam which was 'now a lake'.[87] The windmill may have supplemented the waterwheel before the steam engine was installed. The tall brick stack with stone dressings was linked to the steam engine, but the engine and boiler houses no longer survive. Scars recorded on the south base of the stack are thought to mark their position. Photographs from the 1920s show the mill dam with its stone parapets and a wide pool in front which has since been filled in.[88]

John Boughey died in 1885 having been miller for 67 years[89] and by 1891 the mill had passed to Henry Hinton, who in 1896 advertised that the mill 'has been recently fitted up with a powerful gas engine'. One of several mills owned by Joseph Long in 1899,[90] the

81 SA, MI8200/1; SA, 6000/19478.
82 SA, 4791/1/1, Thomas Jeffreys, miller, policy no. 217.
83 SA, DP199/2, see Fig. 2 above. Also depicted on: SA, 1096/7, Robert Baugh's map of Shropshire, 1808, and SA, 800, bdl 138.1.
84 HER 05520; HER 16819.
85 Woodward, 58–9.
86 *Tibnam's Salop Dir.* (1828), 128; SA, 8611/3/15; Bagshaw, 322.
87 SA, MI7225.
88 SA, PH/W/8/5/11; PH/W/8/5/14; PH/W/8/5/16.
89 *Montgomeryshire Express*, 20 Jan. 1885; *Wellington Jnl*, 3 Jan. 1885.
90 *Kelly's Dir.* (1891), 464; *Wildings Dir. of Shrewsbury & District* (1896), 453, (1899), 469. 'Long's Provender mills and stores, Birkenhead, Seacombe and Wem', postcard with photograph of mill (undated): SA, 8540, Wem album no. 2.

Figure 10 *Wem mill and mill pool in the 1920s.*

Figure 11 *Wem mill converted to apartments.*

complex was sold in 1919 to Wem Mills Ltd which continued the production of animal feeds there until 1985 when the mill finally closed.[91]

Another watermill, or mills, formerly existed at Wem Pool. A deponent in 1622 referred to two water corn mills standing in Wem Pool and a third built more recently. Another recalled two corn mills adjoining Wem Pool on the main drainage channel ('strind').[92] A mill may have existed here by 1553, when an agreement to begin draining Wem Pool referred to the lord's two watermills;[93] alternatively it may have been constructed as part of the drainage works undertaken *c.*1586. In 1648 the mill was valued at £40 per annum, but the surveyor recommended that it should be removed to improve the drainage of the Pool lands.[94] Some masonry visible in the river bank, and rubble blocks on the river bed, about 150 m. upstream from Mill Dam Cottage, may relate to this structure.

Creamore mill, off the Whitchurch road at the northern limit of Wem township, was established shortly before 1851 by Thomas Jebb, the son of a Whitchurch miller.[95] By 1871 Henry Hinton, a former employee, had taken over from Jebb as master miller and when offered for lease on Jebb's death in 1875 it was described as a steam corn mill with up to 38 a. of land and a substantial residence. It was offered for auction in 1877.[96] By 1891 Hinton had moved to Wem mill and Creamore mill was in the hands of Messrs Wycherley when it was sold in 1901.[97] The mill closed around 1960 on the death of one of the Wycherley brothers. The premises were used for various light industrial purposes in the later 20th century, including a wheelwright and steel fabrication workshop. After the present owners acquired the premises in 1986, they repaired and extended the mill buildings to suit their woodturning business, which trades as Creamore Mill.[98]

Crafts and Industries

The various crafts and industries carried on in Wem were generally linked to the agricultural economy and reflected the function of a small market town serving its hinterland. It is the wide range of occupations of its inhabitants that differentiates Wem as a market town from the surrounding villages.

Hemp and Flax

In 1776 Edward Maurice of Petton (about five miles (8 km) south-west of Wem) observed that 'Every cottager and every farmer has hemp; a farmer generally 2 acres, and a cottager all he can spare from potatoes and beans; they dress, spin, and weave it

91   *Strong's* (1925), 'Mill Street'; Woodward, 112, 124–5.
92   TNA, E 134/20Jas1/Mich5.
93   *Survey 1561*, 52–3.
94   ACA, MS 508, f. 3v.
95   Jebb's death was reported in *Eddowes's Jnl*, 28 July 1875.
96   *Census*, 1851, 1871; *Eddowes's Jnl*, 8 Sept. 1875; *Oswestry Advertiser*, 5 Sept. 1877.
97   *Wellington Jnl*, 16 Nov. 1901.
98   SA, DA27/710/3/44; pers. comm. Sam Buckland, Creamore Mill, June 2017; http://www.creamore.co.uk (accessed 4 Mar. 2019).

into cloth in the country.'[99] By the 16th century there was a 'Flax Pool meadow' beside the river near Spenford bridge in Horton,[100] and regular presentments were made to the court leet for retting flax and hemp.[101]

Flax and hemp, tow and spun yarn are recorded in 13 of the 117 probate inventories for Wem township in the period 1535–1648.[102] For instance, the probate inventory of the wheelwright John Sherratt (d. 1636/7) listed hemp and flax worth 10s., and John Pidgin of Wem, husbandman (d. 1640), had hemp and flax worth 3s. 4d. Combing and spinning tow into yarn was typically women's work: an inventory of 1602 included two spinning wheels and 'other things of housewifery' worth 1s. 8d.[103] An exception was John Cowper (d. 1592), described as a 'spinner', who left two spinning wheels, tow and yarn. Probate inventories of widows often include significant quantities of yarn: in 1607 Margaret Richardson of Trench Farm left 11 slippings of hemp yarn and flax worth 10s., two spinning wheels, a hatchel, a pair of combs and a pair of cards worth 2s. 8d.

Weaving was a specialist skill. Lawrence Sandland (d. 1641), who left a loom and weaving implements to the value of 10d., is the only weaver identified in the probate inventories, although in the parish register for burials, 'weaver' is a common occupation in the early 17th century: 11 men are identified as weaver in 1599–1608 and ten in 1609–18, compared with just five in 1653–62. A list of trades in Wem in the early 18th century names six weavers. There was also normally a dyer in the town: William Lawrence (d. 1695), dyer, left 'furnaces?, dyeing stuff, shears, tainters, press, and other implements of trade' worth £12 11s. 6d.[104]

A new one-day fair established in 1636 was described in the mid 18th century as being the outlet for 'great quantities of linen cloth', presumably of local production.[105] John Chidlowe (d. 1602) may have been a dealer: he left tow cloth worth 16s., flaxen cloth worth 12s. and hempen cloth worth 10s. He had no farm stock and was owed several debts. Richard Southall, mercer (d. 1666), left bundles and bails of different varieties of hemp and flax by the hundredweight, which was assessed separately from his 'shop stock' of cloth, lace, hose, ribbon, etc. A few farmers left sheep and/or wool but there is little evidence for the production of woollen yarn or cloth.

Brewing and Malting

In 1829 Wem was praised for its 'many … good malting concerns'; 'perhaps no town for its size, has so many excellent inns'.[106] The Drawwell brewery, off Noble Street, originated with domestic brewing: the ales of William and Hannah Cooke, tenants of Drawwell

99   A. Young, *Tours in England and Wales (abridged from Annals of Agriculture)* (London, 1912), 162.
100 *Survey 1561*, 81, 83, 85, 91; shown on the Arundel map. At the court held on 1 Oct. 1590 there were presentments for watering flax ('bissum') at Spenford ('in Pensford'): SA, 167/3.
101 E.g. SA, 167/5A, 19 Oct. 1612, 28 people were fined 4d. each for watering hemp in the Roden in Wem township.
102 'Wem wills'.
103 Robert Wyddowes of Edstaston, yeoman, 1602.
104 Wem Parish Registers; 'Wem wills'; SA, 9043, File A, 15.
105 Below, Economic History (Markets and Fairs). The rest of this paragraph is based on 'Wem wills'.
106 *Pigot's Dir.* (1828/9), 697.

House from 1781, were particularly praised.[107] By 1824 the property was owned by Thomas Ireland, whose tenant, Joseph Cooke, was a maltster in 1821 and 'retail brewer' in 1828.[108] The site was advertised in 1845 as 'an excellent Malt House, Brewery and Dwelling House at the Drawell' and in 1862 as a 'maltkiln, compact brewery and three-stall stable called "The Drawwell Brewery".[109]

The Talbot inn and brewery supplied other public houses with its 'Shropshire Ales' and by 1890 it was managed by William Hall, owner of the Circus Brewery, Shrewsbury, who also owned the White Lion and the Bull's Head in Wem.[110] In 1898 Hall joined with C.H. Kynaston, owner of the Drawwell brewery, to form the Shropshire Brewery Co. Ltd; renamed the Shrewsbury & Wem Brewery Co. Ltd, all of its brewing and bottling operations had been moved to the Drawwell site by 1920.[111] The brewery became one of the town's largest employers,[112] owning eight public houses in Wem in 1901.[113] Greenall Whitley & Co. of Warrington purchased the business in 1951; it closed the bottling plant in 1959 but retained the site as an administrative and distribution centre and brewed draught ale at the Drawwell brewery until it closed the whole Wem operation in 1988.[114]

Brewing was supported by local malting.[115] An early 18th-century list of trades in Wem names nine maltsters, and the same number are listed in a commercial directory in 1822.[116] In 1841 there were seven malt kilns in Wem but by 1870 there were just three: at Bank House, on Noble Street and at the Drawwell brewery.[117] Bank House, at the west end of High Street, probably originated as a maltings or corn store. The building served as the parish poorhouse between 1805 and 1838 but afterwards it was converted (back) to a maltings, which was still in operation in 1975 when it was owned by United Malting Co.[118] Constructed of brick on a stone plinth, the building has a three-storey gabled front with central doorways to the ground and second floors, and windows with segmental brick heads which may be later insertions. Continuing to the left is a range of three bays divided by shallow buttresses, originally single-storey but raised later with an upper level doorway under a gabled hoist canopy.

To meet the growing demand from his Drawwell brewery, in the 1890s C.H. Kynaston extended the Noble Street maltings, a six-bay, three-storey range with kiln at the east end under a hipped roof. He also erected a new maltings in 1897 on the site of a sawmill

107 Edwards, 12.
108 SA, P295/B/2/1; 'Wem, Chapel St. Independent Chapel, 1785–1836' [transcribed by A.M. MacLeod], in *Shropshire Parish Registers. Nonconformist and Roman Catholic Registers, Pt 2* (Shropshire Parish Register Society, 1922), years 1815, 1819, 1821, 1825; *Pigot's Dir.* (1828/9), 697.
109 *Shrews. Chron.*, 28 Feb. 1845; *Eddowes's Jnl*, 30 July 1862, advertisements.
110 *Kelly's Dir.* (1890); SA, QA/9/3/1 (1891).
111 *The Globe* (London), 15 Feb. 1898; R.G. Dakin, 'The Shrewsbury & Wem Brewery Co. Ltd: Brewers of Real Ale' (typescript, 1977: SA, I 28.3 v.f), 'History of Wem'; http://www.wemlocal.org.uk/wempast/industry/brewing.htm (accessed 4 Mar. 2019).
112 Dakin, 'Shrewsbury & Wem Brewery Co.'; Plans for extensions of the brewery, 1907–30: SA, DA14/700/12, nos. 1–3, 7, 11, 12, 17, 18.
113 SA, QA/9/3/1 (1901).
114 Dakin, 'Shrewsbury & Wem Brewery Co.'; Woodward, 100, 112, 122.
115 *VCH Salop.* IV, 141–50. Reference to a malt kiln in Wem township, 17 Oct. 1578: SA, 167/1.
116 SA, 9043, File A, 15; *Pigot's Dir.* (1822).
117 TNA, IR 29/29/334; *PO Dir.* (1870); *Eddowes Jnl*, 30 July 1862, advertisement.
118 Woodward, 100, 112.

Figure 12 *The former Kynaston's maltings on Station Road, destroyed by fire in 1977.*

near the station, where the building with its two large towers became a landmark for rail travellers.[119] Shrewsbury & Wem Brewery Co. Ltd ceased malting in Wem in 1968;[120] ironically, another landmark in the town – the cowl of the old Drawwell brewery maltings with its malt-shovel weathervane – was adopted soon afterwards as the trademark of the brewery company.[121] The Station Road maltings was acquired by Whitchurch Seed & Corn Co. and used as a grain store until it was destroyed by fire in 1977.[122]

Leather Production

The whole production cycle of the leather trade, from skinning and tanning to finished goods (gloves, footwear, breeches, saddles) was carried out in Wem until the late 19th century, especially the production of tanned hides. The lord of the manor controlled the trade by requiring leather produced for sale to be sealed; two leather-sealers were appointed annually by the court leet for this purpose.[123] Defaulters were liable to be

---

119 *Kelly's Dir.* (1900). Noble Street: SA, PH/W/8/8/43. Station Road: SA, DA 14/700/13; photograph at
      Historic England, Card reference no. 5115/66: https://historicengland.org.uk/images-books/photos/
      englands-places/gallery/ (accessed 4 March 2019); Woodward, 126 and fig. 15.
120 Dakin, 'Shrewsbury & Wem Brewery Co.'
121 Ibid., reproduction of trade advertisement, *c*.1977; Woodward, 100, fig. 14.
122 SA, PH/W/8/8/7–24; *Shropshire Star*, 20 June 1977; Woodward, 126.
123 Leather sealers are named in the earliest extant record of the court leet, SA, 167/1, 17 Aug. 1578, and
      subsequently.

presented to the court and fined, though there are few such cases in the court records.[124] In 1613 the court prohibited washing hides or dyed cloth in certain marl pits as it was a nuisance to cattle.[125]

The probate inventories of six tanners, in the period 1535–1650, suggest that they carried on farming alongside their trade. In the same period there were seven shoemakers and a glover, Allan Mose (d. 1634), whose wealth was considerable, being £120 3s. 4d., and another glover, Robert Hill, who was wealthy enough to set up a charity for the benefit of the local Nonconformists in 1697.[126] John Barnes, a tanner, who died in 1645, had 18 dickers of leather (bundles of 10 hides) worth £103 plus quantities of hides worth £140. Catherine Forgham of Wem (1644), the widow of a tanner, had leather and bark in stock and in the tanhouse. Later, another tanner's widow, Hannah Drury, was in 1805 the individual who owned the largest number of houses, gardens and other commercial premises in the town.[127]

Tanneries are recorded at several sites. Thomas Adams, father of the school founder, had tan pits on the banks of Wem Brook near where it was crossed by the High Street.[128] The eastern part was taken over by the school grounds c.1670, but tan yards remained in operation on Wem Brook.[129] The New Pool Bank tannery was operated from the 1830s by the Gough family and then by John Everall and son.[130] Another tan yard on the brook, just south of the bridge, was part of the endowment of the grammar school. In 1805 it was a 'skinner's yard'.[131] It was transferred to The Grove estate in 1828, in exchange for land near the school in Noble Street:[132] in 1831 it was operated by Messrs Pritchard and Wood and from 1849 to 1871 by Philip and Stephen Gough.[133]

The tannery of the Forgham family was established by 1631 near the Well House, at the bottom of Chapel Street. In 1599 William Forgham, tanner of Wem, left leather, bark etc. belonging to the tan house worth £20. James Forgham, in 1638, left stock of seven dickers of leather and four hides worth £54 4s. and bark worth £10. The tan yard was leased by William Forgham to Henry Burton and William Gough in 1824 but had apparently ceased to operate by 1842.[134] There was a tan yard on the north side of the British School site on Leek Street before 1839, described as a currier's shop in 1846 and as a 'valuable tannery' in 1873; by 1880 it had been replaced by Thomas Gough's foundry and ironworks.[135]

---

124 SA, 167/5A, 14 Apr. 1614.

125 SA, 167/5A, 15 Apr. 1613.

126 Below, Social History.

127 Yalden, 'Landownership', 2.

128 SA, 167/5A, 5 May 1617; SA, 167/4, May 1623; Garbet, 175, 217, 333; inventory of Thomas Addams, 1607.

129 Garbet, 175.

130 SA, 3994 box 2; SA, D3561/B/151/3, Robert Gough of Wem, tanner, to John Everall of Wem, tanner, 13 Sept. 1848; SA, 1416, box 45: lease by Adams Grammar School Trustees to John Platt, 7 Apr. 1879.

131 SA, 8611/3.

132 SA, 1186/124.

133 SA, 7577/36/8, 30 July 1831; SA, 1186/126–31, 134–8, 141, 145. Shown on 1882 map, SA, DA14/701/7; *Shrews. Chron.*, 12 May 1865, 1.

134 SA, MI6508/1A, probate inventory of James Forgham, tanner (d. 1638); SA, 1848, box 167: lease dated 11 Aug. 1824.

135 Title deeds to 17 Chapel Street, in private possession; SA, 1848, box 22, Drury deeds, notice of sale 15 Oct. 1846; SA, 1848, box 167, bill for sale of various properties, 17 Feb. 1873.

John Everall, father and son, and the Gough family dominated the tanning industry in Wem for most of the 19th century. The former ceased business around 1872, when all but one of Wem's tanneries appear to have closed. The last remaining tannery, on Noble Street, was in operation by 1805.[136] The Gough family continued to operate it until 1898, when it was advertised for sale with 'a massively built bark bay with tan pits beneath, engine and boiler house, numerous drying, rolling, scouring, lime and store houses; offices, curriers shop, bark mill ... covered and open tan pits and bark spenders'.[137] The tannery had reopened by 1909. By 1925 it shared the premises at 43 Noble Street with Moss Bros. motor garage, which had taken over the old tannery site by 1941, bringing to an end the tanning industry in Wem.[138] The closure of the tanneries on Wem Brook in the 1870s, and complaints of noxious effluent from the Noble Street tannery in the 1880s,[139] indicate that carrying on leather trades within the town was incompatible with late Victorian standards of public health.

Timber

Timber was abundant in the parish up to the mid 18th century.[140] Commercial dealing in timber had begun in the town by the mid 17th century: 'Mr Thorp of Wem, timber merchant' supplied timber to rebuild the school house a few years after the great fire of 1677.[141] Timber was sourced from a wide area: in 1668 George Allen of Newtown (Wem) had timber at Tilstock, Stanwardine and elsewhere worth over £100.[142] George Walford of Wem, who supplied timber to the Navy between 1768 and 1773,[143] was still active in 1797 when he contracted for the purchase of trees from Andrew Corbet of Shawbury.[144] The Noble Street site of the National School had been until 1811 a timber yard belonging to Philip Ireland, timber merchant, and the tannery on the eastern bank of Wem Brook south of the bridge was temporarily a timber yard in 1842 and reverted to that use after the tannery closed.[145]

The arrival of the railway attracted the timber trade to Aston Street. By 1925 Jones & Son specialised in agricultural supplies such as oak field gates and posts, but as wooden items were superseded by other materials the business closed in 1960.[146] There were two sawmills beside the railway by 1880.[147] One belonged to Thomas Gough, who also sold coal at the station yard and operated an iron foundry in Leek Street; it was replaced by

136 SA, 3994 box 2; *Pigot's Dir.* (182829), 697, 698; *Cassey's Dir. of Shropshire* (1871), 377; SA, DA14/100/3, 98, 296; coloured blue on 1882 map, SA, DA14/701/7; depicted in a watercolour of 1889: SA, PR/2/524.
137 *Wellington Jnl*, 15 Dec. 1898; obituary of Stephen Gough: *Shrews. Chron.*, 5 Jan. 1900.
138 Woodward, 100.
139 SA, DA27/994/1/1, 382, 384, 396, 399, 411 (1881); DA27/994/1/1, May 1884.
140 Garbet, 8.
141 Garbet, 200–1. Also Richard Pay of Wem, timber merchant, *c.*1703: Garbet, 306–7.
142 'Wem wills'.
143 TNA, ADM 106/1173/188, ADM 106/1206/255, 296, 304, 398, ADM 106/1212/115, 116, 119, ADM 106/1222/306.
144 SA, 166/7/24.
145 TNA, ED 49/6433, draft of conveyance to school trustees; 1842 Tithe Apportionment; Bowcock, 'Wem of the past'.
146 Woodward, 100; *Strong's* (1925), advertisement; inf. from Tom Edwards.
147 Trinder, *Ind. Archaeol.*, 47–8; OS Map 25", Salop. sheet XIV.15 (1880 edn); SA, DA14/701/7.

Figure 13 *Wem station sidings and Isherwood's timber yard in 1966. Kynaston's maltings stands in the distance.*

1891 by Kynaston's Station Road maltings.[148] The other belonged to John Thorniley & Son and was steam-powered by 1890.[149] By 1900 Thorniley's timber yard had been sold to John Cooper & Sons of Wem and Bolton,[150] and in 1909 it was taken over by Albert Isherwood & Co. Ltd, trading as the Railway Saw Mills, which flourished for decades as a family-owned business. In 1955 it employed 50 men and women in the sawmill and another 30 in the adjacent tree nursery and in felling and transportation.[151] In the early 1970s, with modern kilning facilities and a nationwide trade in 'high quality joinery and butchers' blocks', the sawmill was the town's largest employer.[152] The business's fortunes declined, however, and it closed in 1991 with the loss of 30 jobs.[153]

Clay-Pipe Making

Clay pipes were produced in Loppington parish and six pipemakers are named in Wem parish registers between 1681 and 1703.[154] This cluster of pipemakers is not readily explained, for instance, by any known deposit of suitable clay. Based on occupations recorded in parish registers, however, there were more pipemakers in Wem than in Shrewsbury in this period.

148 SA, DA27/994/1/2, May 1891.
149 SA, DA27/994/1/2, Nov. 1890; *Slater's Dir.* (1880), 134.
150 SA, DA14/100/2, 58; DA14/100/3, 62, 178; *Kelly's Dir.* (1900), (1909).
151 *The Shropshire Mag.*, Oct. 1954, 16–18, Apr. 1955, 24–7.
152 SA, DA14/154/1; SA, PH/W/8/9/7–8; Woodward, 100, 112; photographs taken in 1985 and 1990: SA, 8540, Wem album no. 3.
153 Woodward, 123.
154 Inf. from David Higgins. D.A. Higgins, 'The interpretation and regional study of clay tobacco pipes: a case study of the Broseley district' (unpublished Univ. of Liverpool Ph.D. thesis, 1987); D.A. Higgins, 'A brief introduction to the Shropshire clay tobacco pipe industry', *TSHAS*, 79 (2004), 157–66.

Markets and Other Services

As a market town Wem offered services to the surrounding agricultural area, such as retailing, hospitality and legal services, as well as, for example, schools, medical treatment and entertainment.[155]

Markets and Fairs

Wem is a typical market town, indeed the market is probably as old as the town. A royal charter of 1205 has been cited as the authority for both the weekly market and the annual fair on St Peter's day (26 June). The attribution of this charter to Wem was however an uncharacteristic error by the antiquary Edward Lhuyd (or Lloyd); the charter that Lhuyd noted for Wem was for Highworth (Wilts.).[156] In the late 13th century the lord of Wem claimed a market and fair by charter of Henry III,[157] but no such charter has been found. Both the market and fair appear rather to be prescriptive, implying an early creation – in the 11th or 12th century – before royal licence was generally required to exercise such prerogatives.

By 1292 the weekly market was held on Sundays with a three-day fair on the eve, the day, and the day after the feast of St Peter and St Paul (26 June).[158] The market place was a widening of the High Street in front of the castle, with a market house provided by the lord of the manor.[159] Toll was taken by the lord's officers from traders at the fairs; in 1370 fair tolls came to 40s.[160] Burgesses enjoyed customary exemption from the toll which in 1589 was charged on 'standings' and merchandise valued at more than 1s. sold by strangers and other tenants.[161]

Two additional fairs were established. The Martinmas fair, established before 1589, was 'chiefly remarkable for vast numbers of the best hogs, most of which are bought on the eve of the fair, and in droves sent to London for victualing the navy', as well as 'horned cattle, horses [and] linen cloth'.[162] A third fair was granted by Charles I in 1636; held on St Mark's day (25 April, then 6 May after 1752), it specialised in the sale of linen cloth,[163] in 1788 'horned cattle, horses, sheep, linen, flax seed' were traded.[164]

By the mid 19th century the lord's three fairs were still held, as well as five more which were held by the 'landowners, tradesmen and farmers of the town of Wem and the surrounding district'. Around 1858 some 90 of them petitioned the duke of Cleveland

---

155 Below, Social History.
156 Garbet, 29, 227; SA, 6001/108, 6001/5705; see J. Everard, 'Wem Market Charter', forthcoming, *TSAHS*.
157 SA, 6000/2651; Eyton, *Antiquities*, IX, 172.
158 Shropshire eyre of 1292, cited in Lloyd: SA, 6001/108; T.F. Dukes, *Antiquities of Shropshire from an Old Manuscript of Edward Lloyd* (Shrewsbury, 1844), 130. See TNA, JUST 1/739–41.
159 For the market place see above, Landscape, Settlement and Buildings. For the court house/market house see below, Local Government..
160 TNA, C 135/157/4; C 135/206/15; C 136/14/11.
161 TNA, LR 2/225.
162 Garbet, 228; *Owen's New Book of Fairs* (London, 1788), 55–6.
163 Garbet, 228; TNA, C 202/18/1.
164 J.A. Chartres, 'The marketing of agricultural produce', in J. Thirsk (ed.), *The Agrarian History of England and Wales*, V, II (1985), 427; *Owen's New Book of Fairs*, 55.

as lord of the manor for the rationalisation of the eight fairs due to the arrival of the railway.[165] They asked for seven fairs, to be held on the first Monday of March, May, June, August, September and November, and on the second Monday of December, and thereafter Wem's livestock market was duly held on the first Monday of the month.[166] When Lord Barnard transferred his market rights to Wem UDC in 1905 the lord's fair rights were not transferred, being deemed of no value.[167]

The market held on Holy Thursday (Ascension Day) was especially large and was even classed as a fourth annual fair.[168] It had probably developed from a springtime hiring fair; having been 'much frequented by maids, dressed all in white, and often appearing twenty or thirty in a body; whence it is commonly called Rig-fair'.[169] A winter hiring fair, known as the 'gawby' fair, took place at the first Thursday market after Christmas and survived into the early 20th century.[170]

A weekly market was held by the late 13th century. The market day is recorded variously as Thursday, Saturday or Sunday; it had settled on Thursday by 1589. It was described in 1673 as 'a great Market on Thursdays for Cattle and Provisions'; and in the early 18th century it did 'not take off any quantity of corn', but in autumn it was 'very remarkable for swine', with 30 or 40 hogs sold every market day from the beginning of September until Christmas.[171]

In 1290 market tolls were worth 20s. per annum to the lord of the manor; in 1361 the market and fair together came to the same amount, but in 1370 the market was worth just 6s. 8d. Although in 1589 the market was said to be 'free',[172] by the mid 18th century the town bailiffs collected 1d. from 'every stranger that pitches a standing, or hawks, or sells anything in the streets'.[173] The lord also held the assize of ale, of bread and finally of all provisions sold in the market. The two town bailiffs kept standard weights and measures and had the authority 'to seize all false measures and weights' and also underweight merchandise.[174]

There was a market house on the market place from at least the 15th century.[175] It was referred to in 1561 as the lord's court house, with shops beneath, occupying the same site as the present 'old town hall', which dates from 1702, when it was constructed with open arcades to house a covered market and corn exchange. By the 1880s townspeople were calling upon the lord of the manor to upgrade the market facilities; in 1896 the rector described the building as being 'cold and draughty'. He believed the market was dominated by two dealers who forced down prices, and many farmers avoided

165 Undated petition, Raby Castle, Shropshire and Staffordshire deeds box 6.
166 Below, Economic History.
167 SA, DA14/100/2, 11; SA, Raby Estate, box 8.
168 E.g. in *Owen's Book of Fairs* (London, 1756) and *Owen's New Book of Fairs*, 55.
169 Garbet, 227–8; Bodleian, MS Blakeway 21, f. 80b, note; *First Report of the Royal Commission on Market Rights*, 198.
170 L. Etherington, 'The memories of Alice Edge of Whixall', *The Wemian*, 2002, available at http://www.wemlocal.org.uk/wempast/memories/edge.htm (accessed 4 Mar. 2019). cf. J. Wright, *The English Dialect Dictionary* (London, 1900), II, 530–1.
171 Blome, *Britannia*, 194.
172 TNA, C 135/157/4; C 135/206/15; C 136/14/11; LR 2/225.
173 Garbet, 145.
174 Garbet, 144.
175 Below, Local Government.

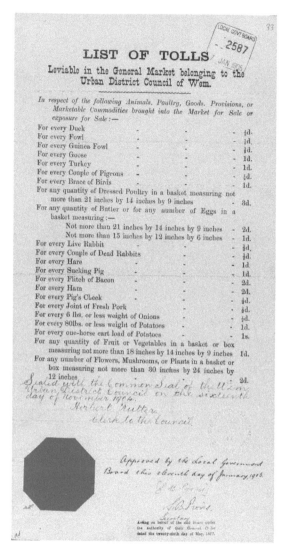

Figure 14 *List of tolls levied at the general market in the new town hall, 1904.*

selling there, even preferring to drive to Shrewsbury.[176] In 1890 G.H. Birch drafted plans for the duke of Cleveland to extend the existing building southwards into the church yard, trebling the market hall in size.[177] These plans were not implemented and the duke's successor, Lord Barnard, agreed to transfer his market rights to Wem UDC,[178] which in 1905 replaced the old market house with the present town hall, incorporating a ground-floor market hall.[179] In 2019 a weekly produce market was still held on Thursdays in the town hall.[180]

Josiah Franklin claimed to have established 'Wem Smithfield' by conducting an auction of cattle, sheep, pigs and horses at the fair in November 1858.[181] In 1859 Franklin's sales yard was 'nearly adjoining the Wem Station', the railway having arrived the previous year.[182] From 1867, Franklin's Smithfield was situated behind the Castle inn,[183] where livestock sales were held monthly, and fortnightly by 1890.[184] 'Wem Smithfield' did not have a monopoly of livestock sales – another was conducted at the Talbot inn

176 SA, Raby Estate, box 9, esp. letter from G.H.F. Vane to his brother, Lord Barnard [1896]; SRO, B/C/12/1/530.

177 SA, Raby Estate, box 9.

178 SA, DA14/100/1, 16, 55, 138, 167; SA, Raby Estate, boxes 9 and 34; See *Shrews. Chron.*, 5 Feb. 1904, 5.

179 SA, DA14/100/2, 56, 224, 226; DA14/135/5, no. 33; *Wellington Jnl*, 21 Jan. 1905; Etherington, 'The memories of Alice Edge of Whixall'.

180 Wem Civic Society: http://www.wemlocal.org.uk/wempres/siw/markets/wemmark.htm (accessed 4 Mar. 2019).

181 *Chester Chron.*, 20 Nov. 1858; *Wellington Jnl*, 29 Sept. 1883, advertisements.

182 *Eddowes Jnl*, 2 Mar. 1859, advertisement.

183 A plaque above the former entrance, behind the Castle public house, bears this date; hence perhaps *Shrews. Chron.*, 6 Sept. 1867, 'Re-opening of Wem cattle fairs … at Wem Smithfield'; SA, DA14/100/1, 46.

184 *First Report of the Royal Commission on Market Rights and Tolls* (London, 1889), 19; *PO Dir.* (1870); *Kelly's Dir.* (1890). Monthly fairs were reported in *Shrews. Chron.*, e.g. 18 Oct. 1872, 7: about 500 sheep and a large number of pigs sold at the fair on 14 October.

yard in the 1870s.[185] Josiah Franklin retired in 1887, handing his 'Smithfield' business on to auctioneers Hall, Wateridge & Owen.[186]

The provision of a public livestock market was an ambition of Wem UDC from its inception.[187] In 1913 the council negotiated the purchase of a site behind the Talbot inn, owned by the Shrewsbury & Wem Brewery Co., with 'the stand' to be leased by Hall, Wateridge & Owen.[188] Unable to raise the necessary funds, Wem UDC finally resolved in 1923 that the Smithfield project was beyond its means.[189] Hall, Wateridge & Owen then purchased the site, operating 'Wem New Smithfield' by January 1925.[190] Livestock markets at Wem ceased in 1962, largely due to the opening in 1959 of the new Shrewsbury livestock market at Harlescott.[191]

The western end of the High Street was known as the Horse Market in the 18th century,[192] although the evidence for a horse market there is circumstantial.[193] In 1613 the court leet banned the tying up or shoeing of horses in the street between High Street and Noble Street and Simon Allenson was fined for 'collecting horses in the street' there, measures perhaps intended to prevent the horse market encroaching on the town centre.[194] In the mid 19th century there remained a cluster of public houses at the western end of the town, including the Horse and Jockey, formerly the Packhorse, which had stabling provision second only to the town's premier coaching inn, the White Horse.[195]

Retailing

By the mid 16th century retailing was being carried out from permanent shops around the market place. There were three shops beneath the courthouse in 1561 and another 'next to the grave yard', while on the opposite (north) side of the market place was a blacksmith's shop and another shop or workshop (*opella*) beneath the old courthouse.[196] By 1612 another shop – a house with a '*pergula*' – had been opened on the north-west

185 E.g. *Wellington Jnl*, 19 Aug. 1876, advertisement.
186 *Wellington Jnl*, 29 Oct. 1887.
187 SA, DA14/100/1, 196, 220.
188 SA, DA14/100/2, 125, 174, 196, 199–200, 219; DA14/100/3, 149, 150, 181; DA14/100/4, 433, 501, 508, 534, 542.
189 SA, DA14/100/4, 582, 618, 635, 655; DA14/700/17; DA14/100/5, 1182, 1198, 1203–4.
190 *Strong's* (1925); OS Map 25", Salop. XXI.3 (1926 edn); 'Brock', 'Wem livestock market', *The Wemian*, Spring 2011.
191 Shrewsbury Corporation Markets and Fairs Committee, *The Shrewsbury Smithfield. Official Handbook* (Shrewsbury, 1959); Woodward, 113; 'Brock', 'Wem livestock market'.
192 Garbet, 245; SA, 1848, box 15, 13 Oct. 1738, 'Horse Markett Street'; SA, 1848, box 121, 29 Apr. 1752; SA, 167/27, f.1, 17 Apr. 1801, the parish poorhouse in 'the Horse Market'.
193 cf. P.R. Edwards, 'The horse trade of Shropshire in the early modern period', in J. Chartres and D. Hey (eds.) *English Rural Society, 1500–1800: Essays in Honour of Joan Thirsk* (Cambridge, 1990), 227–49.
194 SA, 167/5, 15 Apr. 1613, 21 Oct. 1613.
195 SA, P295/B/3/1/2, 1773/4; *Shrews. Chron.*, 17 June 1775: notice of a sale at the Packhorse; SA, 7577/36/8, 3 Mar. 1831. Above, Economic History.
196 *Survey 1561*, 21, 33; Garbet, 235; 'the shop beneath the courthouse' in 1596–7: SA, 167/4, ff. 129, 154.

of the market place.[197] In 1648 the lord's demesne included seven shops in the town, one 'newly built',[198] forming a row of shops with 'chambers over' in front of the church.[199]

A list of traders in Wem in the early 18th century names ten innholders, nine maltsters, nine tailors, nine shoemakers, seven barbers, six bakers, six butchers, six chandlers, five grocers, three glovers, three mercers, two tallow chandlers, one haberdasher and one hatmaker, along with a wide variety of crafts.[200] By 1795 there was greater diversity and more specialisation, especially in personal apparel and consumer goods: four tailors, six shoemakers, two hairdressers, two bakers, four butchers, two grocers, four drapers, two millers (corn dealers), two stay makers, a hatter, a milliner and mantua maker, a breeches maker, a clock maker, an ironmonger, a liquor merchant and a Staffordshireware dealer.[201] In 1822 the same trades and retailers were represented, with the addition of two confectioners, two grocers dealing in hosiery, an upholsterer, a tinman, a clothes dealer and a glass and cutlery dealer. Geoffrey Franklin, who published Garbet's *History of Wem* in 1818, was a valuer, bookseller, printer, jeweller and agent to the Shrewsbury Fire Office.[202] By 1827 he and T. Green, a grocer, occupied two newly built houses with shops on the market place near the Black Lion inn.[203] Another notable Wem printer and publisher was Thomas Gregory, who in 1824 published *The Shropshire Gazetteer* illustrated with plates of market towns, including Wem.

Some of these businesses were situated in the buildings that extended along the High Street in front of the church.[204] By the early 19th century they had deteriorated and become an affront to civic pride. Such was the importance of this central site that the Wem Improvement Society was formed *c.*1829 with the aim of purchasing the buildings, demolishing them, and erecting in their place 'a row of neat shops'. A shares issue raised £1,250, the balance being raised by mortgage.[205] The Union Buildings, with a High Street frontage of 144 ft (44 m.) from the corner of Mill Street almost to the church gate, contained 13 shops with a newspaper reading room above.[206] Trading had commenced by August 1831.[207] In 1842 the shareholders sold the Union Buildings to John Griffiths of Shooter's Hill, Clive.[208] Ownership finally passed to W.J. Evans, a grocer and tobacconist who occupied three of the shops.[209] By 1936 Evans had retired, his business carried on

197 SA, 167/5A, f. 8.
198 ACA, MS 508, f. 36–36v.
199 ACA, MS MD 59, pp. 52, 56, 59, 82. On one sketch map (SA, 9043, File W), Garbet noted, 'The court house stood on the north of the church yard, where the L[or]d has shops now'; these shops already appear on the 1631 survey. Garbet's sketch map of the town in his own day shows them as small tenements, each marked 'F', for freehold.
200 SA, 9043, File A, 15.
201 *Univ. Brit. Dir.*, 718–19.
202 *Pigot's Dir.* (1822).
203 *Chester Courant*, 13 Mar. 1827, 3.
204 SA, 167/47 (1805), p. 128, 'Houses adjoining the Church Yard'.
205 SA, 1848 box 165, indenture, 3 June 1830; SA, 3994 box 1; SA, 7577/36/8, 2 Oct. 1830; 'The Story of the Union Buildings', *Shrews. Chron.*, 8 Mar. 1940.
206 SA, 1848, box 166, building contract, 17 May 1830; J. Wood, *High Street, Wem, Shropshire: Archaeological Watching Brief*, Cotswold Archaeology, May 2014.
207 SA, 1848 box 165, ledger book with treasurer's accounts, 1830–40, printed advertisement for sale of the Union Buildings as one or several lots on 22 Dec. 1842.
208 Ibid.
209 *Strong's* (1925), advertisement.

by Colin Wright.[210] The Union Buildings were demolished in 1943 to widen the High Street–Mill Street junction.[211]

From the initial focus on the market place, shops and businesses extended both east and west.[212] By 1890 both sides of the High Street from Mill Street to The Grove were filled with shops, businesses, public houses and dwellings.[213] The demolition of the Union Buildings in 1943 proved detrimental to the shops west of the church which became isolated from the town's retail centre.

Aston Street remained largely undeveloped until the late 19th century. When the railway arrived in 1858 there were gardens and smallholdings there, extending as far as a public house near the junction with Aston Lane and the Soulton Road toll gate. It was not until the early 20th century that the road to the railway station was fully built up with new houses, shops, light industry, businesses and institutions, such as the Primitive Methodist chapel and the Morgan Library.[214]

From the 19th century onwards the independent traders in Wem were supplemented by local and regional chains. Hunters Tea Stores, a cash grocer founded in the late 19th century and spreading across much of northern England, had a branch in Wem, on the corner of Chapel Street and High Street, by 1909.[215] There was also competition from nearby towns: Morris's grocers in Shrewsbury had so many customers from Wem that in 1899 a trap was sent to the town monthly.[216] Melia's Ltd, a nationwide grocery chain, opened at 24 High Street in the 1930s.[217] From the 1960s consolidation of regional and national chains became significant, together with the rationalisation of their shops. Melia's amalgamated with Home & Colonial Stores and, together with Hunter's, withdrew from Wem in the early 1960s.

A concentration of food retailing between the White Horse hotel and the White Lion inn took place in the second half of the 20th century; the ribbon of shops along the High Street became shorter and thicker. Food retailers began to withdraw from Aston Street as they had from the High Street west of Mill Street. More shoppers visited the town by car, which encouraged retail development beside the car park (the former livestock market), away from the High Street. The Co-operative organisation followed this pattern. It was started in Aston Street by 1900, as a branch of the Prees Industrial Co-operative,[218] and had moved to 9 Station Road as part of the Ellesmere & District Co-operative by 1934.[219] In 1973 Wright's Grocery at 11 High Street ceased operating; with the adjoining Obertelli's Café (no. 13) it was demolished and rebuilt as a supermarket operated by

210 *Shrews. Chron.*, 11 Dec. 1936, 13; *Strong's* (1925), (1930), (1941).
211 *Shrews. Chron.*, 5 Mar. 1943.
212 For High Street and Aston Street in the 19th and 20th centuries, see Wem Civic Society's 'Wem Local' website, especially 'Wem's Shopping Centre': http://www.wemlocal.org.uk/wemmap/index.htm and links from that page (accessed 3 Dec. 2018).
213 Wem High Street 1891: http://www.wemlocal.org.uk/wemmap/index.htm (accessed 4 Mar. 2019).
214 *Strong's* (1925), advertisements for H. Williams, shoeing and jobbing forge; T. Jervis, 'Wem Building Supply Stores'; A. Simpson, motor and mechanical engineer and plumber.
215 *Kelly's Dir.* (1909).
216 N. Watson, *Morris & Company: A Family Business, 1869–1994* (Shrewsbury, 1995), 35.
217 *Kelly's Dir.* (1934).
218 *Kelly's Dir.* (1900).
219 *Kelly's Dir.* (1934).

Midlands Co-operative until 1993.[220] The Talbot inn was demolished and replaced in 1971 by a new supermarket and five other shops between the High Street and the car park, with three more developed in Leek Street. Morris & Co. of Shrewsbury redeveloped the part of Isherwood's timber yard nearest the car park as a SaveRite supermarket with post office, four shops and two office suites which opened in 1990/1.[221] The Co-operative, which had withdrawn from Wem, bought SaveRite in 2000 and moved into its Wem store. This shift in retail topography is also reflected in the development of a new outdoor market place adjoining the car park, Jubilee Square, in 2012.

Public Houses

In 1579 the lord's steward ruled that there should be not more than five alehouses in Wem township, but unlicensed brewers and alesellers were undeterred and were presented and fined in numbers at each court leet. Execution of the assize of ale was delegated to the two town bailiffs and two aletasters appointed annually. The bailiffs conducted an annual inspection of the measures used by each maltster and aleseller, having the authority to seize defective measures and merchandise.[222]

In 1612 there were 16 licensed alesellers in Wem township and one in Edstaston.[223] In 1686 the alehouses of Wem offered a total of 40 beds for guests and stabling for 73 horses, figures similar to those for Oswestry (42/76) but much lower than for Market Drayton (127/220) and Whitchurch (84/187).[224] In 1753 there were 15 licensed alesellers in Wem township and one in Northwood,[225] the number falling to 11 inns c.1795 and ten in 1822.[226] Under the Beer House Act 1830, a number of new beer houses were opened in Wem, with 14 public houses and six 'retailers of beer' listed in a commercial directory of 1835.[227]

By 1878 the Buck's Head in Mill Street had become a temperance house, which was still trading in 1930.[228] In 1932 it was purchased by the Barber Trust and converted into offices for Wem UDC and RDC.[229] In 2019 it was a private residence, the building's earlier identity recalled by a plaque, featuring an elaborate deer-head crest, fixed on the south wall.

Public houses required a large amount of yard space, especially for stabling.[230] An example is the beer garden at the Castle inn, which also afforded access to the livestock market, from 1867, through a segmental brick arch wide enough for carts. Behind the

---

220 *Newport & Market Drayton Advertiser*, 'Great Fire of Wem Souvenir', 1977; Wem Chamber of Commerce list, 1993.
221 Watson, *Morris & Co.*, 152, 159.
222 SA, 167/1; Garbet, 144, 145. E.g. of fines: SA, 167/5A, 18 Apr. 1612.
223 Register of badgers, drovers and alesellers, 1613–31: SA, QE/2/2/1, 12 Apr. 1612.
224 TNA, WO 30/48, f. 159v.
225 Register of alesellers, 1753–4: SA, QE/2/1/1, licences held on 17 Sept. 1753.
226 *Univ. Brit. Dir.*, 718–19; *Pigot's Dir.* (1822). See also insurance policies for inns: the Crown, 1780, the Packhorse, 1782 (SA, 4791/1/1, 96, 316), the Black Lion, 1793 (SA, 4791/1/3, 188), the Bull's Head and the Waggoners, both 1824 (SA, 4791/1/11).
227 *Pigot's Dir.* (1835), 385.
228 *Strong's* (1930).
229 SA, DA14/100/6, 250, 267–9; DA27/154/5.
230 Stabling provision is recorded in returns of licensed houses, 1891 and 1901: SA, QA/9/3/1.

former Buck's Head, outbuildings are arranged around a yard. These include a three-bay cart shed, now converted to residential use.[231] Likewise, the long stable range behind the White Lion has been converted to holiday accommodation. To the rear of the former Horse and Jockey, at 90 High Street, is a large 18th-century outbuilding, probably designed as a stable block, constructed of stone and containing doorways with four-centred arches, suggesting the material may be reused from an earlier building; in the late 19th century the inn offered stabling for 12 horses.[232]

If most of the public houses were alehouses catering to farmers on market days, the larger inns served many more functions. In the absence of municipal or public buildings in Wem prior to the 20th century, inns hosted auction sales, balls, celebration feasts, club meetings and theatre,[233] and the White Lion was the excise office.[234] The White Horse was the preeminent establishment, in the most prominent location, with an assembly room for 200 people.[235] The Waggoners and the Castle had opened further east along the High Street by 1822 and vied with the White Horse for the coaching business.[236] Later, passengers arriving in Wem by train still looked to the hotels for local transport. By 1902 the White Horse was offering 'every description of open and closed carriages for hire'. It was a logical progression for these inns to affiliate with national cycling and motoring associations in the 20th century, and to offer motor garaging, repair and hire services.[237]

There were 17 public houses in Wem UD and five in Wem Rural in 1901,[238] and in 1907 Quarter Sessions ordered a reduction in the number of licensed houses, delicensing the Vine Vaults, Lord Hill, Corbet Arms, Seven Stars and Vyrnwy on the grounds that they were surplus to the needs of the neighbourhood, which then had one licensed house per 216 of population.[239] The first three escaped closure, but the closure of the Seven Stars, an old building in poor repair, enabled redevelopment of its High Street site as the new post office.[240] The closure of the livestock market in 1962 removed the main trade of the remaining High Street public houses. A number of edge-of-town pubs fared better: the Albion (renamed the Drayton Gate, but closed in 2018) at the eastern end of the town, the Fox at the western end, the Hawkestone Arms to the north on the Whitchurch road and the Raven at Tilley.

231 SA, PH/W/8/5/1.
232 HER 32607, incl. R.K. Morris, *Field Survey Report, 90 High Street, Wem*, 2003, pp. 4–7, 11, 15–16; County of Salop. Return of Licensed Houses in the Petty Sessional Division of Wem, 1891: SA, QA/9/3/1.
233 Woodward, 70–2. Below, Social History.
234 *Pigot's Dir.* (1835), 385; *Slater's Dir.* (1850), 58; Bagshaw, 321.
235 *Shrews. Chron.*, 24 Feb. 1860, notice of auction sale; *Strong's* (1925), advertisement for the White Horse hotel.
236 Above, Landscape, Settlement and Buildings. *Shrews. Chron.*, 23 Mar. 1832, 3; *Salopian Jnl*, 15 July 1835, sale of contents of the Castle; *Eddowes's Jnl*, 12 Oct. 1859, 4.
237 *Strong's* (1925), advertisements for the White Lion, Horse and Jockey and Castle.
238 Return of licensed houses, 1901: SA, QA/9/3/6.
239 *Shrews. Chron.*, 15 Feb. 1907, 8.
240 Register of licences referred, Apr. 1907: SA, QA/9/5/1.

Banking

The Northern & Central Bank of England opened a branch in Wem soon after its establishment in 1834; the business was later taken over by the National Provincial Bank of England, which opened its Wem branch in 1837,[241] with Thomas Ireland as the first manager. Ireland had previously been in partnership with George Walmsley as mercers and drapers at 67 High Street but Walmsley died in 1837 and their business was taken on by a new generation.[242] Ireland himself died in 1847 and was succeeded as manager by John Daniel Lloyd.[243] The National Provincial was the only bank in Wem for many years, although the post office provided a money order facility from 1849 and a savings bank from 1861.[244] By 1874 the bank was located at 21 High Street. In that year, the National Provincial moved into the large Georgian house at 39–41 High Street. Substantial alterations took place in 1965,[245] but what became the National Westminster Bank closed its Wem branch in 2016.

The Birmingham, Dudley and District Banking Co. Ltd arrived in Wem in 1883, under the superintending management of Edward Bygott, who had promoted the venture. The next year the bank leased the premises formerly occupied by the National Provincial Bank at 21 High Street.[246] Becoming the Birmingham District and Counties Banking Co. Ltd, in 1889 the bank purchased land on the corner of High Street and Noble Street (20 High Street) and erected an imposing new building designed by the bank's architects, Thomason & Whitwell of Birmingham, and built by J. Gresty.[247] The insignia 'BDC' is inscribed over the main entrance. It was ultimately acquired by Barclays Bank, which refurbished the premises in 1956 and incorporated the shop next door by 1979. Barclays had vacated 20 High Street by 1992 when the building was temporarily the town's library, but continued to operate from the adjoining no. 16–18 until closing the branch in 2018.[248]

The 21st Century

The major Wem employers all disappeared in the last decades of the 20th century: the ordnance depot in Aston Park, the two cheese factory/creameries, the brewery and the timber yards. Much of the land they had occupied was given over to housing, although

---

241 *Shrews. Chron.*, 18 May 1838. Inf. from RBS Archives, Edinburgh.

242 SA, 4791/1/9, p. 150: insurance policy for Ireland and Walmsley, 1812; SA, D3651/B/102/2; MI1278/2; *Pigot's Dir.* (1842), 49; *Eddowes's Jnl*, 3 May 1843, 3,10.

243 *Eddowes's Jnl*, 22 Dec. 1847; Bagshaw, 322.

244 Above, Landscape, Settlement and Buildings.

245 SA, PH/M/6/14/41; RBS Archives, photographs D3827 (1902) and D2891 (1968); Whitehead, *Wem*, 45.

246 Barclays Group Archive: 3/1349, Board minutes no. 2778, 22 Oct. 1883, 5 Nov. 1883; 1/206, no. 2906, 6 Oct. 1884; 3/984, premises register: lease 25 Sept. 1884; Bowcock, 'Wem of the past'.

247 Barclays Group Archive: 1/206, Board minutes no. 4359, 17 June, 8 July 1889; 1/209, title register; SA, DA27/994/1/2, Dec. 1889; *Kelly's Dir.* (1891); and see *Nantwich Guardian*, 7 Mar. 1916 (obituary of Edward Bygott).

248 Barclays Group Archive: Barclays register of title (ref. 80/621): planning consent from UDC, 1 Mar. 1955, colour photographs of exterior and interior in 1979 and inf. from Barclays Group archivist, Nicholas Webb; Woodward, 137.

the Aston Road creamery site, the Drawwell brewery and the former ordnance depot were all converted to light industrial use. Wem ceased to be a centre of local government with the creation of the Shropshire unitary authority in 2009. Although lacking in employment opportunities, Wem remains a desirable place to live, with the majority of its working-age residents employed elsewhere:[249] in 2011 only 31 per cent of working people who lived in Wem worked in the town. The largest share (46 per cent of workers) commuted to other places in Shropshire, presumably mostly to Shrewsbury, and 9 per cent to Telford; at the same time, 3,639 people (about 60 per cent of workers in Wem) were commuting to Wem from elsewhere. In 2011 the largest employer was Meres & Mosses Housing Association, with 200 employees, and a similar number worked in the town's two schools, followed by those employed in two care homes (68) and two NHS medical practices (37).

249 This section is based on Shropshire Council, *Wem Market Town Profile, Winter 2017/18* (Shrewsbury, 2018). For a detailed contemporary account of the period 1980s–2011, see Woodward, chapters XII–XIV.

Social Character

Medieval

THE DOMESDAY DESCRIPTION OF *Weme* shows that by 1086 it was already different in character from the other settlements which later formed the manor of Wem, and this implies that the castle-town had already been established. There were 12 peasant households in *Weme*, compared with an average of 2.6 in the surrounding estates, and it was the only estate to have both *villani* (more substantial peasant landholders) and *bordarii* (smallholders or cottagers).[1] The eight *bordarii* in *Weme* were more numerous than in the other estates combined (Table 5).

In 1327 the two wealthiest householders in the manor were in Wem township: William le Botiler, lord of the manor, and Alice de Montgomery, the widow of his elder brother; the rector would no doubt have been third. These excepted, the number

Table 5 *Types of tenants recorded in Domesday Book.*

1086 'manor'	servus	villanus	bordarius	radman	bovarius	free man (*liber homo*)	Total per 'manor'
Weme	2	4	8	-	-	-	14
Aston	1	-	2	-	1	-	4
Coton	-	1	-	2	-	-	3
Edstaston	-	3	-	-	-	-	3
Horton	2	-	3	-	-	-	5
Lacon	-	-	1	-	-	-	1
Sleap	-	-	-	-	-	1	1
Soulton	-	-	-	-	-	-	0
Wolverley	-	3	-	1	-	-	4
Total	5	11	14	3	1	1	35

Source: *Domesday*, 703–4. 'Manors' listed are those encompassed in the medieval parish of Wem.

---

1   A. Stevenson, 'From Domesday Book to the Hundred Rolls: lordship, landholding and local society in three English Hundreds, 1066–1280' (unpublished King's College London, Univ. of London Ph.D. thesis, 2014), 123–7, 217–18.

Table 6 *Lay subsidy assessments in the manor of Wem, 1543.*

Township	Value of subsidy assessed, no. of households							
	2d	4d	6d	8d	12d	16d	20d	Total
Wem	13	6	10	1	1		3	34
Aston	3	2	3	5			1	*14*
Coton	7	2	1	4		1	2	17
Edstaston[1]	4	3	1					8+
Horton	2	1	4	1				8
Lowe and Ditches	3	2	2	1				8
Steel	1		2					3
Tilley	2	3	4	3				12
Unidentified[2]		2		3			*1*	6+
	35	21	27	18	1	1	7	*110*

Source: Faraday (ed.), *Shropshire Taxes,* 278–9.

[1]   The first five lines for Edstaston are missing, meaning probably the one or two highest valuations.
[2]   Faraday, no. 961: probably Wolverley or Newtown (cf. no. 986), missing the township name and at least one entry (the first, and probably the highest value).

and wealth of households assessed for the lay subsidy appears broadly similar for all townships.[2] In 1381, however, when poll tax was assessed on all men and women, not just the wealthiest households, Wem was clearly the most populous township.[3] By that time the lord of the manor had ceased to reside in Wem and in 1543 of the seven richest households in the manor just three were in Wem. None was conspicuously wealthy, however; the highest tax assessed was 20*d.* (Table 6).

Despite the proximity to Wales, there is no evidence of a Welsh population within the borough in the Middle Ages, in contrast with the northern parts of the manor directly bounding the border with Wales,[4] where tenants in the 14th century included Thomas Vaghan (Welsh, *bychan*: the younger) in Edstaston and Madoc Moyl (Welsh *moel*: bald) in Coton (fl. 1327), and Nicholas Vaan and John Moyl (fl. 1381). In 1381 Sybil Seys (Welsh *sais*: 'English') lived in Edstaston and Adam le Walsche in Coton.[5] It is possible that Welsh people were excluded from burgage tenure at various times, perhaps during the revolt of Owain Glyndwr (1400–*c.*1412) but by 1561 there were three burgesses with apparently Welsh names: Maurice David, William Yevans and Nicholas Griffin.[6]

2   *Shropshire Lay Subsidy Roll, 1327,* 143–7.
3   Above, Landscape, Settlement and Buildings, esp. Table 1.
4   *Roll of the Shropshire Eyre 1256,* no. 683; *Shropshire Lay Subsidy Roll 1327,* 144, Thomas son of Eddeneuet [in Welsh: Tomas ap Ednyfed]; *Survey 1561,* 103, Thomas Powell, Richard Lloyd.
5   Fenwick, *Poll Taxes,* 392–4; T.J. Morgan and P. Morgan, *Welsh Surnames* (Cardiff, 1985), 58–60, 167, 189–90.
6   *Survey 1561,* 20–1, 26–7.

With an absentee lord, and often absentee rector, the lord's steward wielded considerable authority over the town and the whole manor while, under the steward's authority, the 70-or-so burgage-holders were the core of Wem society, providing the churchwardens and other public officials such as the bailiffs and the town jury.[7] Alongside predominantly agricultural occupations, some townspeople were identified by commercial and craft activities, including, in 1599–1608: clerk, dyer, mercer, chapman (2), shoemaker (3), tailor (5), tanner (7) and weaver (11).[8]

17th and 18th Centuries

From autumn 1643 to spring 1645 Wem gained regional importance as a Parliamentarian enclave in north Shropshire. The failure of the Royalists to take the town, and the resilience of the defenders, was pivotal to the outcome of the Civil War in Shropshire. What was in effect an occupation – there is no evidence that the townspeople favoured the Parliamentary cause[9] – must have had major, even traumatic, effects. The population would have more than doubled, with the influx of troops, prisoners and deserters; the mortality rate spiked at the time when the garrison was most pressed.[10]

In 1672 Wem town was the largest settlement in the parish, with 110 hearth-tax payers in the township, almost 40 per cent of the parish total (Table 7). The mean of 1.68 hearths per household in Wem parish, and 70–78 per cent of households either exempt from taxation on grounds of poverty or taxed on a single hearth, is not exceptional compared with other Shropshire parishes. Wem town had proportionately more households with two or more hearths than elsewhere in the parish. There were few large houses; the largest had nine hearths and only ten in the manor had six or more.[11] Three of these were in Wem town: the rectory with nine hearths, and the houses of the lord's steward, Richard Jebb, and of Richard Higginson, probably Drawwell House, with seven.[12] A few years later many houses were destroyed by the great fire in 1677.[13]

By the mid 18th century Wem shared in England's Georgian 'urban renaissance'. This was reflected in the building, or rebuilding, of town houses in brick; the market house, lauded by Samuel Garbet;[14] and the endowed grammar school. There were annual hunts and race meetings attracting rural gentry from the surrounding area. Resident gentry – such as Sir Thomas Longueville Bt (d. 1759), tenant of one of the 'good' houses on the High Street[15] – and professional men supported a growing retail and service sector which included attorneys-at-law, an excise officer, apothecaries and barber-surgeons, carriers linking Wem with neighbouring towns and villages, nearly a dozen inns, and specialist

7   Below, Local Government.
8   Wem Parish Registers.
9   Gough, *History of Myddle*, 71–5 ('Some accidents which happened in the parish of Myddle in the time of the Warrs'): 'There were but few that went out of this parish to serve the Parliament', after listing about a dozen men who went to serve the king.
10   Watts, 'Mortality in three Shropshire parishes'. Above, Landscape, Settlement and Buildings.
11   *Shropshire Hearth Tax Roll of 1672*, 47–52; *Shropshire Hearth Tax Exemptions*, 254, 263.
12   *Shropshire Hearth Tax Roll of 1672*, 47–8; Arundel map; on Drawwell House, see Garbet, 224–5.
13   Above, Landscape, Settlement and Buildings.
14   Garbet, 235; below, Local Government.
15   Garbet, 234; *Burke's Landed Gentry* (1847), I, 765. Probably on the western corner of Chapel Street, see SA, 9043, File A, 1.

Table 7 *Hearth tax assessments in the manor of Wem, 1672.*

		Number of hearths per household						
	No. illegible	*1*	*2*	*3*	*4*	*5*	*>5*	*Total*
Wem	-	47	34	15	4	6	4	110
Aston	-	14	2	3		1	1	21
Coton	-	19	4	1	1	1	2	28
Edstaston	-	21	1	5	1	2		30
Horton	2	2	3	2				9
Lowe and Ditches	-	12		1	1		1	15
Newtown	3	5	1	1			2	12
Northwood	-	22		2				24
Tilley	-	17	6	2	3	1		29
Wolverley	-	5	1	1	2			9
Total	5	164	52	33	12	11	10	287
Percentage	1.7	57.1	18.1	11.5	4.2	3.8	3.5	100%
Exemption certificates 1662								73
Exemption certificates 1671–2								116

Source: Shropshire Hearth Tax Roll of 1672, 47–52; Shropshire Hearth Tax Exemptions, 51–2, 147–8, 238.

trades including gunsmith, glazier and cane-chair maker.[16] In spite of these indicators of a 'polite' society, civic improvement schemes, as well as cultural activities such as theatre and libraries, do not appear until the first decades of the 19th century.

19th Century to the Present

By 1805 there was a notable socioeconomic divide between the few who received rents from agricultural land as well as property in the town, and the many who owned or rented small, urban residential/commercial properties and made a precarious livelihood from labouring, crafts and trades.[17]

In 1851 about 6 per cent of the population of Wem township had private means; 12.5 per cent of men worked as agricultural or general labourers and 23 per cent of women were employed as indoor domestic servants. Other occupations included 15 drapers, 14 butchers and ten grocers; 12 tanners and six curriers, and 16 farmers. There were 13 publicans and innkeepers, three of whom were women. The most common

16   SA, 9043, File A, 15; Wem Parish Registers, baptisms, 1727–36 (father's occupation); above, Economic History, and below, Social History..

17   Yalden, 'Landownership'.

professional occupation (about 20) was schoolteacher, 14 of whom of were female. The other professionals comprised two Anglican clergy, four Nonconformist ministers, six solicitors and five law clerks, and five physicians, one medical student and two subordinate medical staff. These figures did not change significantly for several decades.

By 1881 the number of agricultural labourers had fallen by more than half, to 5.2 per cent (46 men), although there were still 13 farmers in the township. The numbers of shoe and boot makers and tailors had also halved. In contrast, the number of bricklayers had grown from 19 to 34, and other building trades had expanded. A new category of work had also been created with the arrival of the railway which employed ten people by 1881.

There was a marked increase in retail activity between 1851 and 1881. The number employed in the grocery business rose from ten to 27. In 1881 there were also 12 'general shopkeepers' compared with just two in 1851, and six wine and spirit merchants. Other service activities had grown too: there were more inn/hotel servants and grooms, and five people employed in connection with post and telegraph services.

The social character of the town, and its contrasts, is epitomised in two new streets developed in the late 19th century: Barnard Street and Station Road. The former honours Henry de Vere Vane, ninth Baron Barnard, who became lord of the manor in 1891. The 17 semi-detached houses have a south-facing aspect over the river, their small front gardens enclosed with iron railings. The occupants in 1901 were either retired or in white-collar occupations such as solicitor's clerk and school-master or -mistress, and the average household size was 3.94. The Station Road houses, although also semi-detached, are street houses featuring garish polychrome brickwork. The occupants in 1901 were all skilled and unskilled workers, such as bricklayer, joiner or painter – some almost certainly employees of the developer, C.H. Kynaston – and the average household size was 5.92.

Communal Life

Friendly Societies

Wem Friendly Society and Wem Young Union and Young Friendly Society were formed in 1811, the latter meeting at the Buck's Head inn.[18] Branches of national organisations included the Independent Order of Oddfellows Manchester Unity, 'Refuge of Hope' Lodge, no. 2871, founded in 1841[19] which met at the Castle inn until the Oddfellows Hall (4 Chapel Street) opened in 1905.[20] The Ancient Order of Foresters met at the town hall;[21] and the Rechabites (a temperance movement) 'Walford Tent', no. 1271, established in 1879, met at the former Catholic Apostolic church and later at the Oddfellows Hall.[22] By 1925 the Wem, Clive and Prees Model Building Society had its head office at the Oddfellows Hall; it dissolved in 1948.[23]

18   SA, QE8/1/1; QE/8/1/2, 39.
19   *Wellington Jnl*, 15 July 1899, 8, rules enrolled by Quarter Sessions, 1852: QE/8/1/2, 39.
20   *Wellington Jnl*, 30 Dec. 1905, 2. The Oddfellows Hall had been converted to residential apartments by 2016.
21   SA, DA14/154/13: Jan. 1906, letter agreeing to tenancy of Wem Corn Exchange by Ancient Order of Foresters.
22   *Strong's* (1925), 'Friendly Societies'.
23   *Strong's* (1925), 'Banks'; Building Societies Association, 'Alterations, mainly since 1937, in the official Register of Building Societies', Extract from *BSA Yearbook 2016/17*, 167.

Libraries and Institutes[24]

The Union Buildings, from its opening in 1830, incorporated a newspaper reading room and library on the upper floor.[25] Established in 1856, Wem Literary and Scientific Institution possessed a library, ordering books from Mudie's Lending Library and subscribing to national newspapers and popular journals. Membership, with borrowing rights, was available to men and women. The inaugural lecture was held in 1856 in the National School with the rector as chairman and the Institution was still in existence in 1884.[26] A Conservative Club was opened in Sambrook House, Noble Street, in 1892, with facilities including a library, billiard room and bowling green.[27] A working men's club was formed in 1886 at 4 Chapel Street.[28]

In 1902 Phoebe Ann Morgan bequeathed funds to create a memorial to her late husband, John Morgan, a native of Wem who had made a successful career as a grocer in Oldham (Lancs.) – a free library, to be named the John and Phoebe Ann Morgan Library.[29] F.H. Shayler, the Shrewsbury architect, designed the library and its furniture, creating 'a little Arts and Crafts essay'.[30] The building, 55 Aston Street, constructed of brick and stone, features a round-arched entrance with a stone tympanum, with a carving of two boys each holding a book, beneath an inscription. Shayler's original design depicted a boy to the left and girl to the right, but the design proved too expensive and was simplified.[31] To the left of the entrance is a large canted bay window set forward, lighting the north-facing reading room. The library opened in 1905, offering a lending library, a reading room with newspapers and magazines and a chess room.

In 1920 the trustees conveyed the property and its management to Wem UDC.[32] In 1966 the library was transferred to SCC, reopening in 1967 as a county branch library.[33] In 1992 it was refurbished under the General Improvement Area scheme[34] but in 2001 the branch library moved to Talbot House at 3 High Street. From 2002 to 2019 the Morgan Library building was leased to Mythstories Museum of Myth and Fable, which claims to be the world's first museum of storytelling.[35]

Town Hall and Community Centres

Before the 20th century Wem lacked public buildings for civic and cultural activities.[36] In 1822, when the popular actor William Betty produced and appeared in amateur

24   Recreational activities and social and sporting clubs are addressed, in greater detail than is possible here, in Woodward, passim.
25   *Pigot's Dir.* (1835), 383.
26   SA, P295/G/1; P295/G/1/1, 3 Aug. 1861 and 8 Dec. 1864; *Eddowes's Jnl,* 1 Oct. 1856; 30 Jan. 1884; Bowcock, 'Wem of the past'.
27   *Strong's* (1925), 69; SA, DA14/700/12, 8–10; Bowcock, 'Wem of the past'.
28   Bowcock, 'Wem of the past'.
29   *Wellington Jnl,* 19 Aug. 1905; SA, DA14/135/8/1; SA, 1848, box 79.
30   Newman and Pevsner, 675; SA, DA14/135/8, no. 2.
31   SA, DA14/135/8, no. 5.
32   SA, DA14/100/5, 986; DA14/135/8/1.
33   SA, 7577/6/6/4/2.
34   Woodward, 137.
35   Woodward, 145–6; *Shropshire Star,* 6 June 2012; http://www.mythstories.com (accessed 11 Aug. 2019).
36   See Woodward, 106.

Figure 15 *Morgan Library. Relief carving above doorway as originally proposed by F.H. Shayler.*

dramatics to raise funds for local causes, the venue was 'the Large Room' of the Castle inn.[37] From 1840 the British School and National School offered venues for public meetings, lectures and entertainments, such as cricket club fund-raisers in 1860 and 1869 and annual productions by the Wem Rifle Volunteers, formed in 1859.[38]

After it was opened by Wem UDC in 1905 the town hall, with both the large market hall and the first-floor assembly room seating 500, hosted a range of activities, from dances and whist drives to boy scouts and rifle volunteers drills.[39] The assembly room was in regular use both as a cinema by 1911[40] and from 1919 by Wem Amateur Dramatic and Operatic Society (ADOS).[41]

With the 1905 agreement that the old town hall should not be used for commerce, that building also became available for other community activities. In 1911 Lord Barnard had the ground floor converted for use by the Territorials (formerly the Rifle

---

37   *Morning Post*, 23 Nov. 1822, 2; Woodward, 70. Woodward, 69, however, prints a playbill of 1812 for a 'Theatre – Wem', with boxes and gallery, which has not been identified. *ODNB*, s.v. Betty, William Henry West (1791–1874), actor (accessed 4 Mar. 2019).

38   *Shrews. Chron.*, 9 Dec. 1859, 12 Oct. 1860, 5 24 Dec. 1869, 7; *Eddowes's Jnl*, 24 Oct. 1860, 5; Woodward, 66; *Shrews. Chron.*, 23 Dec. 1864, 7; *Eddowes's Jnl*, 10 Aug. 1864, 5.

39   E.g., SA, DA 14/100/3, 249; DA14/100/7, 108, 116; *Shrews. Chron.*, 3 July 1908, 28 Oct. 1910, 11.

40   Woodward, 106; SA, DA14/100/3, 371, 385; DA14/100/5, 893, 911, 931; DA14/100/7, 108; DA14/154/14.

41   Woodward, 107, 135, 141–2, although Wem Amateur Dramatic Company was active by 1907: *Shrews. Chron.*, 2 Aug. 1907, 8.

Volunteers[42]); the open arches were filled in with ashlar and glazing and the cobbled floor was concreted over. A new two-storey extension with a porch and stairs gave separate access to the upper floor, which was refurbished for use as a parish room.[43] In 1920 Lord Barnard conveyed the premises to the parish, to be managed by the Lichfield Diocesan Trust.[44]

In 1985 ADOS took over management of the town hall assembly room from Wem Town Council. After the town hall was gutted by fire in 1995, ADOS acquired the former Apostolic chapel in Aston Street, renaming it the Stage Door Theatre.[45] Stanier Hall offers another venue, from 1988 hosting the annual sweet pea show organised by the Eckford Sweet Pea Society to mark the centenary of Henry Eckford (1823–1905) cultivating the modern sweet pea.[46]

Amateur Sports

Wem Cricket Club, established by 1854,[47] played at the Castle Field until 1982 when expansion of the brewery forced a move to its present home, the Kynaston Ground on Soulton Road.[48] The club was a founder member of the Shropshire Cricket League and won the premier division of the league in 2018.[49]

Wem Football Club was a member of the Shropshire Amateur Football Association by 1874.[50] Two other football clubs were formed, the Wem White Stars and the Wem Blues,[51] but they amalgamated in 1889 'to have one good football club instead of three inferior ones'.[52] Wem Town Football Club joined the newly reformed Shropshire county league in 1950. The club moved to the new sports complex at Bowen's Field in the mid 1970s.[53] In 2008/9 it entered the West Midlands Regional League (first division) and in 2018 was promoted to the premier division.[54]

Recreational Space

By the 1770s the Wem hunt was held annually in November or early December, meeting at one of the town's inns.[55] The Shropshire hunt, later the North Shropshire, has hunted the Wem area since around 1825.[56]

42 *Shrews. Chron.*, 3 July 1908; Woodward, 98.
43 SA, Raby Estate, boxes 7 and 9; SRO, B/C/12/1/530: faculty granted in 1891 to build on glebe land. See Fig. 34, below.
44 SA, Raby Estate, box 34; SA, DA14/100/3, 237.
45 'Wem theatre group unveils £35k new extension', *Shropshire Star*, 12 Dec. 2011.
46 Woodward, 116, 141–3; *ODNB*, s.v. Eckford, Henry (1823–1905) (accessed 22 June 2019).
47 Woodward, 95–6; *Eddowes's Jnl*, 31 May 1854, 5; 20 Sept. 1854, 6; *VCH Salop.* II, 195.
48 NSDC, *Wem Discussion Paper* ([1981]), 18; Woodward, 122.
49 *Shropshire Star*, 18 Sept. 2018.
50 *Eddowes's Jnl*, 21 Oct. 1874, 5.
51 *Wellington Jnl*, 26 Feb. 1881, 5; 31 Dec. 1881, 7, 23 Oct. 1886, 6; *Eddowes's Jnl*, 18 Nov. 1885, 7, 19 Dec. 1888, 2.
52 *Oswestry Advertiser*, 6 Nov. 1889; *Border Counties Advertizer*, 27 Mar. 1935.
53 Woodward, 122, 130.
54 'History of Wem Town FC': http://www.wemtownfc.co.uk (accessed 4 Mar. 2019).
55 Woodward, 64–5; e.g. *Shrews. Chron.*, 23 Nov. 1772, 5; 19 Dec. 1772, 5; 20 Nov. 1773, 3; 2 Dec. 1775, 2; *VCH Salop.* II, 166.
56 Nimrod, *Hunting Reminiscences...* (London, 1843), 14; e.g. *Eddowes's Jnl*, 10 Dec. 1884, 7, 29 July 1885,

Wem races, accompanied by dinners and assemblies in the town's inns, drew all classes together, allowing the gentry to socialise and patronise the town's tradesmen.[57] A meeting was held in 1774 with two races for a silver cup worth £5.[58] After a break, racing resumed in 1816 with a two-day meeting at the beginning of October at which all the races were 'well-contested'.[59] The racecourse then occupied just over 32 a. of meadow land south of Lyons Wood Farm, about three miles south of the town, in Broughton parish.[60] In 1823 it was reported that 'the course was thronged with spectators and the sport was excellent',[61] but in 1827 a 'calamitous accident' occurred when the stand collapsed and about 18 people were injured, some seriously.[62] The stand was rebuilt by the landowner, Thomas Meares, a Wem maltster, at a cost of £400–£500.[63] Hurdle races were introduced in 1836 to be ridden by 'Gentleman Riders', the first such races to be staged in the county.[64] In 1839 Meares was declared bankrupt and the course was put up for sale.[65] That year's meeting went ahead and was reported a success, but in the wider sporting community the Wem races were regarded as 'very inferior' and thereafter fell into abeyance.[66] Racing on the course became impossible after the Shrewsbury–Crewe railway line was constructed in 1857,[67] and the grandstand was later converted into a house named 'Chase End'. Steeplechase meetings were held from 1847, to the north of the town, but seem to have ended in 1849, after a spectator was thrown from his horse and died from his injuries.[68]

In 1887 celebrations for Queen Victoria's golden jubilee took place at the Alleys field. The annual parish festival was hosted in the grounds of the rectory.[69] In 1842 the Castle inn boasted 'a large walled bowling green with summer house' and flower gardens.[70] A field north of the inn, known as the Castle Field, was used for outdoors sport and recreational activities in the 19th and early 20th centuries, such as the peace celebration in 1919.[71] It was the original home ground of both Wem Football Club and Wem Cricket Club.[72]

In 1919 the War Memorial Committee proposed a public recreation ground for the town. Its successor, the Recreation Committee, acquired 'The Lawns' – the grounds to the rear of The Hall – and in 1926 Wem UDC took over its management as a public park

8; *Shrews. Chron.*, 1 Aug. 1902, 6–7; *Horse and Hound*, 20 Mar. 2008.

57 D. Brailsford, *A Taste for Diversions: Sport in Georgian England* (Cambridge, 1999), 24–8; *VCH Salop.* II, 180–3.
58 *Shrews. Chron.*, 3 Sept. 1774.
59 *Chester Courant*, 15 Oct. 1816; Woodward, 66–7.
60 *Shrews. Chron.*, 7 June 1839, 1.
61 *Bath Chron.*, 28 Sept. 1823.
62 *Berrow's Worcester Jnl*, 4 Oct. 1827.
63 *Salopian Jnl*, 2 Oct. 1833.
64 *Shrews. Chron.*, 12 Aug. 1836.
65 *Chester Chron.*, 28 June 1839; *Shrews. Chron.*, 7 June 1839, 1.
66 J.C. Whyte, *History of the British Turf* (London, 1840), I, 294.
67 *Shrews. Chron.*, 2 Oct. 1857.
68 *Shrews. Chron.*, 19 Mar. 1847, 30 Mar. 1849.
69 Woodward, 93–5.
70 *Shrews. Chron.*, 18 Mar. 1842.
71 Woodward, 95, 105–6; *Eddowes's Jnl*, 25 Oct. 1854, 6; SA, DA14/100/5, 916.
72 *Shrews. Chron.*, 6 July 1866, 8; *Eddowes's Jnl*, 21 Oct. 1874, 5; 7 Nov. 1888, 2; E.W. Bowcock, 'Fifty years in Wem: A Dominie's reminiscences', 6 Feb. 1935, newspaper cutting: SA, 7577/36/8.

and recreation ground.[73] It was a popular amenity for the new Shrubbery Gardens estate and in the 1930s was the playing field for both the nearby senior school and the primary school.[74] In 1949 the recreation committee proposed a new bowling green, tennis courts, children's playground equipment and football and cricket pitches.[75]

In 1967 Wem sports club (later Sports and Social Association) was formed to represent the town's sporting clubs. It took over the management of the recreation ground while promoting the development of a new sports and leisure complex. Bowen's Field, adjacent to the Castle Field, was acquired with the assistance of Wem Urban parish council and NSRDC; a swimming pool was built there in 1972 and the Butler Sports Centre opened in 1975, named after the then chairman of the Wem Sports and Social Association.[76]

Education

Adams' Grammar School

In 1650 Sir Thomas Adams, a native of Wem who became Lord Mayor of London in 1645, founded a school in his home town.[77] It was managed by at least nine trustees, with the ministers of Wem, Whitchurch and Hodnet as school visitors. Free to the sons of parishioners, who paid just an entrance fee and a small charge for cleaning the schoolhouse, the school was held initially in the market house; evicted by Daniel Wycherley (lord of the manor), in 1665 it moved into the church. This motivated the trustees to build the first schoolhouse, in 1670, on Noble Street. It was adjacent to Adams's own house, which was destroyed in the great fire of 1677, and was later replaced by the headmaster's house. The first schoolhouse survived the fire, but was then partly rebuilt in brick by the headmaster, Robert Roe, who also added a chimney. Roe's successor, Francis Williams, was credited with building 'the larger and better part of the school house, being the timber building'.[78]

The school flourished under John Appleton (headmaster, 1724–48), who taught mathematics, astronomy, geography and Hebrew, as well as classics. Under the long headship of John Spedding (1755–1804), academic standards declined, although the school house was rebuilt in 1776.[79] Of brick with stone dressings, it was dominated by a large bell cupola. The two-storey front elevation had round-arched openings to the ground floor but otherwise plain detailing. The central gabled bay was slightly advanced,

73 Woodward, 99; SA, DA14/100/5, 920, 1013, 1020, 1235, 1294; SA, PH/W/8/6/31–4.

74 SA, DA14/100/7, 19 Dec. 1938.

75 Woodward, 99; SA, DA14/100/8, 282, 754, 757–8. Wem Bowling Club: SA, DA14/160/1.

76 Woodward, 115, 129; http://www.gov.uk/government/organisations/charity-commission, no. 522583 and charitable incorporated organisation (CIO) no. 1181598 (accessed 4 Mar. 2019).

77 *ODNB*, s.v. Adams, Sir Thomas, first baronet (bap. 1586, d. 1668) (accessed 4 Mar. 2019); Garbet, 174–80. The school's archives are deposited at SA, ED6266. For the school to 1969, see *VCH Salop*. II, 158–9; see also Garbet, 174–212, and W.J. Creak, *History of Adams' Grammar School, Wem* (Wem, 1953).

78 Garbet, 290–1.

79 For photographs, see SA, ED6266, box L and box 6, respectively.

bearing a date stone recording the founding of the school in 1650 and its rebuilding in 1776.

The curriculum in the 1820s included classics, scripture, mathematics and history, with dancing, drawing and French as optional extras, but attendances were low. In 1830, there were two foundation boys, four or five boarders in the upper school, and 30 boys in the lower school, with only two masters after 1838. The opening of the town's two elementary schools reduced demand still further: the British School, in particular, was preferred by Nonconformist families.[80] In 1864 an inspector found Adams' School 'nearly useless', set in a 'sleepy little town ... [with] not a creature in the streets, except a stray fowl and the loungers at the public-house door'. There were only 11 boys present in the lower school, which was 'dingy', with a stove in the middle. An external staircase led to the upper school room, which was 'dismal' and only ten feet high, with only three boys present.[81] The inspector questioned whether the continued existence of the school was even desirable.[82]

Under a scheme of 1879 the trustees were replaced by nine representative governors. Chemistry and French were introduced into the curriculum, and Greek became optional. Numbers remained low, in spite of free places being provided for boys from local elementary schools, until the headship of Joseph Ohm (1889–1910), a mathematician, under whom a chemistry laboratory was built and a full-time science master appointed. By 1905 the school had been placed under the control of the Board of Education, but there were still only 58 boys in 1906. A new range was added to the front of the 1776 schoolhouse in 1911, resulting in the plan that exists today. This work was funded by a legacy and undertaken by Thomas Pace of Shrewsbury at a cost of £3,353.[83] In this arrangement offices flanked the entrance, with a classroom to the right and a changing room with lockers to the left, whereas the rear (original) range was a central assembly hall surrounded by classrooms.[84] The building's façade, as it existed c.1920, had double panelled doors with distinctive circular glazing motifs.[85]

Further improvements took place from 1925 to 1932 under the direction of the County Architect, G.N. Bailey, carried out by Treasures of Shrewsbury at a cost of £4,735.[86] The front elevation was remodelled in a simple Neo-classical style, with large Venetian windows to the outer gables to light the classrooms. A fives court was built in the school yard and cricket and football pitches in the playing fields, which had been acquired in 1920.[87] The 1911 entrance doors were retained, and a large pediment added above bearing a new stone tablet. 'Enlarged in 1930' was added to the original details, but no acknowledgement given to the alterations of 1911. A clock was mounted above the apex, on a stone piece with scrolled edges. Also of this phase are the fine iron

80   *Abstract of Answers of Returns on State of Education in England and Wales* (1833) (House of Commons Parliamentary Papers), 786; *Schools Inquiry Commission* [3966-XIV], 319, HC (1867–8), xxviii (12).

81   Creak, *History of Adams' Grammar School*, 25–7; *VCH Salop.* II, 158–9.

82   *Schs. Inquiry Comm.*, 318–22.

83   Creak, *History of Adams' Grammar School*, 39.

84   SA, ED6266, box S.

85   SA, ED6266, box L.

86   SA, ED6266, boxes D and S; Newman and Pevsner, 675; Creak, *History of Adams' Grammar School*, 53–4.

87   SA, ED6266, box S.

Figure 16 *Postcard of Thomas Adams' Grammar School, before 1910.*

Figure 17 *Photograph of boys and masters outside Thomas Adams' Grammar School, 'Summer term, 1920'.*

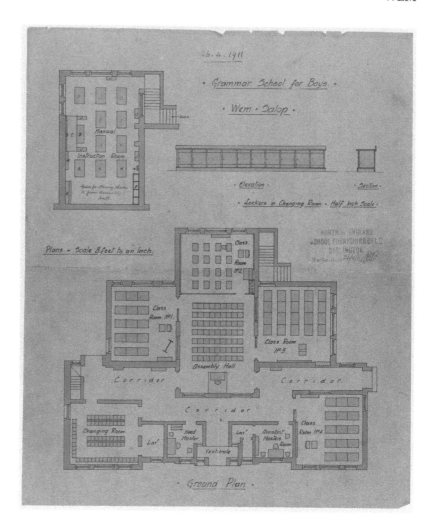

Figure 19 *The former grammar school, now Adams College.*

entrance gates with curved motifs, which were constructed as a war memorial in 1922. A memorial plate formerly fixed to the left gate stated that the gates were a gift of the present boys in memory of the old boys who had given their lives in the First World War.[88]

By 1950 there were 130–140 pupils including almost 30 in the sixth form,[89] and when Stanier Hall was opened in 1969 there were 200 pupils, including 45 boarders.[90] In 1976 the school ceased to be an independent grammar school, merging with Wem Secondary Modern School to become a co-educational comprehensive.[91]

Elementary Schools

Pre-1870

A charity was established by Richard Corbet in 1703 to pay £1 every other year to a 'writing master' to teach four poor boys reading and arithmetic.[92] A Sunday school at the parish church was established by 1802.[93] A subscription charity school was held in the market hall, conducted 'on Dr Bell's plan', with about 100 pupils in 1818.[94] There may have been a small Nonconformist school in Mill Street around 1824.[95] There was a newly established fee-paying infants' school with 100 children by 1833 and the charity subscription school had grown to 186 weekday scholars with 120 attending the Sunday school.[96] In 1837 the latter had 150 pupils, and 400 children attended four Sunday schools in the parish supported by voluntary donations.[97] In 1838 newly appointed trustees purchased a former timber yard on Noble Street and applied for a Treasury grant 'for the construction of a school-house with proper offices, for the instruction of as many poor children of the parish and neighbourhood of Wem as the trustees think fit, in English and the religious principles of the Church of England, to be called Wem National School'.[98] A simple gable-fronted building with raised kneelers and tall central window was erected: 'a commodious brick building with two spacious rooms, erected at a cost of about £1,000'.[99] A stone clock, mounted on the gable apex, is a vestige of the building's original function.

---

88   SA, PH/W/8/8/25; Imperial War Museum, War Memorials Register, no. 13929: iwm.org.uk/memorials/item/memorial/13929 (accessed 4 Mar. 2019).

89   Creak, *History of Adams' Grammar School*, 59–60.

90   *VCH Salop*. II, 159.

91   Woodward, 130.

92   *The Charities in the County of Salop. … Reports of the Commissioners for Inquiring Concerning Charities in England and Wales …* (London, 1839), 332–3.

93   Garbet, 'An Account of the Dreadful Fire of Wem …' (1802), note inside front cover.

94   *Select Committee on Education of the Poor* (1818). Digest of Parochial Returns (Parliamentary Papers), 763; R.L. Kenyon, *Shropshire Charities for Elementary Education. Report of the Endowments Committee of the Shropshire Local Education Authority* (Shrewsbury, 1906), Mary Hankey's Charity, 90; SA, 731/2/1840; 'the National Schools' mentioned in a letter to *Morning Post*, 23 Nov. 1822, 2; SA, 7577/36/8, 17 Nov. 1831; SA, Raby Estates, box 9, letter describing past uses of the market house, 1882.

95   SA, P295/B/2/1: church rate book for Wem (17 Aug. 1824).

96   *Returns on State of Education* (1833), 786.

97   Ibid.; TNA, ED 103/139, 223–8.

98   SA, ED2699/43/18; TNA, ED 49/6433; TNA, ED 103/98, 985–90, 991–6.

99   *Kelly's Dir.* (1895), 252; Bagshaw, 321.

In 1837 the Noble Street and Chapel Street chapels resolved to found their own school,[100] applied for a Treasury grant, and in 1839 purchased a plot on Leek Street for £80, where they built the British Schools: 'two separate school rooms, one above the other, the Upper School having an entrance from the Old Chapel Street otherwise Lick Lane and the Lower School room having an entrance from the Dark Lane ...'[101] The girls' classroom was on the upper floor and the boys' on the lower, but in 1876 the school became mixed, with the infants and younger children on the lower floor.[102]

In 1869 few children in the parish were not attending school. Boys generally stayed to the age of 11 or 12 and would not be regularly employed before the age of 12, whereas girls were more often taken out of school at the age of 10 or 11 to go into domestic service.[103]

Post 1870

Improvements to the National School were carried out in 1861 and 1894,[104] and by 1902 the school had places for 234 pupils, with 227 enrolled, and the infant school, with 62 places, had 90 enrolled, but the average attendance was 50. The staff consisted of the headmaster, six pupil teachers for the mixed junior school, and an assistant teacher and two pupil teachers for the infants.[105] By 1909 the school had become overcrowded and the standard of pupils' work was suffering.[106] The trustees of the British Schools in 1894 purchased the adjacent burgage plot to the south; 17 Chapel Street became the headmaster's house and the Leek Street end of the plot became the school playground.[107] Elijah Wood Bowcock JP was headmaster, 1884–1924.[108] In 1902 there were places for 307, the number enrolled was 264 and average attendance was 211.[109]

In 1911 the trustees of the British Schools asked SCC to take the school over, but it declined due to the cramped site and poor condition of the buildings.[110] In 1914 the SCC Education Committee acknowledged criticisms of both the National and the British Schools and the need to increase provision, proposed a new elementary school with up to 650 places, and in 1915 purchased a site at the end of Barnard Street.[111] Threatened with closure, the National School raised the funds for substantial improvements.[112] SCC continued to plan a new elementary school, now at Shrubbery Gardens, as late as

---

100 TNA, ED 103/139, 223–8; Woodward, 88.
101 Title deeds of 17 Chapel St, Wem, in private possession.
102 Ibid.; SA, ED262/12.
103 *Employment of Children, Young Persons, and Women in Agriculture* (1867) Commission: Evidence (House of Commons Parliamentary Papers), 78.
104 TNA, ED 103/98, 991–6; TNA, ED 21/14950.
105 SA, ED2699/43/18.
106 TNA, ED 21/14950, HM Inspectors' reports, 20 Oct. 1909, 13 Oct. 1910. See ibid., plan of school, *c.*1911.
107 Ibid.; SA, ED2699/43/17, 2.
108 Obituary, *TSAHS*, 1948.
109 SA, ED2699/43/17. See further, TNA, ED 21/38503, Wem CofE School 1923–35.
110 TNA, ED 21/14950, 6 June 1911.
111 SA, DA36/150/WU/4/16; TNA, ED 21/14950–1; *Wellington Jnl*, 1 Aug. 1914.
112 SA, DA14/700/12: National Schools, Noble St: plans submitted to Wem UDC for alterations, 1 Jan. 1912; TNA, ED 21/14950.

1929.[113] Meanwhile the British Schools was repeatedly condemned for its 'deplorable' conditions.[114] After the school-leaving age rose to 14 in 1919, and the Hadow Report of 1926 recommended separate provision for pupils aged over 11, there was a competing demand for a senior school in Wem.[115] The solution was a new senior school at the Shrubbery Gardens site, while the under-12s from the British Schools transferred to the improved and enlarged National School. The British Schools closed in 1931,[116] when the National School became Wem Church of England Junior School for pupils aged 5 to 11. In 1935 Alderman S. Woollam, Lord Mayor of Manchester, and a former pupil of the National School, formally opened the new infant school there.[117] From 1958, known as St Peter's School, it was divided between the old Noble Street premises and the former Senior School in Shrubbery Gardens, the primary and secondary modern sharing the latter into the 1970s.[118] Once the move to Shrubbery Gardens was complete, the Noble Street school site was acquired by Thomas Adams School, initially as a dining hall and craft centre. At the time of writing it is the school's music centre.[119] The former British Schools building was sold in 1960 and demolished in 1973, the site becoming a public car park although the gateway on Chapel Street leading to the 'British Schools' still exists in 2019.[120] St Peter's Church of England Primary School still occupied the Shrubbery Gardens site in 2019. In 2007, 352 children aged 3–11 were enrolled, larger than the Shropshire average, and by 2017 numbers had grown to 416.[121]

Wem Senior School

Wem Senior School commenced in 1931 in a new building in Shrubbery Gardens designed by G.N. Bailey at a cost of £17,700.[122] A long symmetrical two-storey range of polychrome brickwork is flanked by lower wings at right angles and has the county's 'Floreat Salopia' insignia to the centre. The first head teacher was Thomas F. Chard.[123] The school took pupils aged over 11 from Wem and the surrounding villages. More academically able pupils transferred at the age of 11 or 13 to Adams' Grammar School (boys), Whitchurch High School (girls) or Shrewsbury Technical College.[124] The Grove School in Wem also offered secondary education for girls. In 1931 the Senior School had 342 pupils from eight primary schools.[125] Some travelled by bus and in 1934 those from

113 SA, DA14/701/9.
114 SA, ED262/13, 198; SA, DA14/100/5, 1055, 1090, 1123, 1214, 1300.
115 SA, DA14/100/5, 1162, 1214.
116 *Whitchurch Herald*, 31 July 1931.
117 Newspaper report, 6 Mar. 1935, cutting in SA, 7577/36/8.
118 Law, *Draft Wem Planning Policy & Advisory Plan* (1971), par. 42–4.
119 Author's pers. obs.
120 SA, DA36/150/WU/10; SA, NO4950/1/42; *Shropshire Star*, 27 Apr. 1973, cited in Edwards, 84. SA, PH/W/8/6/20.
121 Ofsted Inspection Report, 27 Sept. 2007 via https://reports.ofsted.gov.uk/provider/23/123589 (accessed 4 Mar. 2019); Shropshire Council, *Wem Market Town Profile*, 41.
122 *Whitchurch Herald*, 31 July 1931. The site had been purchased for an elementary school by Sept. 1923: SA, DA14/100/5, 1214; cf. Woodward, 105.
123 *Whitchurch Herald*, 31 July 1931; SA, ED2782/29, 40–3; Woodward, 105.
124 SA, ED2782/29, 42, 66, 139–40; SA, DA14/100/8, 370–1.
125 SA, ED2782/29, 40–3.

Figure 20 *Senior Council School, Wem, in the 1930s.*

Edstaston, Loppington, Newtown, Weston and Wixhill, and Lee Brockhurst were issued
with bicycles.[126] During the Second World War the school admitted a total of 497 evacuee
children and 12 teachers from Liverpool, with a peak attendance of 512 pupils – 326 local
children plus 186 evacuees. Three-week 'potato holidays' were declared in 1943 and 1944
when school staff and pupils worked on the potato harvest.[127] In 1943 SCC purchased a
plot of 1½ a. on New Street which was added to the school grounds and incorporated in
the school's extensive gardens for training in horticulture and agriculture.[128]

Education after 1944

From 1945 the Senior School was renamed Wem Modern School.[129] Thomas Chard
retired in 1948 and was succeeded by G. Stinson, who reported after his first year
as headmaster on the 'problem of backwardness in this area and in this school'.[130]
Absenteeism was a problem, especially at potato harvest time.[131] In 1946 there were 310
pupils from 18 contributing schools,[132] and from 1947 numbers increased, reaching 489

126 Ibid., 4, minutes of 5 Feb. and 28 Sept. 1934.
127 Ibid., 21, 23–4, 27–8.
128 TNA, ED 21/60033; e.g. SA, ED2782/29, 118.
129 SA, ED2782/29, 30; Woodward, 105.
130 SA, ED2782/29, 40–3, 48–9.
131 Ibid., 48–9, 66, 148.
132 Ibid., 32–3.

in 1957 when the school was 'uncomfortably crowded' and more growth was expected due to the post-war baby boom.[133]

In 1954 SCC announced plans for a new secondary school in Wem to take up to 750 pupils.[134] The new school was built off Lowe Hill road in 1957–8 by Frank Hancock, contractors, of Stoke-on-Trent, under the direction of the County Architect, C.H. Simmons. The overall cost, including furniture and a caretaker's house, was £128,000.[135] In 1958 the school began to move to its new site where initially there were places for 330 pupils.[136] In 1961 it was reported that, since the last inspection in 1952, the school had addressed the 'basic problems' it then faced, materially with new buildings, and educationally with mastering basic literacy and mathematics.[137] Results continued to improve; in 1964 the school achieved above the regional average in English CSE.[138]

In 1976 Wem Modern School merged with Adams' Grammar School to form a comprehensive school, initially known as Adams School and, since 2004, as Thomas Adams School.[139] It is one of two state boarding schools in Shropshire. The sixth form, Adams College, occupies the former grammar school building on Noble Street, while the lower school is located on the adjacent Lowe Hill site. In 2014 there were 1,420 pupils, aged 11–18, including 361 in the sixth form and 52 boarders.[140]

Private Schools

The Nonconformist congregations sought educational provision in keeping with their religious principles. William Hazlitt, minister of the Noble Street chapel from 1787, operated 'a model crammer for the dissenting rationalist' where his son William Hazlitt, the essayist, was educated to the age of 15.[141] Around the same time, a Mrs Swanwick had a schoolhouse built in Noble Street – probably The Hollies (no. 22) – where she kept a girls' day and boarding school.[142] The daughters of the Congregationalist minister, Peter Edwards, took over Mrs Swanwick's school after her death and ran it from 1806 until the 1840s.[143] Edwards's successor at Chapel Street, Joseph Pattison, took the lead in founding the British Schools as a means to educate children from poor families.[144] His daughters

133 Ibid., 38, 56, 66, 106, 126.
134 SA, CP173/21/14/1.
135 SA, ED6266, box S; SA, PH/W/8/6/36; Pevsner, 675.
136 SA, ED2782/29, 144; SA, PH/W/8/6/36; programme of the official opening of the school, 7 Nov. 1958 (in possession of Tom Edwards).
137 TNA, ED 109/9055/2, ED 109/9502/4; SA, ED2782/29, 181.
138 SA, ED2782/29, 238.
139 Woodward, 116–17, plate 15. The name was changed to avoid confusion with Adams' [Grammar] School in Newport (Salop).
140 Ofsted report, 16–17 Jan. 2014 via https://reports.ofsted.gov.uk/provider/23/123589 (accessed 4 Mar. 2019).
141 D. Wu, *William Hazlitt. The First Modern Man* (Oxford, 2008), ch. 2.
142 SA, 4791/1/2, insurance policy no. 1270, 20 July 1788; *Salopian Jnl*, 17 June 1835. For the Swanwick family, see *Eddowes's Jnl*, 15 June and 14 Dec. 1887; *Wellington Jnl*, 27 Dec. 1879; Garbet, 234. Joseph Swanwick was a school friend of William Hazlitt: Wu, *William Hazlitt*, 44.
143 *Salopian Jnl*, 27 May, 24 June 1835; *Robson's Dir.* (1840); Woodward, 87–8.
144 TNA, ED 103/139, 223–8.

kept a girls' school at their home, Islington Villa, from 1856 to 1889.[145] Islington Villa continued as a girls' private school, being advertised in 1895 as an 'old established day and boarding school' under the Misses Grove.[146]

In 1833 there were six private day schools with a total of 66 boys and 84 girls, and two private girls' boarding schools with a total of 40 pupils.[147] The Hall was a girls' school from c.1863 until 1866, when Mr Rogerson, the headmaster of Belle Vue Academy, Shrewsbury, advertised that he had taken the lease of The Hall and would commence a school there.[148] The Hall day and boarding school for boys flourished until the premises were sold in 1878.[149]

Tilley House, south of the river, housed three private schools at different periods. The first was Tilley House Classical Academy, advertised in 1824. In 1830 its proprietor announced that he was moving the school to Flintshire.[150] In 1911, P.J. O'Dea, a former master at Adams' grammar school, opened a school for boys and girls at Warwick Villa in New Street, but when numbers increased he moved the school to Tilley House in 1918. Some 850 pupils were said to have attended the school in its 27 years.[151] The school closed when O'Dea retired in 1938.

In 1902 a day and boarding school for girls was opened at The Grove by two sisters, Frances and Mary Wrench.[152] Between 1917 and 1922 the headmistress was Miss A.R. Eglinton, formerly headmistress of the High School for Girls, Barnard Castle (Co. Durham).[153] When Tilley House became vacant in 1938 the school moved there. Under the headship of Nora A. Freeman, The Grove School offered secondary education for girls and a mixed kindergarten and preparatory school.[154] The school closed in 1962 when Miss Freeman retired. Tilley House was then demolished and the site redeveloped as the Roden Grove housing estate.[155] The school reopened as Grove House School, first at 94 High Street and then at Foxley, and finally closed in 1974. At that time the need for private education for girls to achieve university entrance level in Wem was relieved by the admission of girls to the sixth form at Adams' Grammar School.[156]

145 *Slater's Dir.* (1856); *Slater's Dir.* (1859), 58; *Eddowes's Jnl*, 9 July 1856; *Shrews. Chron.*, 25 Sept. 1863; *Oswestry Advertiser*, 21 Mar. 1866; *South Wales Daily News*, 2 Jan. 1880; *Wellington Jnl*, 11 May 1889.
146 *Wellington Jnl*, 28 Sept. 1895.
147 *Returns on State of Education* (1833), 786.
148 *Shrews. Chron.*, 18 Sept. 1863; *Manchester Courier and Lancashire General Advertiser*, 13 July 1864; *Eddowes's Jnl*, 10 Jan. 1866; *Oswestry Advertiser*, 8 Aug. 1866, 19 Dec. 1866. For these and other, more ephemeral, private schools, see Woodward, 88, 105.
149 *Wellington Jnl*, 28 Apr. 1866, 12 Jan. 1867; *Eddowes's Jnl*, 21 Jan. 1874.
150 Woodward, 88; *Pigot's Dir.* (1828/9), 79; *Chester Chron.*, 10 Dec. 1830. Reid, *Tilley*, 190–2.
151 SA, DA14/700/21; *Shrews. Chron.*, 11 Nov. 1938; P. Cooney, 'The (relatively) unchanging face of Wem', *Shropshire Mag.*, July 1971, 36–7.
152 *Wellington Jnl*, 28 Dec. 1901; *Census*, 1911; *Kelly's Dir.* (1913), 289, 291; photograph: SA, PC/W/6/30.
153 *Kelly's Dir.* (1917), 272; (1922), 283; *Strong's* (1925), advertisement.
154 *Kelly's Dir.* (1934), 309; 'Grove House', advertisement for school: http://www.wemlocal.org.uk/wemmap/grove.htm (accessed 4 Mar. 2019); Reid, *Tilley*, 191.
155 Woodward, 105, 117; author's pers. obs.
156 Woodward, 117; pers. comm. Tom Edwards.

Social Welfare

Charities for the Poor

Benefactions to the parish church and the poor were recorded on a board in the church by c.1730.[157] It was replaced in 1827 with four new boards, repainted in 1855, which are still displayed in the church.[158] Missing from these, however, is the charity founded by a Nonconformist glover, Robert Hill, who in 1695 conveyed to trustees several houses in Mill Street and land known as 'Rownhill', the latter charged with £4 per annum to pay the minister of the dissenters' meeting house, the balance for other charitable purposes.[159] Of the Anglican charities, Richard Corbet, by deed of 1703, appointed a rent-charge of £10 per annum on land at High Hatton to clothe poor persons and educate and apprentice selected poor boys.[160] Thomas Spendelow or Spendlove of Tilley, by his will of 1705, left £50 for the poor, including in Wem township, which in 1716 the churchwardens and overseers of the poor of the parish invested in the purchase of pasture land, Stanley End Pieces in Whixall, charged with 50s. to provide bread for the poor of the parish every Sunday. In 1830 £10 8s. was spent on distributing bread and £3 given in coin out of the proceeds of the Spendelow and Corbet charities.

In 1726 Richard Hill bequeathed £100 to the poor and Rowland Whittingham later bequeathed £10. In 1765 these funds were invested to purchase three houses in Wem adjoining the church yard, the rents to be applied for poor relief. In 1810 the vestry decided to demolish them and in 1822 the land was added to the church yard. In lieu of the rents from these houses, £2 per annum was paid out of the church rate and distributed to the poor.[161]

Sir Richard Hill, by his will dated 1808, bequeathed £300 in trust to apply the interest to the poor of Hodnet, Prees and Wem.[162] Sir Andrew Corbet's Charity was established in 1817 by the gift of 25 guineas for the poor. The capital sum paid for rebuilding the church and thereafter 25s. per annum was paid from the church rate for bread. Hankey's charity, established by the will of Mrs Mary Hankey in 1818, used the interest on £40 to support the charity subscription school and the interest on a further £40 for bread at Easter.[163]

The Mill Street houses of Robert Hill's charity were rebuilt between 1879 and 1884 (now 6–8 and 12–16 Mill Street). The charity was subject to a scheme of the Charity

---

157 SA, SA-IMG1998, original drawing in Univ. of Birmingham, Cadbury Research Library, MS MYT/7.
158 Pers. obs.; Woodward, 133.
159 'Re Robert Hill's and Noble Street Chapel Charities, Wem. Summary of the history of the charities', typescript in possession of Tom Edwards; Garbet, 212.
160 The paragraph, unless otherwise stated, is based on *Commission of Enquiry into the Charities of England and Wales, 24th Report (1831)*, 231 XI.1.11, 328–35. There is no other record of 'Minshull's Charity', 334.
161 SA, P295/B/3/1/2–3; P295/Q/8/2/18.
162 SA, P295/Q/3/1; SA, 7577/36/8, 21 Jan. 1832.
163 The £40 benefaction to the charity school does not appear in the 1831 report. See SA, P295/Q/1/1 and 2; Woodward, 44–5. Above, Education.

Commissioners of 1886 with purposes to assist local individuals and organisations in education, training and relief of poverty.[164]

The Corbet, Hankey, Sir Richard Hill and Whixall Estate charities were administered as the Wem United Charities from c.1895.[165] In 1896 the trustees of the Wem Parish Charities stated that more than half of the income was being distributed in money at Easter: in 1895 they had paid £13 5s. 4d. in coin and £8 1s. 4d. in bread, and in future they wished to discontinue cash payments and distribute relief in kind to avoid 'crowding, jealousy, loss of self-respect and drunkenness'.[166]

Later charities included that of Miss Sarah Mary Beetenson (d. 1894) of Islington House, New Street, which distributed coal to individuals and paid a subscription to the Wem Parish Nursing Association.[167] The Nickson Charity, founded by Mary Walford, née Nickson, before 1901, provided flannel petticoats for deserving women.[168] The Harley Harries charity was established in 1921 for the benefit of poor church-goers and remains a registered charity to make annual grants to poor elderly people of the parish of Wem.[169] The Barber Trust, established in 1931, supports projects to benefit the town.[170]

Poor Relief before 1836

An almshouse existed in 1561, on Mill Street opposite the church yard.[171] Around 1625 the parish was burdened by 'poor cottagers', mostly residing on the lord's demesne; the employment that had been found for the men by the lord's officers, first in the demesne woods, and latterly draining Wem Pool, had come to an end and the overseers of the poor and other concerned residents petitioned the countess of Arundel for some allowance to relieve their poverty.[172] Paupers receiving parish relief in Wem were obliged to wear a tin 'P' some years before the Poor Act 1697 made such badges compulsory.[173] There was a poorhouse, or workhouse, by 1739, when 'Widow Patrick, a poor woman from the workhouse' was buried.[174] The poorhouse moved to Bank House, at the western end of the town, c.1801. In 1814 it was well furnished and equipped, with a parlour, dining room, kitchen, store rooms, cellar and 'small beer pantry', brewhouse, bakehouse, milkhouse, barn and cowhouse. The 'school room' appears not to have been in use, but

---

164 Community Council of Shropshire, Charity Review Committee, 'Report of the Review of Local Charities in Shropshire 1975' (SA, C 37.2 v.f), 35; http://www.gov.uk/government/organisations/charity-commission, no. 226135 (accessed 4 Mar. 2019).
165 SA, 4693/192; 'Report of the Review of Local Charities in Shropshire 1975', 35.
166 SA, P295/Q/4/1/2.
167 *Wellington Jnl*, 13 Jan. 1894, 7; SA, P295/Q/2.
168 SA, P295/Q/7; The Administrative County of Salop. List of Local Charities in the North Shropshire District (n.d., c.1974) (photocopy, SA, 6908/16/296).
169 'Report of the Review of Local Charities in Shropshire 1975', 35; http://www.gov.uk/government/organisations/charity-commission, no. 242901 (accessed 4 Mar. 2019).
170 Woodward, 98; 'Report of the Review of Local Charities in Shropshire 1975', 35; http://www.gov.uk/government/organisations/charity-commission, no. 218859 (accessed 4 Mar. 2019).
171 *Survey 1561*, 24–5; Garbet, 242.
172 Cited by Garbet, 58–9.
173 Gough, *History of Myddle*, 258–60; S. Hindle, *On the Parish? The Micro-Politics of Poor Relief in Rural England c.1550–1750* (Oxford, 2009), 436, 436, 442.
174 Wem Parish Registers, 465.

Figure 21 *Bank House: Wem parish poorhouse (c.1801–38), later maltings; with parish lock-up (1815), later the fire-engine house, adjacent on far left.*

Table 8 *Expenditure on the poor by Wem parish, 1776–1835.*

	(to nearest £)
Year ending Easter 1776	330
Average of three years 1783–85	522
Year ending Easter 1803	2718
Year ending 25 March 1822	2455
Year ending 25 March 1823	1960
Year ending 25 March 1824	1375
Year ending 25 March 1831	1569
Year ending 25 March 1832	1539
Year ending 25 March 1834	1718
Year ending 25 March 1835	1322

Sources: 1776, 'Report from the Committee appointed to inspect and consider the returns made by Overseers of the Poor ... (15 May 1777)', in *Reports from Committees of the House of Commons, vol. IX, Provisions: Poor 1774–1802*, 297–539, at 441; 1783–5, Abstract of the answers and returns made pursuant to an act of 43 George III, 414–15; 1822–4, Report on the Select Committee on poor rate returns, 1825, 175–6; 1831–4, 'An account of money expended for the maintenance and relief of the poor, 1829–34', 158; 1835, 'Appendix to the second annual report of the Commission under the Poor Law Amendment Act', 302–3.

Table 9 *Expenditure on the poor by Wem parish, 1825–28.*

	Expenditure £			Number of weekly pensioners
	'Disbursements'	Weekly payments	Total	
1825/6				
Wem Quarter	408	315	723	80
Aston Quarter	317	91	408	30
Edstaston Quarter	221	94	315	35
Horton Quarter	247	42	289	13
Total	1193	542	1735	158
1826/7				
Wem Quarter	575	369	944	83
Aston Quarter	452	95	547	31
Edstaston Quarter	342	101	443	34
Horton Quarter	348	36	384	10
Total	1717	601	2318	158
1827/8				
Wem Quarter	605	329	934	83
Aston Quarter	391	89	480	28
Edstaston Quarter	378	93	471	28
Horton Quarter	350	44	394	14
Total	1724	555	2279	153

Source: Wem poor law accounts 1825/6–1827/8 in private possession. Figures rounded to nearest pound.

there were spinning wheels and spun yarn in a store room; upstairs, six rooms of various sizes contained about 20 beds with bed-linen and other furniture.[175]

Between 1814 and 1828 medical treatment was offered to the poor, funded at least partially through charity via the Women's Club of Wem, which began in 1793 with 12 members who met at the Black Lion public house, paying an initial entrance fee followed by an annual subscription, which funded funerals and donations to 'the sick', but always to female recipients and never for the benefit of members themselves.[176] The Women's Club also contributed to retaining a local medical practitioner, usually Charles A. Beetenson but in some years Edward Gwynn the elder, to attend to the poor, with an annual salary of £7–£10.

175 SA, P265/C/1/1, 22 Aug. 1814.
176 SA, 1848, box 180, 'The accounts of the women's club of Wem', 1813–33.

In the late 1820s the Wem overseer paid for potatoes, flour, meat and coal, presumably for the workhouse, and the poor were still apparently employed in spinning yarn.[177] In 1834 there were 18 men aged 40–80 and eight women aged 30–50 in the workhouse, and about 30 individuals received out-relief.[178] At that time, seasonal unemployment among men and a lack of paid work for women were deemed the chief causes of poverty. Men were given subsidised work in the winter by individuals, the parish sharing the cost, but there was no employment for women or children in the summer or winter seasons and at harvest time they gleaned. A labourer's household typically had potato land and kept a pig; 16 a. of land had been made available for allotments, apparently as a private initiative.[179] In 1869 there was still no more than three months' work for poor women during the year, and it was mainly 'in harvest work, topping and tailing turnips, or picking stones'.[180]

Poor Relief after 1836

In 1836 Wem became the centre of a new poor law union, and a union workhouse was built at Love Lane, north of the town.[181] Inmates had a boring and repetitive diet (Poor Law Commission Dietary No. 1), but received three meals per day in consistent amounts, meat three days a week and cheese on the other four days – a better diet than agricultural labourers could afford.[182] In the early years, special dinners were organised by the Guardians for Christmas and as a reward for good behaviour.[183]

Out-relief payments to permanent paupers, often the old or those permanently unable to work, were quite low, averaging 2s. 6d. to 3s. per week in the early 1870s, at a time when agricultural labourers earned about 12s. per week. Occasional payments were often larger but were generally in kind, reflecting Guardians' concerns about money being spent in alehouses. Relief generally consisted of meat, general provisions, brandy, clothes to enable children to take employment and burial costs.[184]

The cost of placing a family in the workhouse was greater than paying out-relief. In 1839 there were approximately four times as many paupers maintained on out-relief as in the workhouse.[185] Indeed, the workhouse was never extended, implying a preference for maintaining paupers on out-relief. In 1891 the workhouse had capacity for 95 inmates[186] and in 1906 there were 78 indoor (resident) paupers – about a quarter aged under 16 and just over half aged over 60 – and 157 outdoor paupers.[187]

177 Wem poor law accounts 1825/6–1827/8, in private possession.
178 *Royal Commission of Inquiry into the Administration and Practical Operation of the Poor Laws* (1834), App. B1, 'Rural Queries', ans. 22, 23.
179 Ibid., ans. 12, 13, 14, 20.
180 *Employment of Children, Young Persons, and Women*, 78.
181 Below, Local Government.
182 J. Sumbler, 'Child poverty in Victorian Shropshire, 1834–1870' (unpublished Keele Univ. Ph.D. thesis, 2016), 356.
183 SA, PL15/1, 7 Dec. 1837, 176, 21 June 1838, 237.
184 SA, PL15/48.
185 SA, PL15/17.
186 *Kelly's Dir.* (1891).
187 *Royal Commission on the Poor Laws and Relief of Distress*, Appendix 25, Statistics relating to England and Wales, 254.

Wem poor law union also provided medical services to the poor, and some formal education for children aged up to about 11 years, after which they were expected to find employment. From 1915 a separate children's home was established, supervised by a 'foster-mother'.[188]

Medical Services

Early resident physicians include Richard Astley (1671–1754), heir to a cadet branch of the Astley family of Aston Hall, who practised as a surgeon ('chirurgeon') in Wem. His youngest son was the society painter John Astley (1720–87), and he does not appear to have had a successor.[189] William Higgins (c.1680–1727) was a barber and perukemaker, a trade which would typically have incorporated teeth-pulling and other minor surgical procedures. His son Thomas (1713–94) was apprenticed as a surgeon, and in turn took his own son Thomas (1759–1803) as apprentice. Thomas Higgins the younger became a local surgeon/apothecary and man-midwife. In his register he recorded over 1,000 deliveries between 1781 and 1803, one-third of which were within Wem town and the others in the surrounding area; he noted his use of forceps in 1788.[190] Higgins usually charged half a guinea per singleton delivery, although the fee seems to have varied according to the financial means of the parents. He attended deliveries of women of widely varying social status, from women in the workhouse to the wife of the Wem attorney John Lee. Over his career, he attended the births of, on average, 31 per cent of children baptised into the Church of England at Wem each year, besides also undertaking a range of minor surgical procedures such as bone setting, pulling teeth, bleeding and inoculation against smallpox, and as an apothecary, preparing and selling drugs.

The 'Mr Beetenson, surgeon and apothecary' who built himself a new house in Market Street, c.1730–50, was presumably the Samuel Beetenson, surgeon, who in 1752 owned a large property in the Horse Market. He had a large family and at least three of his sons became surgeon-apothecaries: Samuel and Arthur in Wem, and John in Ellesmere.[191] In the next generation, Charles Augustus Beetenson (1773–1858) was a surgeon in Noble Street.[192] Joseph Greene Wilson, from Shrewsbury, was his pupil and joined him in practice as 'surgeons, apothecaries and accoucheurs' in Noble Street until 1844.[193]

The Gwynn family supplied four generations to the medical trade as it transformed into a profession in the mid 19th century. Edward Gwynn (c.1766–1845) was in practice

188 Below, Local Government.
189 SA, P132/Q/8/22. See R.C. Purton, 'The family of Astley of Aston in the parish of Wem', *TSAS*, 4th series, I (1911) 23–8; *ODNB*, s.v. John Astley (1720–87) (accessed 4 Mar. 2019); Garbet, 239, 361.
190 SA, 1848, box 44, 1781–1803; A. Tomkins (ed.), *The Registers of a Provincial Man-Midwife*, Shropshire Record Ser., 4 (Keele, 2000); A. Tomkins, 'Demography and the midwives: Deliveries and their dénouements in north Shropshire, 1781–1803', *Continuity and Change*, 25, 2 (2010), 199–232; A. Tomkins, 'Who were his peers? The social and professional milieu of the provincial surgeon-apothecary in the late-eighteenth century', *Jnl of Social History*, 44, 3 (2011), 915–35
191 Garbet, 241; Tomkins, 'Who were his peers?'; SA, 1848, boxes 15 and 121, title deeds; Wem Parish Registers, vol. 2.
192 *Shrews. Chron.*, 18 June 1858.
193 *Shrews. Chron.*, 29 Nov. 1839; *Aris's Birmingham Gaz.*, 20 May 1844.

by c.1795[194] and around 1830 he and his son, Edward (1794–1873), surgeon and medical inspector of Wem poor law union, were in partnership in Noble Street. In 1851 both Edward Gwynn the younger and Samuel Betton Gwynn, FRCS (1823–80), the third generation of this medical family, were in practice in Noble Street.[195] Samuel Tayleur Gwynn (MRCS, 1848) and Charles Henry Gwynn (MRCS, 1879) established their practice in Whitchurch.[196] Samuel Betton Gwynn's son, Edward Betton Gwynn (1866–1936), studied medicine at Edinburgh before working in the Reading area. Returning to Wem, in 1911 he was engaged at the workhouse, presumably in a medical capacity.[197]

Noble Street was the preferred address of the town's medical men, although a Thomas Walmsley, surgeon, resided in High Street c.1828–59,[198] but from the mid 19th century the medical profession migrated to New Street – Joseph Greene Wilson by 1851 and Samuel Betton Gwynn by 1868[199] – and the street has been the location of Wem's medical practices ever since. In 1870, when Wilson was the victim of attempted murder in his New Street residence, Brunswick House, his son and apprentice was able to call immediately upon Gwynn and John Gill, whose joint practice was next door at 61 The Crescent.[200]

Wem's two general practices developed in New Street in the 20th century. That established by Dr Gwynn continued at no. 61[201] with the other at the Old Hall, where Dr Charles Robert Leader (medical officer of health for Wem union, 1901–13) was succeeded by Dr Vere Somerset.[202] On the latter's death in 1962 the two practices were amalgamated and continued by Dr John Keeling-Roberts and colleagues. The SCC Welfare Clinic was established at The Shrubbery by 1971 and the NHS Wem Medical Practice was built on the same site in 1991.[203]

Wem poor law union paid a subscription to the Salop Infirmary in Shrewsbury in order to send paupers there for treatment, while those suffering from mental illness could be sent to the Shropshire Asylum at Shelton, which opened in 1845.[204] An infirmary or 'hospital' was included in the development of the new Wem union workhouse in 1838 and in 1841 a new 'probationary ward' was added to house new admissions, acting as an isolation unit against the spread of infectious diseases such as typhus and smallpox.[205] Unlike in other localities, such as Whitchurch, this hospital wing of the workhouse did not later develop into a cottage hospital. In 1903 an isolation

194 *Univ. Brit. Dir.*, 718.
195 SA, PL15/1, 1836–40; Bagshaw; *Shrews Chron.*, 13 May 1853, 4.
196 General Medical Council, *The Medical Register 1903.*
197 General Medical Council, *The Medical Register 1911, 1915.*
198 *Pigot's Dir.* (1828/9), *Pigot's Dir.* (1842); Bagshaw; *Slaters Dir.* (1859).
199 'Gwynn, Samuel Betton (1822–1880)', Royal College of Surgeons (London, 2012): https://livesonline.
      rcseng.ac.uk (accessed 4 Mar. 2019); Bagshaw; *Slater's Dir.* (1868).
200 *Oswestry Advertiser*, 20 Apr. 1870; *Shrews. Chron.*, 5 Aug. 1870. The son, Charles Joseph Greene Wilson,
      was tried for attempted murder and acquitted.
201 Woodward, 116; *Strong's* (1925), 'New Street'.
202 Woodward, 116; J. Dromgool, 'Wem in wartime', *The Wemian*, Summer 2016, 13; a photograph of Dr
      Vere Somerset, with his pet monkey, at the Old Hall, is in SA, 8540, Wem album no. 2.
203 Law, *Draft Wem Planning Policy & Advisory Plan* (1971), par. 52.
204 *VCH Salop.* III, 160–2.
205 SA, PL15/1, 7 Dec. 1837, 177; L. Smith, 'Refuges of last resort: Shropshire workhouses
and the people who ran them', *TSHAS*, 82 (2007), 113.

hospital, mainly for tuberculosis patients, opened on Prees Heath. Both were used by Wem patients not requiring the services of an acute hospital.[206]

Legal Profession

There were several attorneys-at-law in Wem manor from the mid 17th century, and legal professionals came to dominate local society in the 18th and 19th centuries, playing a prominent role in economic and civic life in their capacity as trustees, executors, clerks and holders of public office, as well as substantial landholders. Offering legal services to the neighbouring countryside, they fulfilled one of the essential functions of the market town. Family firms tended to form dynasties as attorneys were succeeded by their sons or sons-in-law.

Richard Menlove was an attorney living in Wolverley in the second half of the 17th century.[207] He may have been related to William Manlove and Thomas Manlove of Wem who were admitted to Barnard's Inn in 1678 and 1685, respectively.[208] A near contemporary, Ralph Wilson, was in practice in Wem from c.1700 until 1728, residing at a large town-centre property (now 39–41 High Street).[209]

The first official listing of attorneys-at-law of 1729/30 notes two in Wem: Richard Goldisbrough and John Henshaw.[210] Goldisbrough, whose family seat was at the Ryebank, Edstaston, 'was bred up to the law' having been admitted to Barnard's Inn in 1711. He appears to have moved to Ash Magna (near Whitchurch) by 1740 and left no issue and apparently no successor to his practice.[211] Henshaw, in contrast, joined what was to become a Wem legal dynasty. Born at Longford-upon-Tern (Salop), he was apprenticed to Ralph Wilson in 1722 and married Wilson's daughter and sole heiress, Beatrice, in 1728.[212] Henshaw was succeeded in 1763 by his son, also John, described as 'the community broker' in Wem in the late 18th century.[213] John Henshaw the younger died in 1801, commemorated by a monument in Lee Brockhurst church as having 'practiced [sic] as an attorney [in Wem] for near to 40 years with the greatest reputation and success'; another monument, in the Chapel Street chapel which he founded, proclaims that 'As a lawyer his judgement was oracular, his devotion to the interests of

206 J. Clayton, *Whitchurch Hospitals, Their History and Medical Care* (Logaston, 2004), 39.
207 Garbet, 329. The Menlove family held Aston House and its copyhold estate by the early 16th century; by 1561 branches of the family held estates in Edstaston, Horton and Loppington, and later the New House estate in Wolverley: *Survey 1561*, 91, 107, 137, 145, 185; Garbet, 269, 307, 329, 355–6.
208 C.W. Brooks (ed.), *The Admissions Registers of Barnard's Inn, 1620–1869*, Selden Soc., Supp. Ser. 12 (London, 1995), 110, 112, 123; SA, 103/1/5/190–1.
209 SA, P295/B/3/11, rates for Wem quarter, 1700; Garbet, 250, 357; SA, D3651/B/46/2/1/10; SA, P132/Q/8/16; 103/1/5/222; Wem Parish Registers.
210 *Lists of Attornies and Solicitors admitted in pursuance of the late Act for the better Regulation of Attornies and Solicitors presented to the House of Commons …* (London, 1729); *Additional Lists of Attornies and Solicitors …* (London, 1731).
211 *Admissions Registers of Barnard's Inn*, 127; SA, 306 box 16a (deeds for New Street property, 9 Aug. 1740 and 1 Oct. 1766); SA, 5981/B/1/91; Garbet, 268.
212 SA, 327/2/2/47/2; SA, 5981/B/1/145; *The Registers of Battlefield, Shropshire, 1665–1812* (Shropshire Parish Register Society, vol. XIX ([Shrewsbury], 1899), 11 Dec. 1728.
213 Tomkins, 'Who were his peers?', 922.

his clients unwearied, and his uprightness inflexible'.[214] Henshaw's 'uprightness' extended, however, to a distinctly uncharitable attitude to applicants for poor relief.[215] He left no issue, but his four sisters had all married into prominent local families.[216] The *Law List* for 1802 gives the Wem lawyers as John Lee and John Walford. Lee was Henshaw's partner in the last years of his life and acted as his executor, while Walford was Henshaw's nephew and apprentice.[217] Under Henshaw's will, Walford received the bequest of his uncle's law books and manuscripts;[218] another nephew, Jonathan Nickson, received £40 towards the purchase of law books – Nickson had been apprenticed to Lee in 1797.[219] Henshaw, Lee and Walford appear as partners in the *Law Lists* from 1796 to 1801; but in 1802 Lee and Walford were practising independently and by 1808 John Walford had been joined in partnership by Stephen Hassall and John Lee by Jonathan Nickson. These four men seem to have formed the Wem legal fraternity until new individuals came into the town in the mid 1820s.

John Walford died in 1836 leaving a son,[220] John Henshaw Walford, who married the daughter of Jonathan Nickson in 1832, but as the most prominent individual residing in Wem he chose not to work in the family profession.[221] The birth of his son, John Henshaw Nickson Walford, in 1836 was marked by a public collection for the Wem poor and a dinner for 80 gentlemen and tradesmen at the Castle inn, and his coming of age in 1857 was marked by even grander festivities in Wem and Aston.[222] After succeeding his father in 1865, however, J.H.N. Walford moved to Ruyton Towers, where he died in 1910.[223] The Wem legal practice instead passed in 1828 to a solicitor from Middlewich, Henry John Barker, who married John Walford's daughter Sarah Rebecca,[224] and therefore continued under the Barker name. In 1853 'Messrs Barker, solicitors' comprised Henry John and Charles Frederick Barker.[225] In 1865 H.J. Barker, Thomas John Barker (admitted 1855) and Walford Henry Barker (admitted 1863) were all in practice in the town. The latter died young, in 1869,[226] and perhaps for this reason the practice passed in 1872 to H.J. Barker's assistant, Edward Bygott.[227]

214 SA, 4208/117: 'Monumental inscriptions of United Reform Church, Wem, Shropshire 1844–1953', transcribed by J. Challinor (Shropshire Family Hist. Soc., 1986), part 2.
215 'Who were his peers?', 927–8.
216 TNA, PROB 11/1360, ff. 210v–213; Tomkins, 'Who were his peers?', 922–3.
217 Tomkins, 'Who were his peers?', 925–6. *Univ. Brit. Dir.*, 718. The following paragraphs, unless otherwise stated, are based on the annual Law Lists (initially *Clarke's Law List*): partnerships are evidenced by the names given in newspaper advertisements.
218 Walford was the son of George Walford of Wem, timber merchant (d. 1815).
219 TNA, IR 1/37, f. 109.
220 TNA, PROB 11/1875/361.
221 *Shrews. Chron.*, 26 Oct. 1832. Nickson's son died in 1829.
222 *Shrews. Chron.*, 30 Dec. 1836; 11 Dec. 1857; *Eddowes's Jnl*, 9 Dec. 1857.
223 For Walford's death, see *Eddowes's Jnl*, 1 Nov. 1865; *Shrews. Chron.*, 3 Nov. 1865; *Shrews. Chron.*, 12 Aug. 1910, 5.
224 *Staffordshire Advertiser*, 6 Sept. 1828.
225 SA, 816/5; *Shrews. Chron.*, 4 Apr. 1851, 6; *Eddowes's Jnl*, 31 Aug. 1853, 1; 8 Feb. 1854. By 1866, C.F. Barker had returned to Middlewich (Ches.): *Staffordshire Advertiser*, 18 Aug. 1866.
226 For Walford Barker, *Shrews. Chron.*, 12 June 1863; *Wellington Jnl*, 8 May 1869.
227 See the eulogies of Barker at the Wem county court, reported *Shrews. Chron.*, 14 June 1872.

The Walfords and Barkers never had a monopoly of legal business in Wem. Stephen Hassall appears irregularly in the *Law Lists*.[228] He was Walford's partner in 1809–13 and then disappears for a period. In 1827–30 he had a partner in Samuel Walmsley but then seems to have ceased to practise a second time. Hassall resided at the Old Hall in Wem – the southern wing was built for his office – but retired to Aston Park some time before he died in 1843. Walmsley served as clerk to the trustees of the Preston Brockhurst turnpike in the 1840s and went into partnership with William Lucas, who was said in 1844 to have been Nickson's clerk for more than 20 years, but presumably transferred to Walmsley on Nickson's retirement.[229] Lucas died in 1873 but established his own dynasty; his son was admitted as a solicitor in 1863 in the same class as Walford Barker.[230] Thomas Dickin Browne, a grandson of Thomas Dickin of Wem, established himself as a solicitor in Wem in the early 1830s and succeeded Hassall as tenant of the Old Hall. Browne may have diversified into auctioneering around 1860: he died in 1871.[231]

A new type of lawyer appeared after the 1830s. The opportunities for salaried work as clerk to a public body or court grew enormously after this decade. H.J. Barker was registrar of the Wem County Court but stood down to make way for his son Walford; on the latter's premature death he was reappointed to the position.[232] William Lucas the elder was clerk to the magistrates, petty sessions being conducted at his office at 22 Noble Street. The prime example in Wem of this sort of office-holding lawyer is William Owen who lived at The Shrubbery. Owen first appears as clerk to the Wem union; he also became superintendent registrar and acted as local agent to a number of insurance companies. After his death in 1872, the guardians held an election in which the candidates were Wem solicitors, including Edward Bygott and William Lucas the younger. They elected Owen's partner, H. Ponting Cox, as his successor.[233]

A window in the parish church commemorates H.J. Barker as 'one who had served and supported the town in every way possible'.[234] The same could be said of Edward Bygott.[235] Among numerous public offices, Bygott was registrar of the County Court in Wem for 40 years, and a member of the parish council and of the county council. It could justly be said that, 'there has been no public improvement in Wem in which Mr. Bygott has not taken a prominent part', including the water supply and sewerage schemes, the opening of a second bank in the town, the formation of Wem UDC and the construction of the town hall. He served as clerk to the Whitchurch bench of magistrates and to Wem RDC. In 1912 Bygott made his former managing clerk, Albert George Eccleston, a partner,[236] and the firm merged with the Whitchurch practice of Henry Lee shortly after the deaths of Lee in 1915 and Bygott in 1916.[237] In time another generation of Bygotts

---

228 He was apprenticed to Thomas Hilditch attorney of Nantwich in 1781. TNA, IR 1/62 f. 77.
229 Lucas was admitted as solicitor in 1827 (*Law Lists*); for his career, *Eddowes's Jnl*, 7 Aug. 1844. Nickson died in 1846.
230 *Shrews. Chron.*, 12 June 1863.
231 Woodward, 56–7; SA, 306 box 16B; *Chester Chron.*, 1 Sept., 29 Dec. 1843; *Eddowes's Jnl*, 1 Feb. 1871; *Shrews. Chron.*, 8 Feb. 1871. For his ancestry, *Eddowes's Jnl*, 4 Mar. 1891.
232 *Shrews. Chron.*, 14 June 1872.
233 For Owen's offices see the *Law Lists*, passim. *Shrews. Chron.*, 17 May, 14 June 1872.
234 SA, 731/2/3257 and 3271; SA, 1848, box 167; *Shrews. Chron.*, 3, 10 and 17 May 1872.
235 The following is from his obituary, *Nantwich Guardian*, 7 Mar. 1916, 3.
236 *Chester Chron.*, 8 July 1940, 8 Feb. 1941.
237 For Lee, see *Chester Chron.*, 24 Apr. 1915.

joined the firm, Edward Bygott being admitted in 1920, followed by his son, Edward Vere Bygott who took over the practice in 1961 and retired in 1988.[238] The firm continued to operate as Henry Lee, Eccleston and Bygott for a few years but finally ceased in the 1990s.

Another firm continued the practice of William Lucas. In 1925, W.J. Creak of Lucas, Butter & Creak was clerk to the magistrates, who still sat at the firm's office at 22 Noble Street. The Wem office was still in business in 1962.[239] Around 1980 Paul F. Harfitt commenced a new solicitor and property agent practice, occupying the former Barclays Bank building on the corner of Noble Street and High Street. Since 2011, the Shrewsbury firm Hatchers has also conducted regular weekly surgeries in Wem.[240]

238 Pers. comm. Edward Bygott, 14 May 2018.
239 *Strong's* (1925); SA, 3994: account and letter books, 1906–51; SA, SC/48/17.
240 http://www.harfitts.co.uk/about-us; http://www.hatchers.co.uk/celebrating-five-years-in-wem/ (both accessed 4 Mar. 2019); pers. comm. 4 Mar. 2019.

RELIGIOUS HISTORY

COMPLETELY REBUILT IN THE 19th century apart from the medieval tower, the parish church has always been closely tied to the lordship of Wem. It was apparently founded and endowed by early lords and the very large ancient parish was almost identical in extent with the manor. Moreover, the lord of the manor always held the advowson, often appointing a kinsman as rector. Nonconformity thrived in the parish from an early date, with large Congregationalist and Primitive Methodist congregations; of several substantial chapels built by various denominations, at least two are still in use.

Church Origins and Parochial Organisation

The parish church was probably founded by William Pantulf or his immediate successors as lords of Wem, although it is not attested until the 1260s.[1] The early dedication to St Peter and St Paul is suggested by the annual fair being held on their feast day (29 June) by 1292 and a dedication to St Peter is mentioned in 1366.[2]

The ancient parish of Wem was similar in extent to the manor. Two chapelries – St Mary, Edstaston, and King Charles the Martyr, Newtown – became separate ecclesiastical parishes in 1850 and 1861,[3] hence the current ecclesiastical parish is about half its former size. Wem has been held in plurality with Lee Brockhurst since 1947, and in 2016 Weston-under-Redcastle became the third parish in the benefice.[4] Within the diocese of Lichfield, Wem parish alternated between the rural deaneries of Salop and Newport until 1837 when the archdeaconry of Salop was divided into eight new deaneries, one centred on Wem.[5] Wem deanery united with that of Whitchurch in 1962. In 1888 the suffragan see of Shrewsbury was revived and, since the creation of episcopal areas in the diocese in 1992, Wem has been in the Shrewsbury Episcopal Area.[6]

1   Papal dispensation to Master John of Alvechurch, rector of Wem, 1262: *Cal. Papal Reg., I*, 1198–1304, ed. W.H. Bliss (London, 1893), 380. See also Ivo Paunton, below.
2   Above, Economic History; *Cal. Papal Reg., IV*, 1362–1404, ed. W.H. Bliss and J.A. Twemlow (London, 1902), 56; Garbet, 230.
3   *Lichfield Diocesan Dir.* (1938), 238; Youngs, *Admin. Units* II, 396.
4   'Church Time Line', Parish church of St Peter and St Paul, Wem: http://www.wemcofe.co.uk/time_line. html (accessed 4 Mar. 2019).
5   Youngs, *Admin. Units* II, 379.
6   *VCH Salop*, II, 5–6; *Crockford's Clerical Dir.* (2016–17), 1033.

Advowson and Church Endowment

The advowson has always pertained to the lord of the manor, who often presented a kinsman. Ivo Paunton (an English form of Pantulf) was named in 1277 as a former rector of Wem.[7] Almaric le Botiler was presented by William le Botiler in 1313 and Master Edmund le Botiler by another William le Botiler in 1362.[8] John Dacre was rector of both Greystock and Wem (1520–67) during the lordship of William, Lord Dacre.[9] Daniel Wycherley presented his younger son George (rector 1672–89) in succession to Daniel Wycherley DD (1670–2).[10] Harry Vane Russell, appointed in 1873, was a kinsman of the duke of Cleveland and formerly chaplain to the duchess.[11] In 1895 Lord Barnard presented his younger brother, the Hon. Gilbert Holles Farrer Vane.

Endowment

Valued at £13 6s. 8d. in 1291, the rectory of Wem was one of the more valuable rural livings of the archdeaconry.[12] In 1535 the annual income was declared as £26 13s. 4d. but in 1589 it was estimated to be worth £100 per annum, and £350 per annum in 1648, with a purchase value of £1,400.[13] The glebe lay within Wem township, with land on Mill Street and about 40 a. of pasture and arable land in the three open fields. After enclosure, 15 a. was held as two adjacent parcels beside the road to Lowe (Great and Little Chapel fields); the rectory house was relocated there in 1808. The most distant field, at Creamore beside the Whitchurch road (at the tithe commutation known as Rector's Field), was exchanged for the Fridays fields, closer to the rectory, and part of Foxley field was sold to LNWR. In 1884 the glebe consisted of the rectory house site and about 20 a. of land.[14]

In 1696 the parishioners paid tithes in kind and Easter dues apparently in coin. In 1836 the great tithes were worth around £1,650, the small tithes £50 and the glebe £59, a total of £1,759. The tithes were commuted for £2,100 in 1842, by which time Easter dues had ceased.[15] Wem was one of the most valuable benefices in England in 1900: the gross income was £1,482, of which just £58 was from rents and £18 from fees. The net income after the payment of fees and other outgoings was £739. The financial burdens – including the cost of maintaining the rectory – were so great that, unless the tithe rent-

7   SRO, Magnum Registrum, cartulary of Lichfield Cathedral, ff. 252v. and 254v. Quoted in Eyton, *Antiquities*, XI, 177, n. 5, but with an erroneous transcription.

8   *The Register of Walter Langton, Bishop of Coventry and Lichfield, 1296–1321*, I, ed. J.B. Hughes, Cant. & York Soc. (2007), I, no. 965; Eyton, *Antiquities*, IX, 177–8.

9   SRO, B/V/1/2 and 5 (Liber Cleri); *Survey 1561*, 15; Garbet, 151–2.

10   SRO, B/A/1/17. For Wycherley's abuse of his rights as patron, see SA, 6000/18101.

11   *Wrexham News*, 6 Dec. 1873.

12   J. Denton *et al.*, *Taxatio* database, University of Sheffield: https://www.dhi.ac.uk/taxatio/ (accessed 4 Mar. 2019).

13   *Valor Ecclesiasticus tempore Henrici VIII* (Record Commission, 1810–34), III, 187; TNA, LR 2/225; ACA, MS 508, f. 35v.

14   S. Watts (ed.), *The Glebe Terriers of Shropshire: Part 2 (Llanyblodwel to Wroxeter)*, Shropshire Rec. Ser., 6 (Keele, 2002), 154–6.

15   Ibid.

charge was increased, the rector wrote that 'the next rector of Wem cannot expect to live in the style to which the parishioners have become accustomed'.[16]

Rectory House

The medieval rectory was located on the east side of Mill Street, its precinct extending from Drawwell Lane in the south to the almshouse opposite the church in the north. In 1589 it was described as a fine mansion house, with two large barns, a stable and ox-house; a large two-storey house with gable ends and a central gable or dormer was depicted there in 1631.[17] In 1672 the rector was assessed for tax on nine hearths, making his the largest house in the town.[18] In 1696 the rectory was a four-bay house, with bakehouse, two large barns, garden, orchard and yard.[19] It was substantially rebuilt around 1716 by Edward Chandler 'at great expense, and in a new taste', and the outbuildings and gardens were 'much enlarged, and improved' by his successor, Robert Eyton (rector 1718–51).[20]

Edward Tucker Steward (rector 1804–46) built a new rectory house on glebe land west of the town, on Lowe Hill road, c.1808.[21] The fine Neo-classical brick residence has a hipped roof, stone eaves cornice and tall sash windows under rubbed brick heads. The imposing entrance has a stone portico on pairs of Tuscan columns, while the south-facing garden front has a prominent central full-height bow.[22] An additional wing was constructed on the north side, increasing the accommodation to include three studies and 20 bedrooms. On the retirement of P.R. Turner (rector, 1931–61) the Ecclesiastical Commissioners sold the rectory to his son, retaining a plot on the edge of the grounds beside Ellesmere road for a new house which has served as the rectory since c.1962.[23] The old rectory was sold and converted to a restaurant in 1981, and in 2019 was a hotel and restaurant.[24]

Religious Life

Middle Ages to the Reformation

Little is known about the medieval religious life of the parish. Pluralism and non-residence of the rectors were commonplace: in 1262 Wem was one of several benefices held by Master John of Alvechurch,[25] and Almaric le Botiler was given leave of absence

16   *Wellington Jnl*, 9 and 16 Sept. 1905.
17   TNA, LR 2/225; Arundel map.
18   *Shropshire Hearth Tax Roll of 1672*, 47. Within the parish, only Soulton Hall, with ten hearths, had more: ibid., 50.
19   *Glebe Terriers*, 154.
20   Garbet, 159–60, 242. See also 'Visitation 1799', 35.
21   SA, 2495, box 55, no. 166; SA, 167/27, 63–5; *Glebe Terriers*, 155–6; Green, 'A Georgian rectory', 40–1.
22   Newman and Pevsner, 677; HER 16816; NHLE, no. 1055437, Deer Stalker Restaurant in the Old Rectory (accessed 4 Mar. 2019). Drawing of the Rectory, dated 1900: SA, 6805/3/59.
23   Woodward, 117; inf. from William Price.
24   Green, 'A Georgian rectory'.
25   *Cal. Papal Reg.*, I, 512–27; *Cal. Pat.*, 1292–1301, 29.

to study from 1313 to 1316.[26] The last of the pre-Reformation rectors, John Dacre, was not always resident, although he was in Wem in 1561.[27] Curates may have served in the rector's place, but none is recorded prior to 1558, and then in circumstances that reflect the upheavals of the Reformation, when the curate, Bernard Hastie, became involved in a dispute over the burial of a Protestant fugitive.[28]

A chantry chapel in the parish church dedicated to the Virgin Mary was funded by rents from a burgage in the High Street near the church.[29] At the western limits of Wem township was the wayside chapel of St John, endowed with rents from arable land in Lowe township, 'St John's innage' in Noble Street, and a house in Wem, whose income was to be expended on the maintenance of a chantry priest and for alms to be distributed on the anniversary of the founder, whose identity is unknown. The chapel was suppressed in 1548 and by 1606 a house had been built on the site.[30]

Reformation to 1840s

The Reformation brought a new regime of resident, married rectors: Peter Sankey, rector of Baschurch and of Wem (1585–1605) was succeeded by his son Richard (rector 1606–15). The next rector, William Roe, lived with his wife Robina and 'many children' at Wem rectory, where he died in 1637.[31]

The Parliamentarian seizure of Wem in 1643 coincided with an unsettled period for the lordship of the manor and hence for the parish. Nicholas Page, DD, apparently presented by Charles I in 1639, died at Wem in 1643. A successor, Nicholas Metcalfe, may have been instituted, but the Parliamentarians ejected him and in 1646 formally sequestered the rectory, presenting to it a zealous reformer, Andrew Parsons.[32] Parsons fell foul of religious change, being convicted of sedition and imprisoned at Shrewsbury in 1660. Released with the aid of Lord Newport, Parsons returned to Wem where in November 1661 he hosted Philip Henry and other Puritan ministers.[33] On St Bartholomew's day (24 August) the next year he refused to wear a surplice or read the service from the Book of Common Prayer, and was removed by the churchwardens. Deprived of his living, Parsons was replaced by Rees Hughes, instituted in November 1662. After the church was badly damaged by the great fire of 1677, which destroyed all

26   *Reg. of Walter Langton*, nos. 971, 980.

27   *Survey 1561*, 15.

28   John Foxe, *The Unabridged Acts and Monuments Online (1576 edition)* (The Digital Humanities Institute, Sheffield, 2011), Book 11, p. 1646: https://www.dhi.ac.uk/foxe/index.php (accessed 22 Aug. 2019); retold in Garbet, 164–5.

29   *Survey 1561*, 31. See also A. Hamilton Thompson, 'Certificates of Shropshire chantries', *TSAHS*, 3rd ser., 10 (1910), 379.

30   TNA, E 178/4436; *Survey 1561*, 67; Garbet, 246; HER 05527, 01640.

31   TNA, E 331 Coventry&Lich/12; SRO, B/V/1/32; W.K. Boyd, 'Institutions of Shropshire incumbents', *TSAHS*, 3rd ser., vol. 5 (1905), 355; Garbet, 153.

32   *Calamy Revised*, 381–2; *ODNB*, s.v. Parsons, Andrew (1615/16–1684) (accessed 4 Mar. 2019). For restoration of the church, see below.

33   M.H. Lee (ed.), *Diaries and Letters of Philip Henry, MA, of Broad Oak, Flintshire, AD 1631–1696* (London, 1882), 100–1; Garbet, 154–5.

the timbers and melted the bells, Parsons, now living in London, wrote and published a tract on the subject.[34]

From the mid 17th century the rector was routinely assisted by curates or chaplains serving the chapels of ease at Edstaston and Newtown. The latter was entitled to £10 per annum levied on the parishioners living in Newtown, Northwood and Wolverley, but this proved insufficient and the rector was contributing £20 to his stipend by 1718. The office of curate was often combined with that of second or third master at Thomas Adams' School, as for example, Samuel Garbet, curate of Edstaston, 1713–52.[35] Non-resident rectors also provided curates for Wem[36] who, in addition to the care of souls, were responsible for 'transacting the business, and managing the concerns of this large parish … he received, and disbursed money, set, and gathered tithes, employed workmen, paid taxes, and the curates' salaries, and accounted to the rector for the overplus'.[37] The financial difficulties of George Wycherley led to the profits of the rectory being sequestered in 1684 for payment of the curates.[38] A distinguished absentee, Henry Aldrich, DD, dean of Christ Church, Oxford, and rector of Wem 1689–1710, farmed the rectory to a curate for £120 per annum. It was estimated to be worth about 15 times as much but was charged with payment of all the curates' stipends and repairs.[39] One of these, Moses Hughes (d. 1711), came into conflict with the town's growing Nonconformist movement, and popular ill-feeling against the dissenters turned to violent protest in 1715.[40]

Edward Chandler was presented to Wem in 1711. Already rector of St Nicholas, Worcester, where he usually resided, he spent a month or two each summer in Wem until 1717 when he became bishop of Lichfield. During his short early career in Wem, Chandler 'lived in a very handsome manner … He was the first rector of Wem that kept his coach' and he 'almost wholly rebuilt' the rectory.[41] There were then just two, long-lived rectors for the rest of the 18th century: Robert Eyton[42] and Samuel Smalbroke, son of Richard Smalbroke, bishop of Lichfield. By 1799 Smalbroke spent most of the day in bed, neglecting his duties and the fabric of the church.[43] His energetic successor, Edward Tucker Steward, oversaw both the relocation of the rectory house to Lowe Hill road and the almost complete rebuilding of the church.[44]

34 Garbet, 153–5; *ODNB*, s.v. Parsons, Andrew (1615/16–1684), nonconformist minister (accessed 13 Mar. 2018); SRO, B/V/1/67; *An account of the dreadful fire of Wem … by the Rev Samuel Garbet. With an interesting address to the inhabitants by the Rev Andrew Parsons, M.A. their minister of the Established Church* (Wem, 1802).
35 *Glebe Terriers*, 155–7.
36 Ibid., 155. Lists of curates: Garbet, 164–74, 278–80, 321–5.
37 Garbet, 169–70.
38 SA, P295/B/3/11, 6 Apr. 1686; Garbet, 156, 231.
39 *ODNB*, s.v. Aldrich, Henry (1648–1710), dean of Christ Church, Oxford (accessed 4 Mar. 2019). For Aldrich as rector of Wem, see SRO, B/A/1/19; Garbet, 147–8, 156–9, 167–8.
40 SRO, B/A/1/18 (Register); Garbet, 167–9.
41 *ODNB*, s.v. Chandler, Edward (1668?–1750), bishop of Durham (accessed 4 Mar. 2019); Garbet, 159–61. For the rectory house, see above.
42 Garbet, 161–3; TNA, SP 44/150 (1718); SRO, B/A/1/21.
43 SRO, B/A/1/21 and 28; 'Visitation 1799', 35; Garbet, 163; Woodward, 81.
44 SRO, B/A/1/28; TNA, PROB 11/2049/201.

1840s to Present

By 1840 further seating was required and the galleries were remodelled by George Jenkin, architect, of Whitchurch. New galleries were added to the north and south, and the west gallery was altered, giving the current three-sided arrangement, increasing the seating capacity to almost 1,000.[45]

On Census Sunday in 1851 attendance in the parish church was 492 (including 151 children) in the morning; 392 (including 148 children) in the afternoon; and 398 in the evening. The rector, J.W.D. Merest,[46] noted that it had been a 'showery, stormy day', which always reduced the numbers attending, and that the average Sunday attendance was: 570, including children, in the morning; 440, including children, in the afternoon; and 470 in all in the evening.[47] The next rector, Harry Vane Russell,[48] at his own expense and in memory of his daughter, Winifred Barbara, had the chancel taken down and replaced in 1886 by a new, larger chancel, in the Gothic style, by G.H. Birch.[49]

After Russell's death in 1895 the Revd and Hon. Gilbert Holles Farrer Vane, younger brother of the then Lord Barnard, moved from the vicarage of High Ercall to Wem.[50] The Hon. Archibald Parker was appointed as the next rector by Lord Barnard in 1905.[51] Percy Reginald Turner became rector in 1931 and also vicar of Lee Brockhurst in 1947, creating the Lady Chapel, dedicated in memory of his wife, Sara Violet, in 1959.[52] Basil Morson (rector 1962–79) was the first to live in the present rectory house on Ellesmere Road. He introduced a weekly Sung Eucharist, Eucharistic vestments and reservation of the Blessed Sacrament, observances maintained to the present.[53] Neil MacGregor was rector 1980–2001;[54] Christopher Stephen Cooke was priest-in-charge from 2001 until his retirement in 2013; the present rector is Nicholas Peter Heron.[55]

Church Architecture

The Medieval Church

Wem's parish church, *St Peter and St Paul*, is situated centrally within the town. The earliest datable feature extant is the early 14th-century west doorway into the tower, which has four orders of continuous roll mouldings with fillets in the Decorated style; unusually, the mouldings turn out towards the base of the arch, but this may be due to

45 SA, P295/B/5/2/2, P295/B/5/1/2; 1841 plan at Lambeth Palace Library, ICBS 2575.
46 *Clergy List* (1848), 166 (1864), 56, 241; *Crockford's Clerical Dir.* (1868), 454.
47 *Church and Chapel*, 105–6; original: TNA, HO 129/363.
48 *Crockford's Clerical Dir.* (1878), 820.
49 SA, P295/B/5/2/3; M. Keeling-Roberts, *A Short History of the Parish Church of S. Peter & S. Paul, Wem* (Wem, 1987), 5–6; SRO, B/C/5, 29 Mar. 1878.
50 W.G.D. Fletcher, 'Gilbert Holles Farrer Vane. A biographical sketch', in *Wem Parish Registers*, IX, preface; *Crockford's Clerical Dir.* (1897), 1381.
51 Woodward, 104; *Crockford's Clerical Dir.* (1931), 989.
52 Woodward, 117; *Crockford's Clerical Dir.* (1932), 1330, (1961–2), 1216; pers. inf. William Price.
53 Woodward, 117; *Crockford's Clerical Dir.* (1963–4), 854; pers. inf.
54 Woodward, 133; *Crockford's Clerical Dir.* (1980–2), 639, (2002–3), 480.
55 *Crockford's Clerical Dir.* (2004–5), 166, (2014–15), 182; St Peter and St Paul's, Wem.

Figure 22 *Tower and west door, the oldest features of the parish church (late 14th century).*

later alteration. Older masonry exists in the lower courses of the tower, including the plinth, but it is unclear whether this is contemporary with, or earlier than, the doorway. The church was damaged by a great storm in 1366 and a papal indulgence was issued for alms to repair it.[56]

Above the level of the entrance, the tower is Perpendicular in style but with Decorated elements, placing it in the late 14th century.[57] Architectural features include diagonal buttresses, string courses bearing gargoyles, battlemented parapets and pinnacles with crockets. In the centre of the west front is a niche containing a statue of a man carrying a truncheon. It stands on a corbel, under which is a head, in the style of a misericord. On the east side of the tower, offset to the right, is a second statue in a niche, this time of a robed figure. Garbet suggested that the west-facing statue represents Ralph, Lord

56   *Cal. Papal Reg*, IV, 56.
57   Newman and Pevsner, 674; Cranage, 731.

Greystock, whom he credited with building the 'steeple' and rebuilding the parts of the church in white Grinshill stone.[58] The east-facing statue, which is more eroded, has been variously identified as the wife of Lord Greystock, a priest or St Chad, the patron saint of the diocese of Lichfield.[59] Beneath the west statue is a window opening filled in with masonry and a smaller, somewhat crude two-light window said to have been made in 1667.[60] Although the hood mould of the original opening has been partly reconstructed, an eroded head boss is similar to that beneath the statue corbel and may therefore be contemporary. The upper stage of the tower is pierced by two-light louvre openings with foiled heads, as shown in 1631.[61]

The tower arch, with plain chamfered mouldings, is said to have been reconstructed in 1667 together with the exterior west window, now obscured by the Georgian entrance.[62] After the great fire of 1677 parishioners and local gentry gave £200 for repairs; dates of 1678 and 1680 were inscribed on roof timbers in the tower,[63] and the chancel is said to have been rebuilt in 1680.[64]

The internal dimensions of the medieval church, as measured in the early 18th century, were: 28½ yd in length from the altar to the 'belfrey', but 24 yd 'from the east window of the aisle to the lower window' (i.e., the shorter south aisle); the nave varied from 14¼ yd at the east end ('from the vestry wall to the south wall') to 14¾ yd in the middle and 15 yd 6 in. at the west end; the chancel was 6¼ yd wide, the base of the tower ('belfrey') was square, 5 yd in length and breadth.[65] As depicted in 1631, the church had a doorway at the west end of the tower and one in the north wall of the nave.[66] An undated engraving of the church from the north-east shows a north porch; the north aisle may represent the original nave as it is aligned with the tower. In the angle of the north and south aisles is a small gabled vestry, while the south-east end has a large Perpendicular window. This depiction appears inaccurate, however, in showing the north aisle as shorter than the south aisle.[67]

Depictions of the south side of the church show, in agreement with the measurements given above, that the north aisle was longer than the south. A 1791 watercolour by the Revd Edward Williams carefully marks details, alterations and additions.[68] A south porch abuts the nave, which has large three-light Perpendicular windows and battlemented parapets, the clerestory lit by dormer windows.[69] The chancel has lower eaves, a two-light window and a small priest's door. Williams marked an irregular joint in the masonry above the left side of the porch, with white stone to the left, possibly the Grinshill stone attributed to the early 15th-century phase, and red sandstone to the right, which appears to be later. A plan of the church c.1809 shows the walls thicker at the west end than at

58   Garbet, 231, 233.
59   Garbet, 233; Newman and Pevsner, 674; Cranage, 732, respectively.
60   Garbet, 231.
61   SA, 7381/240/1517A; Arundel map; Garbet, 310–11.
62   Garbet, 231; Cranage, 732.
63   Garbet, 231; SA, 484/240.
64   SA, P295/C/1/1; Garbet, 231; Cranage, 732.
65   Noted by Samuel Garbet for William Mytton: SA, 7381/240/1517A; Garbet, 230–3.
66   Arundel map, sheet 5.
67   Fig. 23.
68   Fig. 24. See also Fig. 33.
69   Cranage, 731.

Figure 23 'Wem Church: Taken down in 1811.' View of the parish church from the
north-east, engraved from artwork by David Parkes. The south aisle is inaccurately
depicted as larger than the north aisle.

the east; a line can be drawn from the east side of the north porch to the west side of the
south doorway which correlates with the masonry joint drawn by Williams.

By 1808 there were two chancels, the lord's (south) and the rector's, separated by
a 'Gothic arch'.[70] The north and south aisles were separated by a wooden arcade with
square-section piers, probably installed after the great fire of 1677.[71] Wem was one of
only five churches in Shropshire with a timber arcade.[72] Galleries were located at the west
end and south side, the latter having been added after the fire.

In 1808 a report on the church fabric was produced by the architect William Turner.
The south wall was near collapse despite being buttressed, and there were structural
problems with the arch between the chancels.[73] In July 1809 the vestry decided to
undertake repairs costing £575. A faculty was granted, stating that the church 'was very
much out of repair and the seats, pews, galleries … were very ancient, un-uniform and
decayed'. The roof would be repaired and the pews and pulpit rebuilt.[74] Soon afterwards,
however, the decision was taken effectively to rebuild the church.

The Present Church

The parishioners initially decided to rebuild the nave, at a maximum cost of £2,000 plus
Turner's fee of 100 guineas.[75] In 1810 the lord of the manor surrendered his right and
interest in the lord's chancel and a new faculty was granted to rebuild the church on

70   SA, P295/C/1/1, first page of report by William Turner, 1808.
71   Garbet, 231–3; Cranage, 732; SA, P295/C/1/1; SRO, B/C/5/1809/325.
72   Mercer, *English Arch. to 1900*, 288.
73   SA, P295/C/1/1.
74   SRO, B/C/5/1809/324–5.
75   SA, P295/B/3/1/3, 18 Oct. 1809, 10 Apr. 1810.

Figure 24 *Medieval parish church, from the south, 1791, by the Revd Edward Williams.*

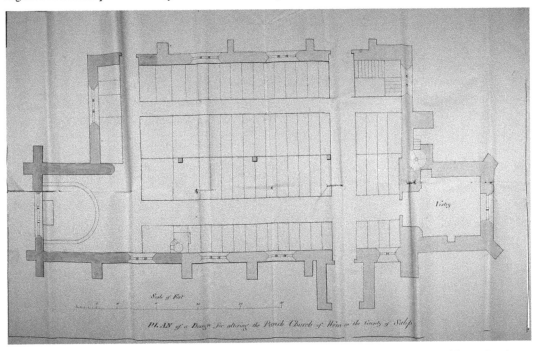

Figure 25 *Plan of proposed alterations to parish church, 1809. The thicker walls at the west end (on right of plan) correspond to the paler stone depicted in Figure 24. The alterations shown on this plan were not carried out, instead the nave and chancel were rebuilt.*

the same foundations as the old one.[76] The tower was retained and the west doorway reinstated as the principal entrance. Its conversion from doorway to window and then back to doorway may explain the unusual turned-out form of the lower mouldings.

The new building had a wide nave with a west gallery of three banks of pews surrounding an organ. The building contract did not run smoothly and there was dissatisfaction with both the architect and the contractor.[77] A new contractor, John Simpson of Shrewsbury, was engaged to complete the nave. Simpson went on to rebuild the chancel in 1812, with a square end with small flanking porches, and in 1813 a single-storey vestry was added south of the tower, probably to Simpson's design.[78] In the same year alterations were undertaken to increase the number of pews, particularly for the poor.[79] Although commodious, the plain style of the church was more like a Nonconformist chapel and it was not popular with the parishioners. A later rector observed, 'The thing was done, which the parishioners since wished undone.'[80]

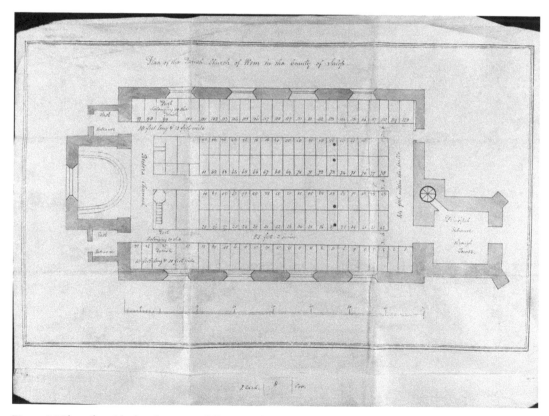

Figure 26 *Plan of parish church in 1813, following rebuilding, showing seating plan.*

76   SA, P295/B/5/1/1/3; SRO, B/C/5/1810/154–5.
77   SA, 306 box 1a: indenture, 15 Mar. 1811.
78   Ibid.; SA, P295/B/3/1/3; SRO, B/C/5/1813/125.
79   SA, P295/B/3/1/3, P295/B/5/1/1; SRO, B/C/5/1813. SA, 7675/212, 'Wem church', undated sketch by D. Parkes (d. 1833), shows the rebuilt church without the vestry.
80   G.H.F. Vane, 'Accounts of the churchwardens of Wem', *TSAHS*, 3rd. ser. 4 (1904), 237–58.

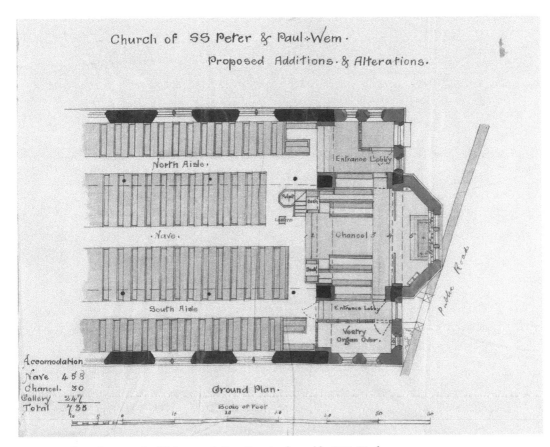

Figure 27 *Plan of proposed additions and alterations to chancel by G.H. Birch.*

Figure 28 *Parish church, from south-east.*

Figure 29 *Parish church, nave and galleries.*

The church acquired its present form in the late 19th century. In 1885–6 the chancel was taken down and replaced by a larger one in the Gothic style by the architect G.H. Birch; at the same time new traceried windows of Harmer Hill stone were inserted into the original openings and the current cusped roof structure was installed on stone corbels.[81] The wide four-window nave is of ashlar, the only decorative feature being the corbel table beneath the eaves; the chancel, also of ashlar, has a hollow-moulded eaves cornice and string course. The east end, with canted corners and a shallow gable, is flanked by small porches. A priest's door to the south is no longer used due to the siting of the organ.

The interior of the church has been little altered since the addition of the chancel in 1886, although some pews have been removed at the east and west ends of the nave. The chancel arch has several orders of mouldings resting on decorative corbels, to the south of which is the Lady Chapel, lined with 16th-century oak panelling.[82] The nave remains dominated by the three-sided galleries, their wood-panelled fronts supported on narrow cast iron columns. The impressive pulpit was presented to the church in 1887, and the organ, by Harrison and Harrison of Durham, was built in 1923. The carved oak memorial screen, by Oakley and Sanville of Manchester, was installed at the new

81   SA, P295/B/5/2/3.
82   Keeling-Roberts, *Short History*; Newman and Pevsner, 674–5.

entrance to the vestry in 1934.[83] The font was moved to a central position at the west end of the nave in 1963.[84] A new altar was placed in the sanctuary in 1996 and the font was moved once more, to the chancel end of the north aisle, in 1999. There is a ring of eight bells cast in the late 18th and 19th centuries.[85]

Church Furnishings

Medieval Church

In 1553 there were two 'great' bells and a 'santes' bell.[86] The bells destroyed in 1677 were replaced by five new ones cast in 1680, and a clock was installed in 1726.[87] Two coats of arms in the east window of the south aisle were recorded in the 17th century, one being the arms of le Boteler.[88] A detailed description exists of the interior and decorations in the mid 18th century, including paintings above the chancel arch dated 1680.[89] Monumental inscriptions dating between 1687 and 1732 and a board listing charities are recorded.[90]

Present Church

The interior of the chancel is highly ornate with a ribbed and painted vaulted ceiling, mosaic floor and two-tier arcaded reredos of Caen stone. The lower tier contains statues of saints in cusped niches, the upper tier of the reredos is transparent, with three ornate cusped arches allowing light to flood in from the east window, which was reused from the chancel of 1812. Flanking the window are wall paintings of saints, Old Testament figures and angels, beyond which are side balconies. At the front of the nave is a low three-sided chancel screen of coloured alabaster surmounted by brass scrolls, the central wrought-iron gates bearing an inscription in pierced copper. Adjacent to the screen, the pulpit of iron and brass open-work is dated 1887, and is mounted on short polychrome marble pillars.[91] In Birch's building specification of 1885, the font was to be restored not replaced, but there is no evidence of the original.[92] The font has an octagonal bowl with inlaid circular marble panels, in a similar style to the pulpit pillars. The stained glass in the east window is by Ward and Hughes, 1873, and shows biblical scenes, including the Presentation of Christ in the Temple and the Ascension in the central lights.[93]

The nave windows were designed without stained glass as they were bisected by the galleries, but there is now a town window to the south-east, celebrating people and events, and symbols of the royal family in the north-east window.

83   SA, P295/B/6/4/1.
84   Keeling-Roberts, *Short History*, 8.
85   H.R. Walters, *The Church Bells of Shropshire* (Oswestry, 1915), 321–3; http://www.wemcofe.co.uk/bells. html (accessed 4 Mar. 2019).
86   TNA, E 117/8/21.
87   Garbet, 233; Walters, *Church Bells*, 322–3.
88   Bodleian, MS Ashmole 854, p. 217.
89   Garbet, 232.
90   Copies of papers of William Mytton: SA, 7381/240/1517, 1519, 1520.
91   Newman and Pevsner, 675.
92   SA, P295/B/5/2/3.
93   Newman and Pevsner, 675.

Figure 30 *Parish church, chancel.*

In the centre of the nave, a brass chandelier in the form of branches is ascribed to Michael Reynolds of Shrewsbury, although the style is considered to be a copy of London work. Made at a cost of £15, it was a gift of the curate George Tyler, following a bequest by his aunt, Mrs Ann Walford (d. 1733). It was installed in the old church in 1737.[94] A large Crown of Light, originally fitted with candles, was transferred from the mortuary chapel in Aston Street in 1886.[95] At the west end is a monument with draped urn commemorating Wine Field Tracey, wife of the advocate general of Jamaica, who died at sea in 1840 aged 27 years.

94   R. Sherlock, 'Chandeliers in Shropshire churches', *TSHAS*, 57, pt. 3 (1964), 247–50; Garbet, 171–2; Cranage, 732.
95   Keeling-Roberts, *Short History*, 8.

Church Yard

The main entrance to the church yard is from the north-west, through a Neo-classical gateway, with rusticated ashlar piers, and large moulded decorative capstones surmounted by draped vases. The decorative wrought iron gates with overthrow were brought from Shrewsbury in 1814.[96]

As Birch's chancel encroached onto the highway boundary, the paths in the church yard had to be re-aligned, including that linking the north entrance with the south gateway.[97] The latter has square-section piers, which were surmounted by large classical-style urns until at least 1976, now replaced by ball finials.[98] As well as 18th- and early 19th-century headstones and tomb-chests, there is a sundial south of the church: a shaped stone pillar on a large circular three-tier plinth, the dial missing. It was erected in 1728 at a cost of £9 9s. 8d.[99] Located south-west of the tower is a small ashlar engine house for blowing the church organ, erected in 1922 by Lloyd Oswell and Iredale of Shrewsbury.[100]

The war memorial, dedicated in 1920, is located north of the chancel in a prominent position overlooking the town. A stone cross, decorated with a crown, foliage and a shield in relief, stands on a pedestal with crenellated top on a four-tier octagonal plinth. It has slate tablets on each side, bearing the names of those who fell in both world wars.[101] Steps lead up to the war memorial from the High Street, with memorial lamps of steel open-work, designed in 1986 by Antony Robinson, evoking the arms of the fallen reaching up to heaven. The material and design of the lamps and handrails also evokes 'swords into ploughshares'.[102] The open aspect of the church here is modern, following demolition of the Union Buildings in 1943. Gravestones and memorials were cleared from the north side of the church, and repositioned in the late 1950s to create the present lawned area.[103]

Nonconformity

In 1676 eleven people in the parish were identified as 'dissenters',[104] and the early Methodist movement gained many supporters, yet it was Primitive Methodism,

96   SA, P295/B/3/1/3, 18 Oct. 1809, 10 Apr. 1810; SA, P295/B/3/1/4, Wem quarter disbursements, 1813–14. cf. Woodward, 42.
97   SA, P295/B/8/1/1.
98   SA, PH/W/8/3/32.
99   Cranage, 733.
100   SRO, B/C/12/1/530.
101   HER, 20321; Imperial War Museum, War Memorials Register, no. 13861: http://www.iwm.org.uk/memorials/item/memorial/13861 (accessed 4 Mar. 2019).
102   War memorial lights, St. Peter's Church, Wem, Shropshire: http://www.forgerobinson.com; Wem Civic Society, Wem war memorial: http://www.wemlocal.org.uk/wempres/wcs/mem.htm (both accessed 4 Mar. 2019); Revd David Smith, pers. com; *Wem and Lee Brockhurst Parish Mag.* (Nov. 2010), 15.
103   SRO, B/C/12/1/530 (1957); photograph of grave stones in situ, in possession of Tom Edwards. Woodward, pl. 7, shows the Union Buildings in front of the church.
104   *Compton Census*, 442.

along with Congregationalism, that became an enduring presence in the parish.[105] Nonconformists were always a minority: in 1800, when the curate took a census, 351 people, or just over 10 per cent of the population of the parish, identified as either 'confessed Methodist' (294) or 'Presbyterian' (57).[106]

Congregationalism: the Chapel Street and Noble Street Chapels

A house in Wem was licensed as a 'meeting house' in 1692 and more followed.[107] Around 1700, 'provoked by the continual invectives of the curate', the Nonconformists abandoned the church and acquired a barn in Leek Lane (now Chapel Street) where they met until it was destroyed by rioters in 1715.[108] With compensation from the Treasury, the Nonconformists purchased a garden in Noble Street and built a new chapel there in 1716. In 1747 the house next door, now Hazlitt House, was purchased for the manse.[109]

After the death of the minister, Thomas Holland, in 1753 the congregation split over doctrine. Those who had left the chapel met for worship in the room over the market hall, until a new building on Chapel Street was licensed as an Independent chapel in 1756.[110] Later, John Henshaw began to hold religious meetings at his house, where John Wesley preached in 1771.[111] Henshaw then funded a new Independent or Congregationalist chapel at the rear of his property, on Chapel Street, which opened in 1775.[112] In 1799 Archdeacon Woodhouse found 'many dissenters' in Wem; the Presbyterians had a meeting house but, he observed (perhaps optimistically), 'these decline'.[113] The Noble Street chapel returned to Congregationalism around 1817 and the two chapels cooperated thereafter.[114]

The Chapel Street chapel was almost doubled in size in 1834, to seat 500. The eastern parts of the brick side walls are those of the 1775 chapel, including a central round-arched window with keystone in the south elevation, the brick joint where the chapel was extended can be seen in the north elevation. The imposing ashlar façade was also added at this time:[115] the two-storey, three-bay front has classical-style detail, including a pediment, shallow pilasters and blind lunettes to the gables, and the central porch canopy

105 Lists of Nonconformist clergy: Garbet, 213–16; Woodward, Appendix C. See too D. Garratt, 'Primitive Methodism in Shropshire, 1820–1900' (unpublished Univ. of Leicester Ph.D. thesis, 2002), esp. 147–9.
106 Wem Parish Registers, 778–9.
107 O. Wakeman et al. (eds.), *Orders of the Shropshire Quarter Sessions, 1638–1889* (Shropshire County Records, n.d.), I, 139; SA, QS/2/7, Jan. 1694 and Oct. 1695.
108 TNA, E 178/6907; Garbet, 168, 213–14, 239.
109 G.E. Evans (ed.), 'The Register of Wem Presbyterian Chapel 1755–1814', in *Shropshire Parish Registers: Nonconformist Registers*, Shropshire Parish Register Society (1903); A. Brown (ed.), 'Noble Street Presbyterian Chapel, Wem, Register of Burials 1822–1837 [from] PRO RG4/1533' (typescript, SFHS, 1984); Garbet, 171–2, 212–13, 239–40.
110 SA, QS/1/3, ff. 203, 277v.; QS/6/3/269.
111 N. Curnock (ed.), *The Journal of the Rev. John Wesley A.M.*, 8 vols (New York, n.d.), V, 402.
112 SA, 6000/18089; J. Bickerton Williams, 'Memorials pertaining to Wem, in Shropshire, with a history of Chapel Street chapel', *Evangelical Mag.*, 33 (Oct. 1855), 565–71, at 567–9.
113 'Visitation 1799', 35.
114 Woodward, 82.
115 Bickerton Williams, 'Memorials pertaining to Wem', 571; Bagshaw, 320; D.D. Evans, *Memorials of the Late Rev. Joseph Pattison, Minister of the Church in Chapel Street, Wem ...; sermons recently preached by him; and a sketch of his life* (2nd edn, Bridgnorth, 1868), 18–20. See SA, PH/W/8/3/42.

Figure 31 *Former Presbyterian Chapel, Noble Street, used as a garage, 1990s.*

is supported on Tuscan columns, flanked by round-arched windows with keystones. In 1844 a plot on the other side of Chapel Street was donated to the chapel, on which a new building was erected along the street frontage for a lecture room and weekday services and the rest used for a cemetery. The lecture room was restored in 1969 and later converted to a house, now 15 Chapel Street.[116]

On Census Sunday in 1851, attendance at the Noble Street chapel was 140 in the morning and 170 in the afternoon; at Chapel Street it was 266 in the morning and 207 in the evening.[117] In 1874 the two congregations reunited in the Chapel Street chapel,[118] and in 1888 the chapel interior was transformed from 'the old barn-like appearance' to a Doric design, the old box pews were removed and re-used as wall panelling, and the wooden stairs to the gallery replaced with a stair wing added to the south-east,[119] with an east gallery and semi-circular organ arch to the west.[120]

---

116 Bickerton Williams, 'Memorials pertaining to Wem', 571; Woodward, 118. This was the western part of the plot whose eastern half had been acquired in 1839 for the British Schools. See above, Social History.
117 *Church and Chapel*, 109.
118 Edwards, 23, 30.
119 Bagshaw, 320; *Whitchurch Herald*, 3 Mar. 1888, quoted in Edwards, 26–7, and see photograph, ibid., 80.
120 C. Stell, *An Inventory of Nonconformist Chapels and Meeting Houses in Central England* (London, 1986), 109; Newman and Pevsner, 675. Photographs of the chapel: Edwards, 32, 80. For the monument, see SA, 4208/117: 'Monumental Inscriptions of United Reform Church, Wem, Shropshire 1844–1953' (SFHS, 1986); Bickerton Williams, 'Memorials pertaining to Wem', 570–1.

The redundant Noble Street chapel was advertised for sale in 1892. By the 1990s it was in a derelict state, having been converted to a garage; a contemporary photograph shows it reduced in height with a mono-pitch roof and blocked windows, but recognisable from the stone quoins and string course.[121] In 1986 the chapel was recorded as a brown brick building with sandstone dressings including rusticated quoins. The entrance had been at the north end, above which were traces of three lights, one with a pointed head. The east and west walls had three windows each, damaged by the insertion of garage doors, and the south end had three arched windows, two flanking the former pulpit. No internal features were preserved.[122] The chapel has since been substantially restored to its former external appearance and converted to a dwelling.

Methodism

John Wesley preached twice in Wem, but was preceded by Alexander Mather, who held a meeting in what may have been a barn or warehouse; when Wesley went to preach in the same place he found it 'filled with hemp'.[123] On this first visit, in 1762, finding no arrangements had been made, Wesley preached in the open market house, eventually attracting a crowd of 'two or three hundred', even though it had been snowing and 'the north wind roared so loud and poured in from every quarter'. On his second visit, in 1771, the congregation was so large that Wesley again preached outdoors.[124] In 1799 Archdeacon Woodhouse reported, 'the Methodists increase, preaching in private houses by taking out licences',[125] and some seem to have been content to attend the Independent chapel in Chapel Street.[126] In 1800 there were 294 professed Methodists in a parish population of 3096.[127] In 1823 a Primitive Methodist mission arrived from Burland (Ches.); one of the missionaries much later recalled that William Dawes, a Wem grocer, was so enthused that he built a small chapel for them at the western end of the High Street, 'a small unpretending place' which opened in December 1824.[128] Dawes, however, already owned a small chapel there, at New Pool Bank, by 1813.[129] The Primitive Methodist congregation grew and in 1843 moved to larger and more central premises, while the site of their former chapel was taken over by the gas works.[130] The new chapel, now 5 Chapel Street, with its lateral entrance may be the conversion of an existing house; it has three round-arched windows to the upper storey and a central doorway with moulded lintel. There was an average attendance of 95 for afternoon service and 90 for evening in 1851.[131]

121 Edwards, 30; Woodward, 84; J. Cox, *Shropshire's Nonconformist Chapels*, http://www.users.waitrose.com/~coxfamily/wempresb.htm (accessed 4 Mar. 2019).
122 Stell, *Inventory*, 204; pers. obs. 2019.
123 *ODNB*, s.v. Mather, Alexander (1733–1800), Wesleyan Methodist Preacher (accessed 4 Mar. 2019).
124 *Jnl of the Rev. John Wesley*, IV, 491–2, V, 431.
125 'Visitation 1799', 35.
126 Bickerton Williams, 'Memorials pertaining to Wem', 568–9; Edwards, 103–5.
127 Above, Landscape, Settlement and Buildings; Edwards, 104–5.
128 Edwards, 105–7. SA, 8611/3/15; SA, P295/T/1/95.
129 SA, 4791/1/9, no. 10865.
130 SA, NM4627/1; Edwards, 109–10, 130 (photograph).
131 *Church and Chapel*, 107.

Wem Primitive Methodist circuit was created from the Prees Green circuit in 1878 and the following year the chapel was enlarged by taking over the attached minister's house, and a vestry and schoolroom were added. A new minister's house was built, named Myrtle Villa, on High Street.[132] Land was purchased in Aston Street in 1911 for a new chapel,[133] designed by James D. Mould of Bury (1856–1935) in late Gothic style.[134] The substantial red-brick building with stone dressings has a square tower at the south-west corner incorporating the entrance, and wide segmental-arched openings; inside are plastered segmental ceiling arches and a small font dated 1911. Construction was delayed by the First World War and the new chapel was not completed until 1926.[135] The old chapel was sold in 1927 and used as a warehouse, but it has since been converted to residential accommodation.[136] In 1983 the United Reformed Church congregation joined the Methodists, forming Wem Methodist United Reformed Church at the Aston Street chapel, since 2010 just Wem Methodist Church.[137] A new room for services and meetings was built in 1989.[138]

Baptists

Following a mission to Wem in 1814, a Baptist chapel was built in 1815 on a narrow plot on the corner of Noble Street and Market Street.[139] Additionally, in 1827, the Baptist minister, Walter Gough, had his house in New Street licensed for religious meetings.[140] On Census Sunday in 1851 the attendance was 22 in the morning and 45 in the evening. There were 40 members of the church and 80 'scholars' in 1870 when the chapel was rebuilt, with a schoolroom on the ground floor and chapel above, designed by David Walker of Liverpool.[141] Constructed of dark red brick, its twin-gabled porch fronting Noble Street appears tightly squeezed-in, the entrance in the right-hand return. Above the twin gables is a large decorative rose window in plate tracery, and a narrow circular corner turret to the right. The entrance is through a pointed arch of notched brickwork, but the windows facing Market Street have plain stone dressings, round-arched to the upper floor and flat-arched to the ground floor.[142]

In 1916 there were just 30 members of the congregation,[143] but with the growing popularity of evangelical churches in recent decades the Baptists have thrived. In 1989 the congregation withdrew from the Baptist Union and joined the Fellowship of

132 Edwards, 113–16.
133 Edwards, 129–30.
134 Edwards, 138; A. Brodie (ed.), *Dir. of British Architects, 1834–1914*, vol. 2 (London, 2001), 222.
135 SA, NM4627/4/3; SA, DA14/100/5, 1302; SA, DA14/700/2/6–9; Edwards, 137, 138, 142–4.
136 Edwards, 145; fieldwork, Sept. 2016.
137 Edwards, 88, 175.
138 SA, PH/W/8/3/43–4/46; Woodward, 131–2.
139 A. de M. Chesterman, *A Short History of Wem Baptist Church, 1815–1965* (Whitchurch, 1965), 6–7. The first chapel is shown on John Wood's map of 1834: SA, 8611/3/15. cf. Woodward, 84.
140 SA, QS/1/10, f. 357v.
141 Newman and Pevsner, 676; Chesterman, *Wem Baptist Church*, 17; *The Cambrian News and Merionethshire Standard*, 14 Apr. 1871.
142 For photographs, see Cox, *Shropshire's Nonconformist Chapels*; SA, PH/W/8/3/49, PH/W/8/6/15, PH/W/8/8/45–46; SA, SC/29/82.
143 *Church and Chapel*, 108; Chesterman, *Wem Baptist Church*, 31.

Independent Evangelical Churches.[144] In the late 1980s they acquired the old Chapel Street chapel, modernising and remodelling the interior to create an upper floor. Six stained-glass windows were brought from the Market Street chapel, including two commemorating Henry Eckford, who was an active member of the congregation. The redundant Market Street chapel was sold and converted to residential apartments.[145]

Catholic Apostolic Church

Chapel Lane off Noble Street takes its name from a chapel of the Catholic Apostolic (or Irvingite) Church. Frederick William Hanham Layton, appointed curate of Wem in 1831, was an early convert; in 1835 he became the 'angel' (bishop) of the Catholic Apostolic Church in Islington, London.[146] The Wem chapel was erected in 1839 at the rear of 40 and 42 Noble Street.[147] Its appearance is unknown, but its outline in 1882 suggests buttresses and a corner tower.[148] In 1851 it was reported that the chapel had been closed for about eight years,[149] but a Catholic Apostolic congregation still met there in 1890. By 1895, however, the chapel was used by other organisations,[150] and by 1924 it had been demolished and replaced by Chapel Cottages.[151]

Apostolic or Pentecostal Church

An Apostolic or Pentecostal Church mission hall was built on Aston Street in the early 1920s. The gable-fronted brick chapel is dated 1922 on the gable apex, a plain building with double panelled doors and a moulded pointed-arched opening above, now blind.[152] The Apostolic Church was still meeting in 1975 but *c*.1999 the chapel was purchased by Wem ADOS and converted to a theatre, with a second gable-fronted range added to the right which obscured the three-window west elevation.[153]

Salvation Army

The Salvation Army had a barracks in Noble Street from 1888 and met there until a new hall was built at the western end of the High Street, on land owned by the grammar school, in 1929.[154] By 1950 the hall was being used by ADOS, but by 1975 there was no longer a Salvation Army group, and the hall was demolished in 2002.[155]

---

144 Pers. inf.
145 Woodward, 132; fieldwork, 2016. On Henry Eckford, see Landscape, Settlement and Buildings.
146 J.A. Venn, *Alumni Cantabrigienses*, Part II, vol. 4 (Cambridge, 1952), 120.
147 *Church and Chapel*, 109; *Pigot's Dir.* (1842), 48; OS Map 25", Salop. XIV.15 (1881 edn).
148 SA, P295/T/1/95, Lot 236; SA, DA14/701/7.
149 *Church and Chapel*, 109; Edwards, 21; cf. Bagshaw, 320.
150 *Kelly's Dir.* (1895), 251; (1900); (1913), 287.
151 OS Map 25", Salop. XXI.3 (1926 edn); *Strong's* (1925), 'Noble Street'.
152 SA, DA14/700/2/1–5; SA, PH/W/8/3/48; Cox, *Shropshire's Nonconformist Chapels*.
153 Woodward, 118; particulars of sale, 6 Oct. 1998.
154 *Wellington Jnl*, 7 Apr., 19 May 1888; SA, DA14/700/9, no. 24.
155 *Strong's* (1925), 'Nonconformist churches and religious bodies in Wem'; SA, DA14/700/24, plan; *Wellington Jnl*, 6 Dec. 1930; SA, 8540, Wem album no. 3; Woodward, 103, 118.

Roman Catholicism

Roman Catholicism was rare in post-Reformation Wem. A list from 1592/3 of those suspected of Catholicism names five from the parish: Richard Bannester (of Lacon) and his wife Margaret,[156] William Davies, and Cicilia Heyward and Catherine Gravenor, spinsters. In 1676 there were eight 'papists' in the parish but surveys in 1715 and 1767 did not list any and none were recorded in 1851.[157]

In 1853 the Roman Catholic parish of Whitchurch was created, incorporating Wem. In 1896 the parish priest leased the former Catholic Apostolic chapel for the Wem congregation, but after this arrangement lapsed they reverted to travelling to Whitchurch. Roman Catholics in Wem benefited from the ministry of the Redemptorist community at Hawkstone Hall from 1926 and of Father Piotr Pawel Niemira, priest to the post-war Polish community at Prees Higher Heath. In 1947 Wem joined the newly created parish of Ellesmere. A Roman Catholic church of prefabricated wooden construction was built on donated land off Drawwell Lane in 1962.[158] It was replaced on the same site in 1991 by the present church, dedicated to Our Lady of Perpetual Succour. Built of red brick with blue brick detailing and a pitched tiled roof, it was designed by John Greenough as a multi-purpose church and community hall.[159]

Cemeteries

Burials for the parish originally took place in the church yard. Burial was also permitted at the chapels of Edstaston and (from 1666) Newtown. From 1775 Nonconformist burials took place in the grounds of the Chapel Street chapel, but when the chapel was extended in 1834 it built over the graves.[160] A burial ground had been laid out on the opposite side of the road by 1844, where the last burial took place in 1953.[161]

By the early 19th century population growth outstripped the capacity of the church yard to receive new burials. The removal of three old houses enabled an extension to the south; this 'new ground' was used for burials from 1824,[162] but extending the church yard was not a long-term solution. Land for a new burial ground, which opened in 1852, was purchased by the parish on suburban farmland on Aston Street.[163] In the centre of the

---

156 See Garbet, 365–6.
157 M.M.C. Calthrop (ed.), *Recusant Roll No. I, 1592–3* (London, 1915), 266–7, 272; E.E. Estcourt and J. Orlebar Payne (eds), *The English Catholic Nonjurors of 1715* (London, [1885]); S. Watts, 'The 1767 Return of Papists in the Archdeaconry of Salop', *Midland Catholic History*, 7 (2000), 27–39; Garbet, 269.
158 E. Maurice Abbott, *History of the Diocese of Shrewsbury 1850–1986* (Bolton, 1987), 110; Woodward, 118.
159 http://taking-stock.org.uk/Home/Dioceses/Diocese-of-Shrewsbury/Wem-Our-Lady-of-Perpetual-Succour/ (accessed 4 Mar. 2019); Woodward, 132–3.
160 Evans, *Memorials of Pattison…*
161 'Monumental Inscriptions of United Reform Church, Wem'; SA, 8611/3/15; SA, P295/T/1/95; Edwards, 12–13.
162 Above, Social History. Parish register of burials (1824), see K.J. Bulmer (ed.), 'Parish Church of SS Peter and Paul, Wem: Transcripts of Registers (SRO 2322/1)' (transcript, c.1970).
163 SA, 1848 box 180, 'Re Wem new Burial Ground', draft 'Declaration of Identity [of land]' by Thomas Sands of Wem, innkeeper (n.d.); SA, 4208/32: 'A Survey and Record of Burials at the Cemetery, Aston Street, Wem, Shropshire' (1981).

Figure 32 *Mortuary chapel, Whitchurch Road cemetery (1892) by G.H. Birch.*

rectangular plot is the Victorian Gothic mortuary chapel of 1853, by Richard Dodson.[164] Of grey stone, the gabled front has a pointed-arched doorway with attached columns and decorative mouldings and a trefoil window above. Narrow lancets pierce the east end and side elevations. The Aston Street burial ground became overcrowded and was formally closed to new burials in 1891.[165] In 1898 and again in 1956 the Aston Street frontage was rebuilt behind its original alignment due to road widening.[166] The closed burial ground remained the responsibility of the parish, but by the 1970s the site was overgrown and derelict.[167] The gravestones were subsequently relocated around the boundary walls and the site landscaped as public open space in 2000.[168]

The Whitchurch Road burial ground was established on a site of nearly 3 a. (1.2 ha.) at Barnett's Bank, next to the workhouse, purchased by the Ecclesiastical Commissioners in 1891.[169] It opened in 1892, and included a small mortuary chapel by G.H. Birch, built at a cost of £375 by Edward George of Shrewsbury.[170]

164 Newman and Pevsner, 675.
165 SA, DA27/994/1/2, Mar. 1890; SA, P295/B/8/2/1–3.
166 SRO, B/C/12/1/530.
167 SA, DA14/180/1; SA, P295/B/8/2/2–3; SA, PH/W/8/6/38.
168 Woodward, 147–8.
169 SA, P295/B/8/2/5–8, 10. See generally P295/B/8/2/4–21.
170 SA, P295/B/8/2/5, 9, 19.

The gable-fronted chapel is of rubbed red brick, the timber framing to the upper level hinting at the Elizabethan-revival style. The entrance arch is of notched brickwork over double doors with strap hinges, with a large rose window above. Love Lane cemetery, administered by Wem Town Council, was opened in 1975.[171]

---

171 SA, 4208/253: 'Monumental inscriptions at Love Lane Cemetery, Wem, Shropshire, 1975–2012'; SA, 'A Short Guide to Cemeteries', Short Guide to Sources no. 22.

LOCAL GOVERNMENT

Manorial Government

WEM NEVER ATTAINED INCORPORATION as a borough and the town remained subject to the authority of the lord of the manor under the same seigneurial regime as the rest of the manor.[1] As tenant-in-chief from *c*.1100 the lord held Wem subject to the authority and jurisdiction of the crown, lacking some of the autonomy of his powerful Marcher neighbours such as the earls of Arundel at Oswestry or Clun. In the Middle Ages, however, this burden was light; the crown intervened only to levy occasional 'subsidies' or during the minority of an heir, while the lord provided military service and performed suit of court at the hundred and shire courts on behalf of the manor, which was exempt from county and hundredal jurisdiction.[2]

Wem was controlled by the lord of the manor, who via his steward and officers exercised important and valuable prerogatives and almost exclusive jurisdiction over the inhabitants.[3] It was the lord who held markets and fairs, collected tolls from traders and travellers,[4] enforced the right of warren, and engaged in avowry (*advocaria*), whereby fugitives from the estates of other lords could be received and settled in Wem – hence the 'Vowree Cross' depicted on the Arundel map at the northern limits of the manor.[5]

The seigneurial regime over Wem was not arbitrary, however, being regulated by customary rights and procedures. In 1459 Ralph, Lord Greystock, issued a charter confirming 'certain customs and liberties to the tenants of Wem'.[6] By 1561 the 1459 charter had allegedly been corrupted and a court of survey was held in 1567 to record the customs of the manor as presented by a local jury.[7] If their customary rights were abused, the tenants could seek justice from the crown, as they did in 1673–4, when an old custumal was produced in evidence in the Court of Exchequer.[8] A new custumal was produced by the manor court jurors in 1751.[9]

---

1   S. Watts, 'The unincorporated town and the role of the manor court in the sixteenth and seventeenth centuries', *Jnl of Regional and Local Studies*, 19, 2 (1999), 30–47.
2   *Rot. Hund.* II, 55–9. See *VCH Salop*, IX, 93–7.
3   TNA, E134/10and11Wm3/Hil30 for comments by Richard Jebb; Garbet, 68, 69, citing manor court books.
4   *Rot. Hund.* II, 58; TNA, E149/1; *Cal. Inq. p.m.* II, 470.
5   *Rot. Hund.* II, 58b. See R. Stewart-Brown, 'The avowries of Cheshire', *English Historical Review*, 29 (1914), 41–55; see also SA, 167/5A, 18 Apr. 1612.
6   *Survey 1561*, 12–13.
7   *Survey 1561*, 13. For the 1567 custumal, see JRL, MS GB 133 PHC/3; SA, 6000/5384; SA, 167/48; Garbet, 110–22.
8   Above, Landownership.
9   SA, 3607, box 3/A/11; Garbet, 139–41.

The lords of Wem were usually non-resident after the 14th century, delegating their authority to a steward[10] who appointed a deputy[11] and at least one reeve (*prepositus*).[12] The steward, or his deputy, presided at the manorial courts and acted as the lord's agent, for example, in authorising enclosure of the common fields.[13]

Within this seigneurial regime, the town had its own officers: two bailiffs chosen from among the burgesses annually at the Michaelmas court leet: one by the lord's steward, the other by the town ('within the bars') jury. Their duties were largely conducted as executive officers of the steward: witnessing livery of seisin of borough-hold land, enforcing the assize of bread and ale, 'wait[ing] on the steward at court leets' and 'assisting at the proclamation of fairs'.[14]

Beyond the town and throughout the barony of Wem, serjeants of the peace were appointed to enforce the lord's authority by the second half of the 12th century. Maintaining them as they went around the lordship exercising their authority was an obligation upon the tenants, initially probably rendered in kind as hospitality (*potura satellitum*). In the lordship of Wem (and Oswestry) the term adopted for this service was Welsh *cylch* (meaning circle or circuit) referring to an official going on his rounds. By the late 13th century it had been commuted to a fixed charge on tenements, which totalled 70s. per annum from Wem manor in 1290.[15] By the late 16th century serjeants of the peace had been replaced by constables – two for the borough of Wem and one for each of the townships owing suit of court there – who were appointed at the Michaelmas court leet.[16] The constables' duties ranged from apprehending wrongdoers to arranging for cases to be brought to court.

In *c*.1283/4 it was said that the lord of Wem had long held his 'free court' twice yearly, with jurisdiction in pleas of bloodshed and of hue-and-cry and the right of capital punishment.[17] In Wem, the penalty for 'bloodshed or affrays' – respectively 3s. 4d. or 6d. – was claimed to have been fixed in 1489.[18] The court leet and view of frankpledge for most of the Shropshire members of the barony was held at Hinstock, which was centrally located for them, but Wem was privileged in holding its own courts. Both the court leet and court baron (*curia parva*) for Wem were held in the town by the early 15th century and probably had been since its plantation.[19] Most legal matters concerning the tenants

10   The lord's occasional residence was still contemplated in the early 16th century: *1561 Survey 1561*, 53; TNA, LR 2/225. Roger de Wyke was steward in 1235–6: *Bk. of Fees*, I, 538.
11   TNA, C 3/7/59, Thomas Bates v John Allinson.
12   *Survey 1561*, 115.
13   ACA, MSS W13 and W14; TNA, C 2/Eliz/W12/58.
14   JRL, MS GB 133 PHC/3; Garbet, 143–6.
15   *Cart. Haughmond*, nos. 133, 145, 1204; R. Stewart-Brown, *The Serjeants of the Peace in Medieval England and Wales* (Manchester, 1936), 66–8; Eyton, *Antiquities*, X, 245; XII, 187, 198. For Wem: SA, 322/2/117 (*kilgh*); TNA, C 133/27/9 (*Cal. Inq. p.m.* II, p. 229), E 133/57, no. 3 (*Cal. Inq. p.m.* II, p. 470), C 135/38/31; *1561 Survey 1561*, 92: 'paset sateletes'; Garbet, 35–6, from Shropshire eyre of 1292 (TNA, JUST 1/739).
16   JRL, MS GB 133 PHC/3; e.g. SA, 167/3, 17 Oct. 1588.
17   SA, 6000/2651; JRL, MS GB 133 PHC/3; printed in *Collectanea Topographica et Genealogica*, I, no. XVI, 111–21, cited by Eyton as 'the Bradford Tenure Roll (about 1286)' (e.g. Eyton, *Antiquities*, IX, 172), probably compiled 1283/4.
18   Garbet, 138.
19   *VCH Salop*, XI, 143; ACA, MS W13; SA, 167/1; SA, 327/1/D/1/2–3; SA, 1514/480: copy of court dated 1466.

of Wem were dealt with by the manor court. Homicide and death by misadventure were among the few matters reserved to the crown,[20] but even so the lord exercised the right to confiscate the goods of felons and suicides and to take deodand.[21] The lord also had view of frankpledge, taken at the court leet held twice a year around Easter and Michaelmas, with presentments of all wrongdoings from each of the townships that owed suit of court: not only Wem, but also Aston, Coton, Edstaston, Horton, Lowe and Ditches, Newtown, Northwood, Tilley and Trench, and Wolverley.[22] The court leet dealt mostly with breaches of manorial regulations ('pains'), such as selling ale, bread, meat, or leather without licence; public nuisance such as sawpits left uncovered, and dung in the street or watering hemp in the river; or contravening the lord's prerogatives by catching fish.

In the 16th century misdemeanours were presented to the court by the constables, whose duty was to bring to each court leet men from their township who would present under oath 'what is presentable' to the jury. There were two juries: one with jurisdiction over the town ('the homage within the bar', in effect a borough jury) and one for the rest of the manor ('the homage without the bar').[23] The relevant jury made the formal presentments and recommended appropriate penalties but could also make additional presentments based on jury members' own knowledge or information provided by any person under oath. The penalties they imposed were reviewed by two 'affeerors', one chosen by the steward and the other by the jury. Once the penalty in each case was agreed, the steward made the formal order and had the authority to execute it against the offender's goods.[24] The court leet continued to be held annually into the 20th century, although by 1892 'its business had been negligible for some time'.[25]

Transactions involving copyhold land and disputes between tenants of the manor were dealt with by the manor court – the *curia parva* or court baron – held customarily every three weeks.[26] A recorder sat alongside the steward (or deputy) to keep the court books and prepare the extracts from them that served as evidence of title to copyhold land.[27] In the mid 18th century, the fee for 'surrender' of copyhold land was 17*s*. 6*d*., of which 13*s*. was due to the steward.[28]

Court House/Market House

The town had a booth hall ('le bothall') by 1512,[29] perhaps the same building as 'le Court Howse', which was situated on the north side of the market place, facing the castle, and redundant by 1544 when it was conveyed from the lord's demesne to one Maurice David

---

20   E.g., *Roll of the Shropshire Eyre of 1256* (Selden Soc., 1981), nos. 683, 689.
21   TNA, E 134/10Wm3/Mich27; 11Wm3/Hil30.
22   Described by Garbet, 120–1, 137–8.
23   In early September the parish clerk visited each of the townships of the parish to make out the jury lists: SA, 7577/36/8.
24   Garbet, 129, 137–8.
25   Woodward, 97; *Oswestry Advertiser*, 2 Nov. 1892.
26   Garbet, 118, 119–20, 126, 139, 141; SA, 167.
27   Garbet, 138–9.
28   Garbet, 138.
29   ACA, MS W14, final membrane.

Figure 33 *View of the parish church taken before 1811, showing rear of market house at left. 'Wem Old Church, Salop'. Engraved (in 1818) from artwork by H. Burn.*

as a copyhold tenement.[30] By 1561, the lord had replaced it with a new court house which occupied the site of the present 'old town hall'. Depicted in 1631 as a large timber-framed, gable-fronted structure, open to the ground floor,[31] it had three shops below the court room and a pentice on the east side where documents were stored.[32] The court house was destroyed by the great fire in 1677 and was hurriedly replaced by a temporary wooden structure.[33] In 1699, frustrated by the inaction of successive lords of the manor, a meeting of ratepayers voted to raise the sum of £73 6s. 8d. for the erection of a new 'market house'.[34] Building commenced, on the same site as the one that had burnt down, in 1702, but was not completed until Henry, Lord Newport, donated £50 in 1728. The new building was usually referred to as 'the market house', perhaps reflecting the commercial interests of the burgesses it served. The upper storey had a variety of uses: manor court room, schoolroom, venue for dissenters' meetings and public entertainments. It was described as a fine brick structure with stone dressings under a tiled roof surmounted by a large ornamental cupola. The front was pierced by three arches with monolithic

---

30   *Survey 1561*, 21; Garbet, 235.
31   SA, 972/7/1/49; Garbet, 234–5.
32   *Survey 1561*, 13, 25, 33; cf. Garbet, 235. For the pentice, or penthouse, see above, Landownership (the Wycherley dispute).
33   Garbet, *Account of the Dreadful Fire of Wem*, 1802 (SA, 665/3/117), 8; Garbet, 226, 235.
34   Vane, 'Churchwardens of Wem', 257.

Figure 34 *'The Old Market, Wem.' Photograph of the old town hall as rebuilt in 1848, taken before 1911 when the open arcades were enclosed.*

columns about 7 ft in height, and there were arches to the rear also. The ground floor was flagged, a staircase leading to the upper floor, which was lit by nine windows.[35]

In 1848 the duke of Cleveland spent £347 on 'rebuilding Wem Market Hall' and a further £75 3s. 6d. on 'fitting up' for sittings of the new County Court.[36] The front elevation was rebuilt, with four elliptical-arched openings on Tuscan columns on the ground floor and another to the east elevation.[37] Most of the original brickwork and staircase remains at the rear, however, and the stone columns were reused from the old building.[38] The County Court had apparently abandoned the 'New Market Hall' sometime before 1923, when the court ceased sitting in Wem, by which time the manor court too was redundant. Its role as the town's market hall ceased in 1905, when the lord's market right was transferred to Wem UDC. There were calls to demolish the building to improve the High Street, but it was spared and remained the property of Lord Barnard under a covenant that it should not be used in any way that rivalled the UDC's new market.[39] Since then the building, which has become known as 'the old town hall', has been used for various community activities.[40]

35   Garbet, 106, 235; SA, 731/2/3271.
36   SA, Raby Estate, box 43, books of rentals and accounts 1847/8 and 1848/9, under 'Buildings and Repairs'.
37   Newman and Pevsner, 675; SA, PH/W/8/4/53.
38   SA, Raby Estate, box 9, reports 18 Mar. 1882 and 4 Sept. 1890; *Shrews. Chron.*, 5 Feb. 1904, 5.
39   SA, DA14/100/1, 16, 55; DA14/100/2, 215–17, 277.
40   Above, Social History.

Parish Government

The parish was divided into four quarters for administrative purposes: Wem township and three rural quarters: Aston, Edstaston and Horton. An annual meeting, chaired by the rector (or curate) and attended by the 'gentlemen parishioners' and parish officers, set the lewns for maintenance of the church, and elected churchwardens for each quarter, as well as assessors and auditors of their accounts, which survive, with vestry minutes, from 1684.[41] Disbursements covered all matters concerning the church, such as cleaning and repairs, hosting diocesan visitations, and ringing the bells on special occasions, as well as payments to the poor.[42]

During the 18th century and the first half of the 19th the county assumed greater responsibility for policing, roads and bridges, but much was still organised on a parish basis. The vestry and churchwardens provided civic amenities, such as a fire engine (1780), a workhouse (1801), gas-lighting the streets (1835) and rudimentary sewerage, although most other initiatives, such as the Union Buildings (1830), banks (1837, 1883), the railway station (1858) and livestock market (1867), were accomplished by private enterprise.

Wem Poor Law Union

In 1836 William Day was sent to Shropshire by the Poor Law Commission to organise the county's parishes into unions. He anticipated that Whitchurch, already an incorporation, would become a union centre but, meeting with resistance, he decided instead to establish a small poor law union centred on Wem. The union combined 12 parishes: Broughton, Clive, Grinshill, Ightfield, Lee Brockhurst, Loppington, Moreton Corbet, Prees, Shawbury, Stanton upon Hine Heath, Wem, Weston-under-Redcastle and Whixall, with a total population of 11,353.[43]

The union inherited poorhouses or workhouses in Wem, Prees and Ightfield. These were deemed unsatisfactory and the guardians purchased a newly erected farm house at Love Lane, north of Wem, which was extended with new ranges to the rear, at a total cost of £2,818.[44] All inmates were transferred there in 1838.[45] The fact that Wem, not Whitchurch, became the centre of the union had important consequences for Wem's future role as a centre for local government.

41   SA, P295/B/3/1/1–3.
42   SA, P295/B/3/1/1. Above, Social History.
43   V. Walsh, 'The administration of the Poor Laws in Shropshire, 1820–1855' (unpublished Univ. of Pennsylvania Ph.D. thesis, 1979), 73, 177–9; Smith, 'Refuges of last resort', 14–15, 118; R.A. Lewis, 'William Day and the Poor Law Commissioners', *Univ. of Birmingham Historical Jnl*, 10 (1963/4), 174–6.
44   Smith, 'Refuges of last resort', 110–14; *Returns to an order of the House of Commons*, 21 Feb. 1840, I, *Returns of workhouses and buildings erected*, 54–5.
45   SA, PL15/1: Wem Union Minute Book, 15 Mar. 1838, 205; 16 Aug. 1838, 256.

Rural Sanitary Authority

By the mid 19th century the parish vestry proved unable to take care of public health. A petition of 1871, signed by 20 ratepayers, called on the churchwardens to summon a meeting to consider the establishment of a local board, but there was strong opposition from those unwilling to pay higher rates.[46] Following the Public Health Act 1872, the guardians of Wem union were compelled to constitute a rural sanitary authority (RSA).[47] A medical officer of health and an inspector of nuisances were appointed, with a range of powers to effect improvements.[48] The public health issues of Wem town were different in nature and degree from those of the predominantly rural territory of the union. In order to adopt urban powers, in 1873 the RSA resolved to constitute Wem Statutory Drainage District (SDD), whose boundaries encompassed the built-up area of Wem township, extending south as far as the junction of the Shrewsbury and Shawbury roads at the railway viaduct, east to the railway, and north to Foxley.[49] Wem parish council nevertheless felt the need to hold the RSA to account and lobby for the town's interests, repeatedly asking for a joint committee with the RSA, requests that were firmly rejected.[50]

Post-1894 Rural and Urban Districts

In 1894 Wem RSA was replaced by Wem Rural District Council (RDC),[51] including Wem civil parish with three wards: Wem, Edstaston and Newtown.[52] An inquiry was soon launched into the award of urban powers to Wem town,[53] as promoted by Edward Bygott in the 1880s, seeking to have the lord's market rights vested in a local authority.[54] The duke of Cleveland (d. 1891) and his successor, Lord Barnard, agreed, but it was found that parish councils did not have the power to deal with markets.[55] Hence in 1900 Wem UD was created, removing the town from Wem RD and extinguishing Wem SDD.[56] The new UDC duly acquired the market rights and built a new town hall incorporating a market hall, improved the water supply and commissioned sewerage schemes. A primary objective of Wem UDC was a public livestock market but it failed to attract the necessary popular and financial support[57] and the new Smithfield was eventually provided by private enterprise.[58] After 1918 the council was an enthusiastic builder of houses.[59]

46 *Eddowes's Jnl*, 20 Dec. 1871, 7.
47 SA, DA27/994/1/1.
48 E.g., *Cheshire Observer*, 6 Nov. 1875, 7.
49 SA, DA27/994/1/1, 74; DA27/970/1.
50 SA, DA27/994/1/2 and 3.
51 SA, DA27/994/1/3; D27/100/1.
52 SA, CP325; *Wellington Jnl*, 10 Nov. 1900, 8.
53 *Wellington Jnl*, 22 July 1899.
54 SA, DA27/994/1/1, Mar. 1888.
55 *Wellington Jnl*, 26 Sept. 1896, 7; *Shrews. Chron.*, 5 Feb. 1904, 5.
56 LGB Order 41000; SA, DA14/133/1; *Wellington Jnl*, 26 May 1900, 11; 22 Dec. 1900, 1.
57 Letter from 'Judicious Economy' complaining about the burden of the rates in Wem and arguing that the Smithfield development was an unaffordable burden on Wem ratepayers: *Shrews. Chron.*, 27 Mar. 1908.
58 Above, Economic History.
59 Above, Landscape, Settlement and Buildings.

When North Shropshire RDC was formed in 1967 by the merger of Ellesmere, Wem and Whitchurch RDCs,[60] it was based in Wem, where its new headquarters opened in 1971.[61] At the same time, a new Wem urban parish council was created, with responsibility for matters such as allotments, public toilets, recreation facilities, street lighting and managing the town hall. It was replaced in 1974 by an elected town council with a mayor.[62]

Also in 1974, North Shropshire RDC was united with Market Drayton RDC to form NSDC, with its headquarters still in Wem. The council offices were modernised, extended and named after HRH Prince Philip, duke of Edinburgh, who formally opened the complex in 1989. By the 1990s NSDC was the largest employer in Wem.[63]

In April 2009 NSDC merged with four other district councils and SCC to form a unitary authority, Shropshire Council, which maintained a customer service point in Wem with a small staff. New tenants were found for Edinburgh House including Wem Town Council, Wem Rural Parish Council, and Meres and Mosses Housing Association.[64]

Town Hall

One of Wem UDC's first priorities was to build a new market and town hall. The present town hall, designed by James Brown of Shrewsbury, was built in 1904.[65] The asymmetrical gabled front is of bright red brick with stone dressings and outer doorways. To the left is a square stair turret set forward. A second staircase was set in a stair turret at the centre of the rear elevation. The upper storey was lit by a large Venetian window with stained glass. A carriage entrance on the east side is now filled in with a single-storey shop.[66] On the ground floor was the corn exchange and council offices, with the market hall to the rear; the upper floor was a large assembly room. By the late 1920s the building proved unsuitable for the council's offices and meetings and in 1932 the Barber Trust purchased the former Buck's Head public house on Mill Street for conversion to offices, renamed it Barber House and leased it to the council.[67] In 1962 the council offices moved further down Mill Street to Roden Lodge which was shared with Wem RDC.[68]

Wem town hall was gutted by fire in 1995, when it was owned by NSDC but occupied and managed by Wem Town Council. It reopened in 2000 with modern facilities, little of the original building remaining except the façade.[69] In 2004 NSDC withdrew funding for the town hall and closed it,[70] but it was reopened in 2009 under the management

60   SA, DA30.
61   Woodward, 111, 123–4.
62   Woodward, 111; Shropshire Council, 'Wem Market Town Profile, Winter 2017/18'.
63   Woodward, 123–4.
64   Woodward, 155; *Shropshire Star*, 21 Mar. 2013; Wem Town Council: http://www.wem.gov.uk (accessed 4 Mar. 2019); 'Wem Market Town Profile', 6.
65   SA, DA14/100/1, 177, 214–16, 239–40, DA14/100/2, 56, 189, 224; Whitehead, *Wem*, 49.
66   Newman and Pevsner, 676; SA, DA14/135/5, no. 1; SA, PH/W/8/4/57; PH/W/8/8/60.
67   SA, DA14/100/6, 250, 267; DA27/154/5.
68   SA, DA14/154/12. Roden Lodge has since been demolished and replaced by a sheltered housing complex with the same name: cf. Woodward, 111.
69   Woodward, 139–41.
70   Woodward, 141, 145.

of Wem Town Hall Community Trust, operating as a community centre and arts and entertainment venue.[71]

Public Services

Law Courts

Wem Petty Sessional Division was created in 1836, with petty sessions and special sessions courts held fortnightly at the office of the justices' clerk.[72] Wem was assigned to the 27th circuit of the County Court which sat in Wem from 1846 – initially monthly but from *c.*1860 in alternate months – until it was withdrawn in 1923.[73] The court initially sat in the 'old town hall', which was refurbished for the purpose, but by 1900 sessions were held in the assembly room of the White Horse hotel.[74]

From 1905 magistrates sat monthly in the new town hall, but this proved unsatisfactory and by 1957 part of the Morgan Library was leased to SCC as an office for the magistrates' committee and justices' clerk and as a court room when required.[75] In 1955 Wem was merged with the Market Drayton and Whitchurch Divisions to form the Drayton Petty Sessional Division. Court facilities were incorporated in the North Shropshire RDC office building in Wem when it opened in 1971. The magistrates' court was held fortnightly in the mid 1970s, but had ceased by 2010 when the Market Drayton magistrates' court closed.[76]

Policing

In the 17th century law and order in Wem was increasingly under the jurisdiction of the county magistrates; Wem and Market Drayton were assigned as the two high constableries of North Bradford hundred, Wem constablery being divided into twelve petty constableries corresponding to the townships of the parish.[77] Wem parish rates contributed to the county 'gaol' or 'house of correction' in Shrewsbury by 1684.[78] There was also provision for the summary detention of wrongdoers in Wem; in 1757 Thomas Harris, constable of Wem, spent £2 12*s.* 8*d.* on repairs to 'the pound and stocks', recouped from the ratepayers of the township.[79] In 1815 the county provided a 'lock-up house' with two cells, adjacent to the fire-engine house in the Horse Market.[80]

71   Wem Town Hall Community Trust: http://www.wemtownhall.co.uk/join-in/wth-community-trust/ (accessed 4 Mar. 2019).
72   'Petty Sessions. Return of the Descriptions of Building in which the Justices of the Petty Sessions hold their usual sessions', 31 July 1845, p. 28, in *Parliamentary Accounts and Papers*, 1845, vol. 9, no. 606.
73   SA, DA14/100/5, p. 1209.
74   *Kelly's Dir.* (1900).
75   SA, DA14/100/5, 1087, 1094, 1250; DA14/154/7–8.
76   SA, PS1/24/E/1–5; Woodward, 111; *Shropshire Star*, 18 July 2010, 12 Feb. 2016.
77   Garbet, 10.
78   SA, P295/B/3/1/1.
79   SA, QS/1/4, ff. 21v–22.
80   SA, 7939/A61; SA, QS/1/11, ff. 281v–282v.

When Shropshire Constabulary was established in 1840, Wem was assigned to Division B, North Shropshire, with one constable for the parish.[81] Thereafter the lock-up was repeatedly condemned for its inhumane conditions and ease of escape. In 1860 the county agreed to build a new lock-up house with a constable's residence[82] on Chapel Street – central, respectable and closer to the new railway station.[83] The house, with lock-up, bell and out-offices, was designed in 1860 by the County Surveyor, Edward Haycock. Of brick with stone dressings and typical Victorian detail, a stone canopy over the door supports a tablet reading 'Erected 1861'. In 1891 Wem was assigned two police officers: a superintendent and a constable, increasing to three at times.[84]

Shropshire Constabulary was merged with other county forces in 1967 to form West Mercia Constabulary, which built a new police station on Barnard Street in 1968, when the old police house on Chapel Street was sold and converted to a private dwelling.[85] The Barnard Street police station was vacated in 2010 and demolished in 2015; since 2010 the West Mercia Police officers serving Wem have shared other local authority premises.

Fire Service

The panic and destruction caused by the great fire in 1677 demonstrates the then ad hoc response to urban fires; Drawwell House was saved by the owner and others 'pouring out water and casting off the shingles'.[86] An old firehook is kept at the present fire station.[87] From 1780 many properties were insured with Salop Fire Office.[88] Some houses still display an insurance badge (for example, 41 Noble Street) but as it was impractical for the insurance companies to maintain fire brigades in rural areas, the fighting was left to local efforts.[89] In 1780 a fire engine was purchased 'for the use of the parish of Wem, to which all the principal inhabitants and gentlemen possessing estates therein contributed', including £5 5s. from the lord of the manor.[90] In 1795 the repair and maintenance of the fire engine was made a charge on the parish rates and a stipend paid to an 'Engine Master'. In 1801 a stone 'Engine House' was constructed beside the parish church but in 1808, when proposing restoration of the church, the architect recommended that it be removed, and the engine 'kept under [the church] tower'.[91] By 1815 an 'engine house' had been constructed adjacent to the then parish poorhouse and a new fire engine, costing

81   SA, QA/6/4/6/3/1–2; *Shrews. Chron.*, 3 Jan. 1840. The number of divisions soon increased, with eight
      proposed in 1887: QA/6/4/6/31. See D.J. Elliott, *Policing Shropshire 1836–1967* (Studley, 1984), 19–20.
82   *Shrews. Chron.*, 23 Oct. 1857, 6; SA, 7939/A61; SA, QA/6/1/1, 17 Sept. 1859, 8 Mar. 1860, 26 June 1860,
      14 Mar. 1861; SA, QA/6/2/2, 114, 120; *Shrews. Chron.*, 8 Jan. 1858, 7, 6 Jan. 1860, 7; *Eddowes's Jnl*, 19
      Oct. 1859, 5, 25 June 1862, 4.
83   *Shrews. Chron.*, 16 Mar. 1860, 6.
84   SA, QA/6/4/6/32; SA, 7939/A189.
85   SA, 7939/A61.
86   Garbet, 224–5. Above, Landscape, Settlement and Buildings.
87   Author's pers. obs., May 2017; presumably the firehook referred to by Woodward, 98.
88   SA, 4791/1/1–11, *passim*.
89   Woodward, 98, 113.
90   TNA, C 110/109 (unlisted box), Accounts of Charles Bolas esq. for the year ending Lady Day 1780 [sic],
      m. 19, Payments out of the Wem estate for the year ending at Lady Day 1781, 25 Dec. [1780].
91   SA, P295/B/3/1/3: 17 Apr. 1795, 22 Sept. 1795, 6 Feb. 1796, 14 Nov. 1801, 4 Feb., 30 Mar., 8 Dec., 23
      Dec. 1802, surveyor's report on state of church, 1808.

£142 7s. 6d., was acquired in 1832.[92] After the old lock-up was vacated by Shropshire Constabulary in 1861 it was converted to house the fire engine.[93] In 1886 the parish agreed to the formation of a fire brigade, funded out of the rates.[94] From 1900 a Joint Fire Committee was formed by Wem UDC and RDC and adjacent parishes. In 1905 the fire engine was moved to Wem UDC's own premises at the rear of the new town hall.[95] In 1926, when the space was required for a cheese hall, it was moved to the other side of Noble Street, near the brewery entrance. In 1937 a Merryweather fire engine and trailer pump was acquired, necessitating alterations and extension to the fire station.[96] In 1939 Wem Joint Fire Committee was constituted a fire brigade under the Fire Brigade Act 1938.[97] During the Second World War, the National Fire Service constructed a fire station on the High Street frontage of the Grove meadow; the redundant Noble Street fire station was resumed by Wem UDC in 1944.[98] Since 1948 Wem has been served by Shropshire Fire Service (now Shropshire Fire and Rescue Service),[99] which operated from the wartime fire station until 1963, when the current fire station was built at the western junction of Noble Street and High Street.[100]

Sewerage and Water Supply

Wem's poor natural drainage meant that by the mid 19th century sewage permeated the subsoil, contaminating wells which were the source of drinking water. In wet weather, cellars filled with water into which sewage often leaked from privies or cesspools, especially in New Street and Mill Street. Wem had a rudimentary sewerage system to which some cesspools were connected and which discharged ultimately into the river. The sewers emptied into three open drains: on the north, the south-east and the west sides of the town. In 1853 it was reported that the open drains were noxious and injurious to public health. Local medical practitioners sought the Board of Health's help to bring about improvements.[101]

The problem may have become acute at this time due to population growth since 1800.[102] There were outbreaks of smallpox in the winter of 1826/7 and the summer of 1833, both resulting in at least 20 deaths, when the average number of burials in the parish church yard was 52 per year.[103] In 1853 Thomas Tisdale, borough surveyor of Shrewsbury, was commissioned by the ratepayers to draw up plans for an effective

---

92 SA, 7939/A61; SA, 7577/36/8, 3 Apr. 1832.
93 SA, 8611/3; SA, QA/6/1, 14 Mar. 1861.
94 SA, P295/C/1/2.
95 SA, DA14/100/1, 44, 53, 233; DA14/100/2, 308–9, 328; SA, CP325/6/10. See Reid, *Tilley*, 217–18.
96 SA, DA14/100/5, 1265; DA14/100/7, 32, 43; *Strong's* (1941). Photograph of the former National Fire Service station in 1988: SA, 8540, Wem album no. 3.
97 SA, DA27/154/7.
98 SA, DA14/100/8, 2; *Strong's* (1941).
99 SA, DA14/100/8, 510.
100 SA, DA14/100/8, 79, 631, 639, 644–5, 657; SA, DA14/135/7/44; SA, PH/W/8/6/40; Woodward, 99, 113; http://www.shropshirefire.gov.uk/stations/wem-fire-station (accessed 4 Mar. 2019).
101 TNA, MH 13/241/305, ff. 695–7.
102 Above, Landscape, Settlement and Buildings.
103 'Parish Church of SS Peter and Paul, Wem: Transcripts of Registers', Introduction to burial register, 1813–40.

sewerage system. As the estimated cost of his proposals was £600, the plan was quietly shelved, with piecemeal improvements being made instead, including culverting of the drain that ran from the High Street, opposite the grammar school, down to Wem Brook.[104]

By 1860 the death rate in Wem township was 25 per 1,000 – 31 per 1,000 when counting workhouse inmates – compared with 18 per 1,000 in a 'healthy' town. In 1876, at 26.49 per 1,000, the death rate was 2.5 times higher than for those in the adjacent rural areas.[105] When in 1871 there were increased cases of enteric fever (14 cases, of which three were fatal) water from four of the town's wells was analysed and all were found to be contaminated and unfit for human consumption. It was estimated that 50 people became ill, and five died, every year *entirely* from inattention to sanitary matters'.[106] The sewage was stagnant and in 1873 it was reported by Wem RSA's first medical officer of health, John Gill, that 'the odour is at times most offensive and likely to be injurious to health'.[107] Nevertheless it was understood that 'drinking impure water [is] the great source of disease'.[108] Gill called for a clean water supply to be brought from a distance from the town, as well as a new sewerage system. Samples from nine wells, including that of the Drawwell brewery, were tested at Guy's Hospital in London, where it was found that 'nearly all of them are unfit for drinking purposes'.[109] Complaints were received, including one about an old sewer near the Albion inn which had been blocked by railway construction in 1858.[110] The RSA addressed these problems by installing first a sewerage system and then a clean water supply.

In 1874 the first meeting of the Wem SDD resolved that the RSA should construct new sewerage in New Street, Whitchurch Road, Wemsbrook Road, Aston Street, Chapel Street, Noble Street and Mill Street. A local builder, Henry Tommy, was paid £408 17s. 6d. for the works, which were mostly completed by the end of the year.[111] In the short term, the RSA used its powers to compel the use of box closets, the contents being combined with ashes and street sweepings, and sold to farmers as fertiliser. Old cesspools were removed and drains cleaned. The intention was the removal of sewage to a distance to avoid further contamination of the town's wells.[112]

In the 1870s the town still relied for its water on wells, all of which were contaminated. In 1882, after various locations had been considered,[113] it was agreed to sink a borehole 6 ft wide and 70 ft deep at Preston Brockhurst and to construct a pumping station to convey the water up to a new reservoir on Palms Hill (a vertical rise of 90 ft (27 m.)), from where it would be piped by gravity to water mains supplying the

---

104 TNA, MH 13/241/305, ff. 695–7; SA, P295/C/1/2, minutes of May, Oct. and Nov. 1853, July 1854; *Shrews. Chron.*, 2 Feb. 1872, 3.

105 Ministry of Health report, 1876.

106 *Eddowes's Jnl*, 20 Dec. 1871, 7. See also *Cambrian News and Merionethshire Standard*, 2 Feb. 1872; SA, DA27/994; SA, 1848, box 179: Ministry of Health report, 1873.

107 Ministry of Health report, 1873.

108 *Eddowes's Jnl*, 20 Dec. 1871, 7.

109 SA, DA27/970/1.

110 SA, DA27/994; Ministry of Health report 1873; *Shrews. Chron.*, 2 Feb. 1872, 3.

111 SA, DA27/970/1.

112 SA, DA27/970/1.

113 SA, DA27/994/1/1.

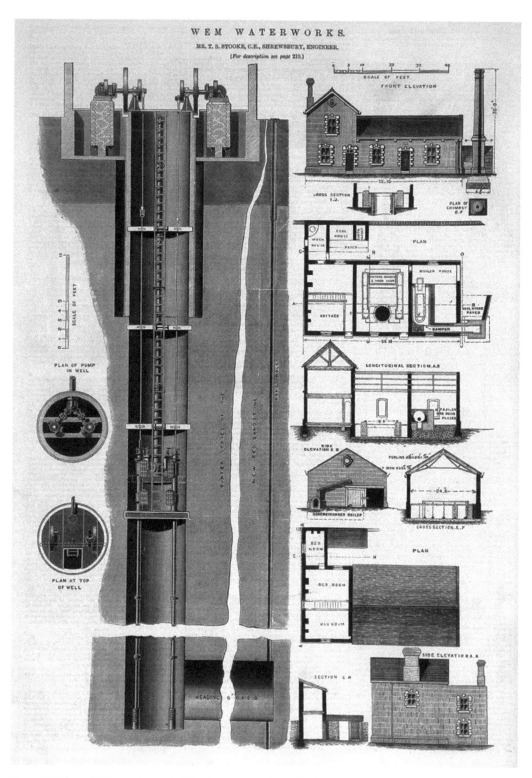

Figure 35 *Plan of Wem waterworks*. The Engineer, *18 Sept. 1885.*

principal streets.[114] This ambitious project, designed by the engineer Thomas Stooke of Shrewsbury, was completed by 1883 and a clean and reliable water supply achieved in February 1884. There was a direct supply to the workhouse, with a water tower for storage, and in the town 15 drinking fountains, two street watering posts, and 36 fire hydrants; 84 houses were connected to the water main.[115] By 1946, 657 houses in Wem UD and part of Wem RD were supplied with piped water from the borehole, but water consumption was beginning to exceed capacity.[116] The Preston Brockhurst borehole is now operated by Severn Trent Water Ltd, although the pumping station and its adjoining house have been converted to a private dwelling. The Palms Hill reservoir site, with its masonry perimeter wall, can still be seen beside the B5063. Wem's water supply is still sourced from ground-water supplies and fed to reservoirs at Sherwood Bank and Prees, where it is treated before being piped into the mains system.[117]

The creation of Wem UDC in 1900 enabled a clearer focus on the infrastructure of the urban area. Improvements had been made to the water supply but the authority was reluctant to develop a comprehensive drainage scheme, its priority being a new public livestock market. The Local Government Board (LGB), however, refused to sanction the Smithfield development until a new sewerage system had been installed. In 1906 Edward Bygott, as chairman of Wem UDC, used his casting vote to adopt a sewerage scheme designed by W.W. Wyatt. At a public meeting, insinuations were made that Bygott's interest arose from his desire to have his housing development at Station Road ('Klondike') sewered at the town's expense. He did not offer himself for election in 1906, but successfully sued another former councillor, G.H. Morgan and a number of others at Shrewsbury assizes. More serious objections were made to the sewerage scheme on grounds of cost and the debt that the council already carried from improving the water supply. At an enquiry into the scheme in 1907, one witness dismissed it as unnecessary and too expensive, and also maintained that there was nothing wrong with the health of the town.[118] Nevertheless, in 1908 the LGB sanctioned a loan of £5,373 to pay for the whole scheme. Wem UDC purchased land between Aston Road and the river to construct sewage disposal works.[119] This was still the location of the plant in 2019, when it was operated by Severn Trent Water Ltd.[120]

Gas

In 1835 the parish vestry advertised for contractors to erect a gas works and to light the town's streets, both contracts being awarded to John Thomas. The cost of street lighting was a separate rate charged on property owners.[121] By 1847, when Thomas sold the

---

114 SA, DA14/701/7; 'Wem Waterworks', *The Engineer*, 18 Sept. 1885, 218–20.
115 SA, DA27/994/1/2; A.H.S. Waters, *Report on Water Supply within the County, 1946, Salop County Council* (Shrewsbury 1946), 27.
116 Waters, *Report on Water Supply*, 27.
117 JRL, GB 133 EMP/3/58, EMP/3/202; inf. from Severn Trent Water Ltd.
118 *Wellington Jnl*, 20 Jan. 1906; 21 July 1906; 9 Mar. 1907.
119 SA, DA14/100/1, 67, 83; DA14/100/2, 335, 403–4; DA14/100/3, 67, 83; DA14/700/24; DA14/725/1.
120 Wallace Evans & Partners, *Wem Sewage Disposal Works extensions stage III*: SA, I 25.9 v.f.
121 E.g. *Eddowes's Jnl*, 10 Apr. 1844, 15 Feb. 1882.

business, it supplied 176 public and 40 private lights, including the church.[122] When the initial lease for the gas works expired in 1860 the Wem Gas Co. was formed to continue it,[123] and when Wem RSA took over responsibility for street lighting in 1892, it awarded the contract to supply gas and lamps to that company's successor, Wem Gas Light & Coke Co. Ltd.[124] The latter company was dissolved in 1949 when the gas works was taken over by the West Midlands Gas Board under the Gas Act 1948.[125] North Sea (natural) gas was supplied in 1969, but the gas holder remained in use as a balancing tank until it was removed in the 1980s. The site is now occupied by a motor vehicle garage and dealership.[126]

Electricity

Electricity first became available for street lighting in the 1920s under the North West Midlands Joint Electricity Authority.[127] It was not widely used; in 1944 the senior school, with its kitchen providing up to 1000 school meals per week, did not have electric power or lighting.[128] The whole town had been supplied with electricity by 1957.

122 *Shrews. Chron.*, 10 and 17 Apr. 1846; *Eddowes's Jnl*, 7 Apr. 1847, 3.
123 SA, 2593/26–38; SA, 4756/4/16; *Cheltenham Chron.*, 10 Aug. 1935, 7.
124 SA, DA27/994/1/2; SA, 1491/86–87.
125 Directors' minutes, 1930–49: SA, 1491; *Register of Defunct Companies*, 2nd edn (Houndmills, 1990), 527. SA, DA14/135/7/44, lot 85. See also the aerial photograph in K.G. Kinrade, 'Tracing the growth of a market town: Some reflections on the early history of Wem', *The Shropshire Mag.*, Oct. 1958, 25, and Woodward, Plate 10.
126 SA, 3221/40 (1962); Law, *Draft Wem Planning Policy & Advisory Plan* (1971), par. 56; Woodward, 111; inf. on balancing tank, Tom Edwards.
127 SA, DP748.
128 SA, ED2782/29, 24–5.

Abbreviations and short titles used include the following:

ACA	Arundel Castle Archive
Arundel map	Map of the manor of Wem, part of a survey commissioned by Thomas, earl of Arundel, 1631: SA, 972/7/1/49/1–9
Bagshaw	Samuel Bagshaw, *History, Gazetteer, and Directory of Shropshire ...* (Sheffield, 1851)
BL	British Library, London
BM	British Museum, London
Bodleian	Bodleian Library, Oxford
Calamy Revised	A.G. Matthews (ed.), *Calamy Revised: Being a Revision of Edmund Calamy's Account of the Ministers and Others Ejected and Silenced, 1660–2* (Oxford, 1988)
Cal. Inq. Misc.	*Calendar of Inquisitions Miscellaneous (Chancery)* (HMSO, 1916–69)
Cal. Inq. p.m.	*Calendar of Inquisitions Post Mortem preserved in the Public Record Office* (HMSO, 1904–87)
Cart. Lilleshall Abbey	U. Rees (ed.), *The Cartulary of Lilleshall Abbey* (Shrewsbury, 1997)
Census	UK Census figures from printed reports and census returns. Returns for 1841–1911 (TNA, HO 107, RG 9–14) accessed via *The Genealogist* website: https://www.thegenealogist.co.uk
Church and Chapel	C.D. Field (ed.), *Church and Chapel in Early Victorian Shropshire: Returns from the 1851 Census of Religious Worship*, Shropshire Record Ser., 8 (Keele, 2004)
Compton Census	A. Whiteman (ed.), *The Compton Census of 1676: A Critical Edition* (London, 1986)
CPAT	Clwyd-Powys Archaeological Trust
CP	Civil Parish

Cranage	D.H.S. Cranage, *An Architectural Account of the Churches of Shropshire: Part 8 – The Hundred of Bradford (North)* (Wellington, 1906)
Dir.	Directory
Domesday	A. Williams and G.H. Martin (eds.), *Domesday Book: A Complete Translation* (London, 2002). Also available at Open Domesday: https://opendomesday.org/
Eddowes's Jnl	*Eddowes's Shrewsbury Journal*
Edwards	P. Edwards and T. Edwards, *A History of the Methodist and United Reformed (Congregational) Societies in Wem* (Wem, 1995)
Excerpta è Rotulis Finium	C. Roberts (ed.), *Excerpta è Rotulis Finium … 1216–1272*, vol. 1 (London, 1835)
Eyton, *Antiquities*	R.W. Eyton, *Antiquities of Shropshire*, 12 vols (London, 1854–60)
Faraday, *Shropshire Taxes*	M.A. Faraday (ed.), *Shropshire Taxes in the Reign of Henry VIII* (Walton-on-Thames, Surrey, 2015)
Fenwick, *Poll Taxes*	C.C. Fenwick (ed.), *The Poll Taxes of 1377, 1379 and 1381: Part 2: Lincolnshire–Westmorland* (Oxford, 2001)
Garbet	*History of Wem … Taken from the Manuscript of the Late Rev. Sam. Garbet, A.M.* (Wem, 1818)
Gelling, *PN Salop.* V	M. Gelling, *The Place-Names of Shropshire, Part 5. The Hundreds of Pimhill and Bradford North* (Nottingham, 2007)
Gelling, *West Midlands*	M. Gelling, *The West Midlands in the Early Middle Ages* (Leicester, 1992)
Gelling and Foxall, *PN Salop.* I	M. Gelling and H.D.G. Foxall, *The Place-Names of Shropshire, Part 1. The Major Names of Shropshire* (Nottingham, 1990)
Gough, *History of Myddle*	D.G. Hey (ed.), Richard Gough, *The History of Myddle* (Harmondsworth, 1981)
HER	Historic Environment Record, maintained by Shropshire Council
Hist. Research	*Historical Research* (1987–)
HMSO	Her (His) Majesty's Stationery Office

ICBS	The records of the Incorporated Church Building Society, images available at http://images.lambethpalacelibrary.org.uk
Jones, *Mr Garbet*	B.M. Jones, *'The Goode Mr Garbet of Wem': The Life of the Revd. Samuel Garbet, M.A. of Wem, Shropshire 1685–1756* (Wrexham, 2001)
JRL	John Rylands Library, The University of Manchester Library
Jnl	*Journal*
JP	Justice of the Peace
LNWR	London and North Western Railway
Lond. Gaz.	*London Gazette*
Mercer, *English Arch. to 1900*	E. Mercer, *English Architecture to 1900: The Shropshire experience* (Almeley, Herefs., 2003)
Moran, *Vernacular Buildings*	M. Moran, *Vernacular Buildings of Shropshire* (Logaston, 2003)
Newman and Pevsner	J. Newman and N. Pevsner, *The Buildings of England: Shropshire* (New Haven and London, 2006)
NHLE	National Heritage List for England, maintained by Historic England: http://historicengland.org.uk/listing/the-list
NMR	National Monuments Record
NSDC	North Shropshire District Council
ODNB	*Oxford Dictionary of National Biography* online (Oxford University Press, 2004–): http://www.oxforddnb.com
OS	Ordnance Survey
PAS	Portable Antiquities Scheme
RCHME	Royal Commission on the Historical Monuments of England
RD	Rural District
RDC	Rural District Council
Rot. Hund. II	*Rotuli Hundredorum, temp. Henr. III. & Edw. I.: in turr. Lond. et in curia receptae Scaccarii Westm. asservati*, vol. II (London, 1818)
Rowley, *Shropshire Landscape*	T. Rowley, *The Shropshire Landscape* (London, 1972)
RSA	Rural Sanitary Authority
SA	Shropshire Archives, Shrewsbury (formerly Shropshire Record Office, amalgamated with

	Shrewsbury Local Studies Library in 1993, renamed Shropshire Records and Research Centre in 1995 and Shropshire Archives in 2003)
SBT	Shakespeare Birthplace Trust, Stratford-upon-Avon
SCC	Shropshire (formerly Salop) County Council
SHC	Staffordshire Record Society (formerly William Salt Archaeological Society), *Collections for a History of Staffordshire*
Shrews. Chron.	*Shrewsbury Chronicle* (1772–)
SFHS	Shropshire Family History Society
Shropshire Hearth Tax Roll	W. Watkins-Pitchford (ed.), *The Shropshire Hearth Tax Roll of 1672*, Shropshire Archaeological and Parish Register Society ([Shrewsbury], 1949)
Shropshire Lay Subsidy Roll 1327	H.M. Auden and W.G.D. Fletcher (eds), *The Shropshire Lay Subsidy Roll of 1 Edward III, 1327* (Oswestry, 1907)
SRO	Staffordshire Record Office, Stafford
Strong's	*Strong's Wem Almanack*
Survey 1561	S. Watts (ed.), *Survey of the Lordship of Wem 1561*, 2 vols (Birmingham University, 2012)
Tax. Eccl.	*Taxation Ecclesiastica Anglie et Wallie … circa AD 1291* (Record Commission, 1801)
TNA	The National Archives, Kew
TSAHS	*Shropshire History and Archaeology. Transactions of the Shropshire Archaeological and Historical Society*
TSAS	*Transactions of the Shropshire Archaeological Society*
UD	Urban District
UDC	Urban District Council
Univ.	University
Univ. Brit. Dir.	*Universal British Directory of Trade and Commerce* (London, 1790– [1798]), vol. 4, *c.*1795.
Welsh Assize Roll	J. Conway Davies (ed.), *The Welsh Assize Roll 1275–88* (Cardiff, 1940)
'Wem wills'	S. Watts (ed.), 'Wem wills of 1535–1660 in Lichfield Joint Record Office' (typescript, SA, C55.5 v.f.)

Woodward	I. Woodward, *The Story of Wem* (1951) reprinted, with additions to 2012 by J. Dromgool (Wem, 2012)
WTC	Wem Town Council
Vane, 'Churchwardens of Wem'	G.H.F. Vane, 'The accounts of the churchwardens of Wem', *TSAS*, 3rd ser., 4 (1904), 237–58
VCH	*Victoria County History*
'Visitation 1799'	'Visitation of the Archdeaconry of Salop [1799–1807] ...' (SA, C 97, transcript of [former] SA, 3916/1/1, now SRO)
Wem Parish Registers	G.H.F. Vane (ed.) *[The Parish Registers of Wem, Edstaston and Newtown], Shrops. Parish Registers, Diocese of Lichfield*, vols IX and X (Shropshire Parish Register Society, 1908), to 1811. A transcript of these volumes is available at http://www.melocki.org.uk/MelockiSalop.html
Whitehead, *Wem*	J. Whitehead, *Wem, Now and Then* (Wem, 1992)
Yalden, 'Landownership'	P. Yalden, 'The pattern of landownership in a small market town: Wem, Shropshire, 1805' (typescript, 'Sydney, Australia, April 1981')
Youngs, *Admin. Units*	F.A. Youngs, *Guide to the Local Administrative Units of England, vol. 2, Northern England* (Royal Historical Society, 1991)

GLOSSARY

The following terms may require explanation. Fuller information on local history topics is available in D.G. Hey, *The Oxford Companion to Local and Family History*, 2nd edn (Oxford, 2010), or online from the VCH website: http://www.victoriacountyhistory.ac.uk. The most convenient glossary of architectural terms is *Pevsner's Architectural Glossary*, 2nd edn (New Haven and London, 2010), available as an app for iOS devices.

A useful dictionary of English dialect words is Joseph Wright's *The English Dialect Dictionary*, 8 vols (London, 1896–1905). For Shropshire dialect, see G.F. Jackson, *Shropshire Word Book: A Glossary of Archaic and Provincial Words, Etc., Used in the County* (Shrewsbury, 1879).

Advowson, or patronage: the right to nominate a candidate to the bishop for appointment as rector or vicar of a church. Often originally held by the lord of the manor of the principal manor within the parish, this right was a form of property which could be bought and sold.

Bay: in architecture, a unit of a building, inside or out, regularly divided from the next by features such as columns or windows. Can apply to a window projecting from a bay.

Burgage: a plot of land in a medieval town occupied by a burgess, usually for a money rent. Burgage plots are characteristically long and narrow, with a row of outbuildings stretching to the rear of the house and shop.

Carucate or ploughland: notionally the amount of land a plough team of eight oxen could plough in a season. In Wem, approximately 144 acres. See **nook**.

Chantry: in the Middle Ages, an endowment for a priest to say regular masses for the donor's soul or anyone nominated by the donor. Some of the most elaborate arrangements provided for a purpose-built chapel, or a side-chapel in the parish church. Chantries were suppressed at the Reformation.

Common (open) fields: communal agrarian organisation under which an individual's farmland was held in strips scattered among two or more large fields, intermingled with strips of other tenants. Management of the fields and usually common meadows and pasture was regulated through the manor court or other communal assembly.

Copyhold: form of land tenure granted in a manor court, so called because the tenant received a 'copy' of the grant as noted in the court records. Often given for several lives (e.g. tenant, wife and eldest child).

Court baron: (Latin, *curia parva*, lesser court) a manorial court which dealt with tenants' services, agricultural regulation and transfers of copyhold land on inheritance or sale. It was usually held every three weeks.

Court leet: a manorial court which dealt with petty law and order and the regulation of agriculture, normally held every six months.

Customary tenure: unfree or copyhold tenure regulated by local manorial custom.

Demesne: in the Middle Ages, land farmed directly by a lord of the manor, rather than granted to tenants. Though usually leased out from the later Middle Ages, demesne lands often remained distinct from the rest of a parish's land.

Enclosure: the process whereby open fields and commons were divided into enclosed fields, to be redistributed among the various tenants and landholders. From the 18th century usually by an Act of Parliament obtained by the dominant landowners; earlier, more commonly done by private agreement, or by a powerful lord acting on his own initiative.

Farm: a fixed annual sum paid as a rent or tax; to hold land or property in exchange for a fixed annual rent; to collect rents, fees or profits due to another in exchange for a fixed annual payment.

Glebe: land assigned to the rector or vicar of a church for his support and the endowment of the church.

Hearth tax: annual tax imposed by central government in 1662–89, assessed on the number of hearths or fireplaces in each house and payable by the occupier. Those who lacked the means to pay could apply for a certificate of exemption.

Hide: unit of land measurement: in the Anglo-Saxon period, the amount required for a family to subsist on; in Domesday Book (1086), a taxation unit; and by the 13th century the sum of four **virgates or yardlands**.

Husbandman: a farmer who generally held his land by copyhold or leasehold tenure. The term husbandman usually denoted less well-off farmers.

Lay subsidy: from the Middle Ages to the 16th century, a periodic royal tax upon the laity, assessed on the value of their moveable goods.

Lewn: a rate or levy.

Manor: a piece of landed property with tenants regulated by a private (manor) court. Originally held by feudal tenure, manors descended through the succession of heirs but could be given away or sold.

Messuage: parcel of land, generally with a house and outbuildings on it.

Nook: notionally one-sixteenth of a carucate. In Wem a nook was defined as the area of land that could be sown with 18 strikes of rye of Whitchurch measure when an acre could be sown with two strikes: it was therefore 9 acres of customary measure.[1]

Parish: the area attached to a parish church and owing tithes to it. From the Elizabethan period it had civil responsibilities, hence a 'civil' as opposed to an 'ecclesiastical' parish. At first the two were usually identical, but from the 19th century, when many parishes were reorganised, their boundaries sometimes diverged.

---

1   *Survey 1561*, 35. For a strike, see G.F. Jackson, *Shropshire Word Book: A Glossary of Archaic and Provincial Words, Etc., Used in the County* (Shrewsbury, 1879), 417.

Radman: 'riding man', term used in Domesday Book for certain tenants, distinctive to the Welsh borders, see M. Atkin, 'A study of "radman villages" recorded in Domesday Book in western Shropshire', *TSAHS*, 89 (2014), 15–26.

Rectory: (1) a church living served by a rector, an ordained minister who generally received the church's whole income; (2) the church's property or endowment (the rectory estate), comprising tithes, offerings and usually some land or glebe.

Recusant: a Roman Catholic who did not attend the services of the Church of England, as was required by law.

Tithe: a tax of one-tenth of the produce of the land, which originally went to the church. It could be divided into great tithes (corn and hay), which went to the rector, and small tithes (livestock, wool and other crops), which supported a vicar.

Turnpike: a road administered by a trust, which covered the cost of maintenance by charging tolls.

Vestry: (1) room in a church where clerical vestments are stored; (2) assembly of leading parishioners and ratepayers, responsible for poor relief and other secular matters as well as church affairs.

Virgate or yardland: (Latin, *virgata*), as the conventional holding of a medieval peasant, one quarter of a carucate, generally 15–40 acres depending on local custom. Most generated surplus crops for sale at market; those with a fraction of a virgate probably needed to work part-time for better-off neighbours.

Yeoman: from the 16th century, a term used for more prosperous farmers, many of them socially aspirational.

This history of Wem was written using a wide range of original sources, some of them printed but mostly manuscript documents. It is this dependence on primary sources (created at the time under study) that makes the VCH series both new and reliable. This list includes the main sources used but is not comprehensive. The most frequently used sources are listed in the List of Abbreviations, while additional sources for specific topics are cited in the footnotes. Shropshire Archives, the principal archive used, is listed first, followed by the other archives in alphabetical order, and then published sources, primary and secondary.

Manuscript Sources

Shropshire Archives, Shrewsbury, holds the records of county government and records from manors, parishes, local government authorities and organisations within the county, as well as collections of family, business and solicitors' papers. Those used for this history are:

167:	Wem manor records
306:	Dickin of Loppington estate
484:	Venables, solicitor
731:	Edward Bygott, solicitor
800:	Longueville, solicitor, bundle 138.1: map of Wem, anon., *c.*1800
972:	Lilleshall Collection
1096/7:	Robert Baugh's map of Shropshire, 1808
1186:	Wright, Hassall & co., solicitors: Wem, estate of William Owen, incl. Dickin estate
1416, 1848, 4756:	Lee, Bygott and Ecclestone, solicitors
1709, 2495:	Sprott, Stokes and Turnbull, solicitors
3607/ III/A/10:	Rental, 1711; extracts from survey of the manor of Wem, 1752; custumal, 1752
3994:	Salt, solicitor, papers
4791:	Salop Fire Office, insurance policy books
6000:	Manuscripts of the former Shrewsbury Public Library

7381/240:	William Mytton papers, copies (originals at Univ. of Birmingham Library)
7577:	John Kynaston's day book, 1830–33 / E.W. Bowcock's scrapbook, 1930s
7939:	West Mercia Police Authority property deeds
8540:	Thomas F. Edwards Collection
9043:	Revd. Samuel Garbet, papers
C110/109:	Accounts of Charles Bolas esq. for Newport estate
D3651/B:	Salt Collection, solicitor
DA14:	Wem UDC, 1900–1971
DA27:	Wem Rural Sanitary Authority, 1872–1899, and Wem RDC, 1888–1971
DA30:	North Shropshire Rural District Council
DP199/2:	Shropshire Quarter Sessions, deposited plans
ED:	County records of schools
HB13:	Wem Highways Board
MI:	Manorial documents
P295:	Wem parish records
PH/W/8:	Photographs of Wem
PL15:	Wem Poor Law Union
PS1/24/E/1–5:	Petty Sessions
QA/6/4/6:	Shropshire Quarter Sessions, Police
QS1, QS2:	Shropshire Quarter Sessions Orders
Raby Estate:	Accounts and correspondence of the Shropshire estates of Lord Barnard
SCC1/K/7 TP70	War Department Depots, correspondence, 1957–65: Aston Park, Wem
TP15:	Map of Wem by John Wood, 1834, photocopy

Arundel Castle, Sussex

MD59:	Register of enfranchisements and sales of demesne by the trustees for sale of the manors of Wem, Loppington and Hinstock, mid 17th century
M508:	Survey of Wem, 1648
W13:	Stewards' accounts for manors of Oversley, Tyrley and Wem, 1409/10

W14:   Stewards' accounts for manors of Wem,
                                              Loppington and Hinstock, 1512–14

Bodleian Library, Univ. of Oxford

Blakeway 21:   Samuel Garbet's 'History of Wem', annotated
                                              ms

British Library, London

Additional MS 24478:   Joseph Hunter, papers
Additional MS 30315:   William Mytton, papers
Harley MS 594:   Diocesan surveys, 1563

John Rylands Library, The Univ. of Manchester Library

GB 133 MS Phillipps Charters, PHC/3:   Late 16th-century custumal of Wem
GB 133 EMP/3/58, EMP/3/202:   Edgar Morton archive, 1945–9, 1962–72

Raby Castle, near Barnard Castle, Darlington

Records of the Vane family, Barons Barnard
Staffordshire and Shropshire deeds, Box 6: Manors of Wem and Loppington
Press 13/41:   Abstract of title deeds relating to manors of
                                              Wem and Loppington

Shakespeare Birthplace Trust, Stratford-upon-Avon

DR 36/182–202:   Piper's Pool (later grounds of The Hall), Wem,
                                              deeds

Shropshire Historic Environment Record, Shrewsbury (formerly the Shropshire Sites
and Monuments Record) holds notes and reports of archaeological sites and features
and listed buildings. An online database is available at https://shropshire.gov.uk/
environment/historic-environment/historic-environment-record/ (accessed 4 Mar. 2019)

Society of Antiquaries, London

MS 477:   James Bowen of Shrewsbury, drawings
                                              of sepulchral monuments, arms, etc., in
                                              Shropshire, by, 1734–7

Library, 57 c: *The History of Wem ... Taken from the
                                              manuscript of the late Rev. Sam. Garbet, ...*
                                              (1818), gift of G.E. Cokayne, annotated by
                                              'G.M.' [probably George Morris of Shrewsbury
                                              (1789–1859)].

Staffordshire Record Office, Stafford

The diocese of Lichfield and Coventry archives contain material on the religious organisation of Wem parish including appointments of clergy and archdeacons' visitations and proof of wills.

MS Magnum Registrum:	The medieval cartulary of Lichfield cathedral
B/A:	Bishops' registers
B/C/5:	Consistory Court papers
B/C/12:	Faculties
B/V:	Visitation books

The National Archives at Kew, London, holds the records of national government from the late 12th century onwards. Calendars of some medieval administrative records which have been used in the history, notably the Close and Patent Rolls, have been published. The classes of documents used in this history include:

ADM 106:	Admiralty correspondence
C 2:	Chancery: Pleadings, Series I, Elizabeth I to Charles I
C 3:	Chancery: Pleadings, Series II, Elizabeth I to Interregnum
C 101:	Chancery Masters' Account Books
C 133:	Chancery: Inquisitions Post Mortem, Series I, Edward I
C 135:	Chancery: Inquisitions Post Mortem, Series I, Edward III
C 139:	Chancery: Inquisitions Post Mortem, Series I, Henry VI
E 112:	Exchequer: King's Remembrancer: Bills and Answers
E 117:	Exchequer: Church Goods Inventories and Miscellanea
E 133:	Exchequer: King's Remembrancer: Barons' Depositions
E 134:	Exchequer: King's Remembrancer: Depositions taken by Commission
E 149:	Exchequer: King's Remembrancer: Escheators' Files, Inquisitions Post Mortem, Series I, Henry III to Richard III
E 178	Exchequer: King's Remembrancer: Special Commissions of Inquiry
E 179:	Exchequer: King's Remembrancer: Records relating to Lay and Clerical Taxation

E 331:	Office of the Governors of Queen Anne's Bounty and predecessors: Certificates of Institutions to Livings
ED 21:	Public Elementary School Files
ED 49:	Elementary Education Endowment Files
ED 103:	Treasury and Committee of the Privy Council on Education: Building Grant Applications
ED 109:	HM Inspectorate: Reports on Secondary Institutions
HO 129:	Home Office, Ecclesiastical census, 1851
IR 29:	Tithe Apportionments
JV 2:	Milk Marketing Board: Minutes and Papers, 1933–98
LR 2:	Office of the Auditors of Land Revenue and predecessors: Miscellaneous Books
PROB:	Prerogative Court of Canterbury, wills proved
SC 12:	Special Collections: Rentals and Surveys, Portfolios
SP 44:	Secretaries of State: State Papers: Entry Books
WO 30:	War Office: Miscellaneous Papers

Printed Sources

Primary Sources

The most frequently cited primary sources, including calendars of major classes in The National Archives, are included in the List of Abbreviations.

Other published primary sources used in this history are:

Antiquities and Memoirs of the Parish of Myddle, county of Salop, written by Richard Gough, A.D. 1700 (Shrewsbury, 1875); and D. Hey (ed.), *Richard Gough, The History of Myddle* (Harmondsworth, 1981). [The parish of Myddle adjoins Wem to the south, hence Gough's history contains numerous references to Wem and its people.]

Auden, H.M. and Fletcher, W.G.D. (eds.), *The Shropshire Lay Subsidy Roll of 1 Edward III, 1327* (reprinted from *TSHAS*) (Oswestry, 1907).

Brown, A. (ed.), 'Noble Street Presbyterian Chapel, Wem, Register of Burials 1822–1837 [from] PRO RG4/1533' (typescript, Shropshire Family History Society, 1984).

Bulmer, K.J. (ed.), 'Parish Church of SS Peter and Paul, Wem: Transcripts of registers (SRO 2322/1) with indexes' [transcript of registers 1813–40] (typescript, Shropshire Family History Society, c. 1970).

Evans, G.E. (ed.), 'The Register of Wem Presbyterian Chapel 1755–1814', in *Shropshire Parish Registers. Nonconformist Registers*, Shropshire Parish Register Society (Shrewsbury, 1903).

Faraday, M.A. (ed.), *Shropshire Taxes in the Reign of Henry VIII* (Walton-on-Thames, Surrey, 2015).

Field, C.D. (ed.), *Church and Chapel in Early Victorian Shropshire: Returns from the 1851 Census of Religious Worship*, Shropshire Record Series, vol. 8 (Keele, 2004).

MacLeod, A.M. (ed.), 'Wem, Chapel St. Independent Chapel, 1785–1836', in *Shropshire Parish Registers. Nonconformist and Roman Catholic Registers, Pt 2*, Shropshire Parish Register Society (Shrewsbury, 1922).

Shropshire Council, *Wem Market Town Profile, Winter 2017/18* (Shrewsbury, 2018): available at http://www.shropshire.gov.uk/media/9454/wem-market-town-profile.pdf (accessed 4 Mar. 2019)

Vane, G.H.F. (ed.), *[The Parish Registers of Wem, Edstaston and Newtown]*, *Shropshire Parish Registers, Diocese of Lichfield*, vols IX and X, Shropshire Parish Register Society (Shrewsbury, 1908).

'Visitation of the Archdeaconry of Salop [1799–1807] … by Very Rev J.C. Woodhouse, Dean of Lichfield as Archdeacon of Salop' (transcript of [former] SA, 3916/1/1, now SRO: typescript, SA, C 97).

Walmsley, J.L., 'Tithe apportionment for Wem parish …' (SA, I 63 v.f.).

Wakeman, O., Kenyon, R.L. and Venables, R.G. (eds.), *Orders of the Shropshire Quarter Sessions, 1638–1889*, 4 vols, Shropshire County Records (Shrewsbury, n.d.).

Watkins-Pitchford, W. (ed.), *The Shropshire Hearth Tax Roll of 1672*, Shropshire Archaeological and Parish Register Society ([Shrewsbury], 1949).

Watts, S. (ed.), 'Wem wills of 1535–1660 in Lichfield Joint Record Office' (typescript, SA, C 55.5 v.f.).

Watts, S. (ed.), *The Glebe Terriers of Shropshire: Part 2 (Llanyblodwel to Wroxeter)*, Shropshire Record Series, vol. 6 (Keele, 2002).

Watts, S. (ed.), *Survey of the Lordship of Wem, 1561*, 2 vols (Univ. of Birmingham, 2012).

Watts, S. and Collingwood, R. (eds.), *Shropshire Hearth Tax Exemptions 1662–1674* ([editors], 2018).

Williams, A. and Martin, G.H. (eds.), *Domesday Book: A Complete Translation* (London, 2002).

The tithe maps for all Shropshire parishes, including Wem, have been privately published by H.D.G. Foxall. Copies of these maps, which incorporate field-names and other material from the tithe awards, are available in Shropshire Council libraries and at Shropshire Archives. Foxall's *Shropshire Field-Names* (Shrewsbury, 1980) contains information about Wem and the surrounding area.

Trade or commercial directories have been used extensively, especially for economic history. A selection of trade directories for Shropshire from 1828 to 1913 is available online at http://specialcollections.le.ac.uk/digital/collection/p16445coll4 (accessed 4

Mar. 2019); more are held at Shropshire Archives. The main directories consulted are: Samuel Bagshaw, *History, Gazetteer, and Directory of Shropshire...* (Sheffield, 1851); *Kelly's Directory*, 1891, 1895, 1900, 1913; *Pigot's Directory*, 1828/9, 1835, 1842; *Slater's Directory of N & S Wales etc.*, 1880. [Part 2: Shrops, Mon, Bristol & Chester]; *Strong's Wem Almanack*, 1899, 1925; *Tibnam's Salop Directory*, 1828; and *The Universal British Directory of Trades, Commerce and Manufacture ... IV* (London, [1795–98]), 'Wem', 417–19. References to these are abbreviated to, for example, *Kelly's Dir.* (1899). The particular volume of each publication cited is that for, or including, Shropshire, unless otherwise indicated.

Secondary Sources

The most important secondary work on the history of Wem, and also an important primary source for the early 18th century, is Samuel Garbet, *The History of Wem, and the Following Villages and Townships, viz. Edstaston, Cotton, Lowe and Ditches, Horton, Newtown, Wolverley, Northwood, Tilley, Sleap, Aston, and Lacon Taken from the Manuscript of the late Rev. Sam. Garbet, A.M.* (Wem, 1818).

Similarly valuable for the 19th and 20th centuries is I. Woodward, *The Story of Wem* (Wem, 1952, second edition, 1976), reprinted with additional chapters by J. Dromgool (Wem, 2012).

The main sources for architectural history are J. Newman and N. Pevsner, *The Buildings of England: Shropshire* (New Haven and London, 2006), M. Moran, *Vernacular Buildings of Whitchurch Area and their Occupants* (Logaston, 1999), and E. Mercer, *English Architecture to 1900: The Shropshire Experience* (Logaston, 2003). The main architectural history of churches is D.H.S. Cranage, *An Architectural Account of the Churches of Shropshire*, of which Part 8, *The Hundred of Bradford (North)* (Wellington, 1906) includes Wem.

Victoria County History (VCH) volumes:

A History of the County of Shropshire: Volume II, ed. A.T. Gaydon and R.B. Pugh (London, 1973).

A History of Shropshire: Volume III, ed. G. Baugh (London, 1979)

A History of the County of Shropshire: Volume IV, Agriculture, ed. G.C. Baugh and C.R. Elrington (London, 1989).

A History of the County of Shropshire: Volume VI.I, Shrewsbury, General History and Topography, ed. W. Champion and A.T. Thacker (London, 2014).

A History of the County of Shropshire: Volume XI, Telford, ed. G.C. Baugh and C.R. Elrington (London, 1985).

Websites

A Vision of Britain through Time: http://www.visionofbritain.org.uk

British History Online: http://www.british-history.ac.uk

British Newspaper Archive: http://britishnewspaperarchive.co.uk

Clergy of the Church of England database: http://theclergydatabase.org.uk

Domesday Book: Open Domesday: https://opendomesday.org

Cox, J., Shropshire's Nonconformist Chapels: http://users.waitrose.com/~coxfamily/
    wempresb.htm

Historic England's Red Box Collection: http://historicengland.org.uk/images-books/
    photos/englands-places/

Oxford Dictionary of National Biography: http://www.oxforddnb.com

Royal College of Surgeons, Lives Online: http://livesonline.rcseng.ac.uk/biogs

UK Medical Registers, 1859–1959. General Medical Council

Wem Civic Society: http://wemlocal.org.uk

Further Reading on Wem

The following is a select bibliography on the history of Wem:

Auden, H.M., 'The fire of Wem', *TSAHS*, 3rd ser., 6 (1906), xxii–xxiii.

Buteux, V. et al., 'Archaeological assessment of Wem, Shropshire', Central Marches
    Historic Towns Survey, 1995.

Cooney, P., 'The (relatively) unchanging face of Wem', *The Shropshire Mag.*, July 1971,
    36–7.

Creak, W.J., *History of Adams' Grammar School, Wem* (Wem, 1953).

Crompton, E. and Osmond, D.A., *The Soils of the Wem District: Soil Survey of England
    and Wales, Wem, Sheet 138* (1954).

Edwards, P. and Edwards, T., *A History of the Methodist and United Reformed
    (Congregational) Societies in Wem* (Wem, 1995).

Edwards, P.R., 'The development of dairy farming of the north Shropshire plain in the
    seventeenth century', *Mid. Hist.*, 4 (1977), 175–90.

Edwards, P.R., 'The farming economy of north east Shropshire in the seventeenth
    century', unpublished Univ. of Oxford D.Phil. thesis, 1976.

E.T.S., '[Wem]', *The Shropshire Mag.*, Oct. 1958, 17–21.

Eyton, R.W., *Antiquities of Shropshire*, 12 vols (London, 1854–1860), especially vol. IX
    (1859).

Gelling, M. and Foxall, H.D.G., *The Place-Names of Shropshire, Part 1. The Major Names
    of Shropshire* (Nottingham, 1990).

Gelling, M. and Foxall, H.D.G., *The Place-Names of Shropshire, Part 5. The Hundreds of
    Pimhill and Bradford North* (Nottingham, 2007).

Jones, B.M., *'The Goode Mr Garbet of Wem': The Life of the Revd. Samuel Garbet, M.A. of
    Wem, Shropshire 1685–1756* (Wrexham, 2001).

Keeling-Roberts, M., *A Short History of the Parish Church of S. Peter & S. Paul, Wem*
    (Wem, 1987).

Kinrade, K.G., 'Tracing the growth of a market town: some reflections on the early
    history of Wem', *The Shropshire Mag.*, Oct. 1958, 23–7.

Meisel, J., *Barons of the Welsh Frontier. The Corbet, Pantulf and Fitz Warin Families (1066–1272)* (Lincoln, Nebraska, 1980).

Reid, A., *Tilley. The Secret History of a Secret Place* (Shrewsbury, 2003).

Riches, A., *Harry Strong, MC: The Story of a Wemian in War & Peace* (Wem, 2018).

Ruscoe, A., *Landed Estates and the Gentry. Part of a Further Study of the History of Landholding in North Shropshire 9. Whitchurch, Wem and Baschurch* (Ormskirk, 2009).

Shropshire Council, *Wem Market Town Profile, Winter 2017/18* (Shrewsbury, 2018).

Smith, L., 'Refuges of last resort: Shropshire workhouses and the people who ran them', *TSAHS*, 82 (2007).

Stamper, P., *'The Farmer Feeds Us All': A Short History of Shropshire Agriculture* (Shrewsbury, 1989)

Sylvester, D. *The Rural Landscape of the Welsh Border Region* (London, 1969).

Sylvester, D., 'Rural settlement in Shropshire: a geographical interpretation', *TSAHS*, 44 (1927–8), 213–56.

Tomkins, A., 'Demography and the midwives: deliveries and their dénouements in north Shropshire, 1781–1803', *Continuity and Change*, 25, 2 (2010), 199–232.

Tomkins, A. 'Who were his peers? The social and professional milieu of the provincial surgeon-apothecary in the late-eighteenth century', *Jnl of Social Hist.*, 44, 3 (Spring 2011), 915–35.

Vane, G.H.F., 'The castle of Wem', *TSAHS*, 3rd ser., 11 (1902), 287–90.

Watts, S., 'The unincorporated town and the role of the manor court in the sixteenth and seventeenth centuries', *The Jnl of Regional and Local Studies*, 19, 2 (1999), 30–47.

Watts, S., 'The significance of colonisation in two north Shropshire parishes: Wem and Whitchurch c.1560–1660', *Midland History*, 25 (2000), 61–77.

Watts, S., 'Some aspects of mortality in three Shropshire parishes in the mid-seventeenth century', *Local Population Studies*, 67 (2001), 11–25.

Whitehead, J., *Wem, Now & Then* (Wem, 1992).

Worton, J., '"A crow's nest": The significance of Wem during the Civil War 1642–1646', *Salopian Recorder*, 86 (2016), 6–8.

Worton, J., *To Settle the Crown: Waging Civil War in Shropshire, 1642–1648* (Solihull, West Midlands, 2016).

Yalden, P., 'The pattern of landownership in a small market town: Wem, Shropshire, 1805' (typescript, 'Sydney, Australia, April 1981') (SA, I 64 v.f.).

INDEX

CPSIA information can be obtained
at www.ICGtesting.com
Printed in the USA
JSHW062301080223
37476JS00004B/31